PRAISE FOR *DOG COMPANY*

"A worthy tribute honoring each member of a small group of volunteers who responded to the call of duty."

—*Kirkus Reviews*

"No World War II historian can tell the story of the U.S. Army Rangers better than Pat O'Donnell. Informative and entertaining, *Dog Company* is a great read."

—Joseph Balkoski, author of *Omaha Beach: D-Day, June 6, 1944*

"*Dog Company* is a super read. It tells a great story of a number of great soldiers I knew personally and uniquely tells the German perspective. Well researched, it is an amazing story of real-life heroism and ultimate success of the good guys."

—Major General John C. Raaen Jr., U.S. Army (Ret.), author of *Intact: A First-hand Account of the D-Day Invasion from a Fifth Rangers Company Commander*

"No historian tells the stories of America's elite infantry and Special Operations troops like Patrick O'Donnell. Expertly researched, he vividly chronicles Dog Company's odyssey across Europe in riveting prose."

—Major General Jack Singlaub, U.S. Army (Ret.), Commanding Officer MACV-SOG, and author of *Hazardous Duty*

"A magnificent story about magnificent men written by a magnificent author—it should be read by all Americans."

—Major General Victor J. Hugo Jr., U.S. Army (Ret.), Landsdale Mission, SOA and SFA

"This is an incredible story of courage under fire, leadership at all levels, and bravery beyond comprehension. This is the story of real American heroes and no one can tell the story better than Patrick K. O'Donnell."

—General Doug Brown USA (Ret.) Commander of U.S. Special Operations Command 2003–2007

"Patrick O'Donnell has set the gold standard for war histories rich in color, drama, and detail. With *Dog Company*, he's hit that high mark once more. World War II comes to life through the eyes of this one company of intrepid U.S. Army Rangers."

—Douglas Waller, author of *Wild Bill Donovan: The Spymaster Who Created the OSS and Modern American Espionage*

DOG COMPANY

THE BOYS OF POINTE DU HOC—
The Rangers Who Accomplished D-Day's Toughest Mission and Led the Way across Europe

Patrick K. O'Donnell

DA CAPO PRESS
A Member of the Perseus Books Group

Cataloging-in-Publication data for this book is available from the Library of Congress.
First Da Capo Press edition 2012
First Da Capo paperback edition 2013
ISBN 978-0-306-82029-8 (hardcover)
ISBN 978-0-306-82159-2 (e-book)
ISBN 978-0-306-82264-3 (paperback)

Published by Da Capo Press
A Member of the Perseus Books Group
www.dacapopress.com

Produced by Marcovaldo Productions, Inc.

Da Capo Press books are available at special discounts for bulk purchases in the U.S. by corporations, institutions, and other organizations. For more information, please contact the Special Markets Department at the Perseus Books Group, 2300 Chestnut Street, Suite 200, Philadelphia, PA 19103, or call (800) 810-4145, ext. 5000, or e-mail special.markets@perseusbooks.com.

10 9 8 7 6 5 4 3 2 1

To the courageous men of
the 2nd and 5th Ranger Battalions whose collective actions
accomplished D-Day's toughest mission and whose
legacy lives on in the next greatest generation of Rangers.

To my many friends of the World War II generation—
your legacy is abiding and inspiring.

To all the Continental soldiers buried in unmarked graves.

For Lily,
the apple of my eye,
the greatest daughter in the world.

CONTENTS

	Prologue	xi
1	Dog Company	1
2	"Rangers? Bullshit!"	12
3	Big Jim	15
4	Fort Pierce and Overseas	21
5	Bude	29
6	The Needles	34
7	The Mission	37
8	Final Preparations	42
9	A Tough Spot for a Landing	47
10	"Into the Valley of Death"	51
11	"The Sky Was Burning"	57
12	The Landing	61
13	The Climb	70
14	Atop the Fortress	74
15	Bunkers and Farms	79
16	The Guns of Pointe du Hoc	86
17	Swimmers	91
18	The First Counterattack	95
19	Nighttime Attacks	102
20	June 7	116
21	The Relief of Pointe du Hoc	123
22	Survivors	126
23	The Assault on Brest	136
24	Hill 63	145
25	The Fabulous Four	151

26	Interlude	158
27	A Factory of Death	161
28	Moving Out	175
29	Bergstein	180
30	Counterattack	182
31	The Church	186
32	The Charge	192
33	Hill 400	198
34	*Their* "Longest Day"	205
35	Nightfall	215
36	December 8	218
37	Final Assault on Bergstein	222
38	Relief Finally Arrives	225
39	The Bulge	227
40	Back to Hürtgen	235
41	Crossing the Roer	237
42	The Last Act	244
	Epilogue	249
	Notes	253
	Acknowledgments	287
	Index	289
	Photographs following page 146	

MAPS

Dog Company at Pointe du Hoc 48
Dog Company in the Brest Campaign 139
Dog Company in Hürtgen Forest 165
Dog Company's Thrust into Germany 229

Prologue

June 6, 1984, Pointe du Hoc, Normandy

Flags fluttered in the breeze as the flash of cameras dovetailed President Ronald Reagan's stirring words. The speech marked the fortieth anniversary of D-Day in a special place, a sacred place. Solemn yet impassioned, President Reagan addressed the watchful crowd and the entire nation:

"We stand on a lonely, windswept point on the northern shore of France. The air is soft, but forty years ago at this moment, the air was dense with smoke and the cries of men, and the air was filled with the crack of rifle fire and the roar of cannon. At dawn, on the morning of the sixth of June, 1944, two hundred and twenty-five Rangers jumped off the British landing craft and ran to the bottom of these cliffs. Their mission was one of the most difficult and daring of the invasion: to climb these sheer and desolate cliffs and take out the enemy guns. The Allies had been told that some of the mightiest of these guns were here and they would be trained on the beaches to stop the Allied advance.

"The Rangers looked up and saw the enemy soldiers—the edge of the cliffs shooting down at them with machine guns and throwing grenades. And the American Rangers began to climb. They shot rope ladders over the face of these cliffs and began to pull themselves up. When one Ranger fell, another would take his place. When one rope was cut, a Ranger would grab another and begin his climb again. They climbed, shot back, and held their footing. Soon, one by one, the Rangers pulled themselves over the top, and in seizing the firm land at the top of these cliffs, they began to seize back the continent of Europe. Two hundred and twenty-five came here. After two days of fighting, only ninety could still bear arms. . . ."

One of the finest speeches of the Cold War, Reagan's words touched each of the veteran Rangers, now senior citizens, who stood shoulder to shoulder before him. Rays of sun gently lit their faces, now lined with age, as the President's words warmed their hearts.

Earlier, sixty-something Ranger veteran Herman Stein had miraculously reenacted the climb. A dozen young Green Berets—all Ranger-qualified and serving in West Germany—scaled the ninety-foot cliffs along with the veteran. His brother Rangers initially tried to dissuade Stein, now a roofer, from attempting this feat. Leonard G. Lomell, Dog Company's first sergeant on D-Day, jokingly chided Stein, "Sixty-year-old Rangers shouldn't try to compete against the Green Berets. We're too old for this nonsense now."

The former Dog Company Ranger didn't listen. He not only scaled the precipice, but also out-climbed the younger Green Berets, easily beating them to the top. The crowd roared. The massive arms of Ranger Captain Otto Masny, who was affectionately called "Big Stoop" during the war, enveloped Stein in a bear hug. After his climb, Stein greeted the awaiting crowd and jokingly spoke a few words: "All these younger guys will be all right if they just stick with it. They hug the cliff too much."

After President Reagan delivered his speech, he approached the line of veteran D-Day Rangers, each dressed in blue blazers with their distinctive, hard-won Ranger patches prominently displayed along with their combat infantry badges and numerous medals. Now, thanks to the President's rousing words, America had finally recognized the extreme bravery and sacrifices of its WWII veterans, acknowledging them as an example of the sacrifices needed to win the Cold War.

The President and First Lady Nancy Reagan hugged each of those Rangers present—Leonard G. Lomell, Tom Ruggiero, Jack Kuhn, L-Rod Petty, Frank South, and the others—but took a particular liking to the last man in line, Herman Stein. "Reagan was all over the moon about my climbing to the top of Pointe du Hoc. I think he wished he could have done it with me."

As the President and the audience thought back on the invasion of Normandy on D-Day, several of the Dog Company Rangers couldn't help but reflect on *their* "longest day," December 7, 1944.

★ ★ ★

December 7, 1944, Bergstein, Germany: Hill 400

"Fix bayonets!" barked Captain Otto Masny, the hulking Ranger officer.

In a scene reminiscent of a World War I battle, both sides stared at each other across a no man's land. Lomell gazed beyond snow-covered ground the size of a football field as his eyes looked up at the ominous mount towering in front of Dog Company. Germans had dug foxholes at the base of the hill and manned bunkers. The icy, flat expanse made an ideal killing field. Germans held their fingers poised on the triggers of their machine guns; with a rate of fire of up to 1,500 rounds per minute, the gunners stood ready to tear the Rangers' bodies to pieces.

BOOM! BOOM! BOOM! BOOM!

A creeping artillery barrage and mortars slowly closed in on Dog Company.

Like a tightly wound, coiled spring, tension within the Rangers' ranks soon reached a breaking point. The acrid stench of cordite assaulted their nostrils. They knew the American artillery exploding in front of them would soon intersect with the German mortars dropping behind them. With Dog sandwiched between the ordnance from both forces, the falling fire would turn the company to hamburger meat within seconds.

Suddenly, a Ranger stood up, raised his tommy gun above his head and screamed: "Let's go get the bastards!"

A Dog Company officer yelled, "Go!"

The Rangers fired a tremendous volley into the German positions facing them. In unison, they stood and let loose a blood-curdling Rebel yell as they charged across the open field.

"WA-WOO-WOOHOO! WA-WOO-WOOHOO! WA-WOO-WOOHOO!"

Shooting from the hip, the Rangers rushed through the snow-crusted field. "We stood up just like in a movie. It was like seeing a wave in the football field.... We went over the field as one," remembered one Ranger.

Mortars and artillery shells exploded next to the men as Dog Company charged into a hail of bullets. Rangers began falling, wounded and maimed in the intense fire. German machine guns opened up from behind a nearby bunker and other positions. Halfway across the field, the Ranger charge grew staggered, as some men ran faster than others. Lomell's heart pounded and his adrenaline surged as he and the other men raced across the field toward Hill 400.

Stunned by the sight of 120 seemingly crazy Americans screaming and yelling as they charged, some of the Germans abandoned their pillboxes and machine gun positions and ran for their lives up the hill.

A Ranger later reflected on the moment: "With bayonets shining, hip firing, and yelling a battle cry that probably goes back into the eons of time, we charged into the jaws of death."

CHAPTER 1

Dog Company

March 1943—Fort Meade, Maryland

"From here over, this is Dog Company, 2nd Ranger Battalion," the captain ordered, parting the group of volunteers with a wave of his hand. Unbeknownst to the men, that moment marked the birth of one of the greatest Ranger companies in American history. However, before earning the honor of being called a Ranger, they would have to engage in grueling training that would test the limits of human endurance.

The men stood at attention, stomachs pulled in, heels together, and eyes fixed forward on the Ranger officer who had just addressed them. With his uncanny resemblance to Lee Marvin, Captain Harold K. "The Duke" Slater made a dashing figure. The Duke possessed an undying spirit to win—at all costs. He was the quintessential Ranger officer. On that clear, sunny day in March, an eclectic group of volunteers had clambered off a 6x6 GMC truck and spilled out into an open field. After meeting their new commander, the men watched as the captain ducked back in the building and returned with another Ranger. The Duke announced, "This is my first sergeant, Leonard Lomell." Cut from the same competitive cloth as Slater, Leonard G. Lomell led by example. The brilliant first sergeant also had a gift for being incredibly lucky.

Slater turned to Lomell. "Find out when we can feed this bunch."

Lomell nodded his head and sent the men over to Fort Meade's chow hall. Fort Meade, named after the famous Union commander and hero of Gettysburg, served as the training center for the U.S. Army. It housed the 76th Division, otherwise known as the "Liberty Bell Division," which served as a training cadre for other Army units. Three and a half million men filtered through the camp. In addition to its combat training facilities, it housed a school for cooks and a special service unit, which trained entertainers and musicians, including the famous swing-band leader Glenn Miller. But during March 1943, the camp gave birth to another legendary band of men.

Slater's volunteers were an eclectic group of desperados drawn from the ranks of the 76th Division. As a newly minted D Company member, Bill Hoffman made his way through the chow line with the other raw recruits. His mind drifted back across the events of that whirlwind, life-changing day. The morning announcements posted on the bulletin board had included a small sentence about the Rangers: "Anybody interested in volunteering for the Rangers should come down to the orderly room." Several of Hoffman's comrades had asked, "What's the Rangers?" One joked, "Hey, maybe we can get a horse!"

Hoffman wasn't completely sure what a Ranger was either, but he knew they were something special. He fought tooth and nail to get into the outfit so that he could escape his old unit. Bill Hoffman knew he was going to war, and he wanted to go into battle with the best.

That March morning after reading the announcements, Hoffman reported to the orderly room. The first sergeant on duty promptly tossed him back out and barked, "Get back to work."

Not easily rebuffed, Hoffman decided to stand outside the orderly room and wait for the company commander. When the commanding officer arrived, he asked Hoffman, "What are you doing standing out here?"

For Hoffman, it was the moment of truth. He explained that he had come down to sign up for the Rangers, but the first sergeant hadn't let him stay.

"Go on inside," the commander instructed, entering with Hoffman.

After looking over some paperwork, the commander told the irritable first sergeant, "I don't see a problem here. Process Sergeant Hoffman."

When the first sergeant chased Bill Hoffman out of the orderly room for the second time that day, it was different: he knew he would return to become a Ranger. "Get your butt out of here. Get back here at 1 P.M. and turn in your gear."

The term "Ranger" goes back hundreds of years. Rangers were first commissioned as an American unit in 1676 during King Philip's War. Vulnerable to hostile Indian attacks and finding European battle tactics unsuited to the wild American frontier, colonists acted as scouts or "ranged," and then struck back at the Indians using stealth hit-and-run tactics. The Americans honed these unique fighting techniques a century later in the French and Indian War. During that war, the colonists implemented numerous concepts that still apply to modern conflicts: irregular warfare, use of proxies, and special operations.

Perhaps the most famous American Ranger was a New Hampshire backwoodsman named Robert Rogers. A debtor implicated in a counterfeiting scheme, Rogers had a checkered past. But he received a British Army commission in what later became known as His Majesty's Independent Company of American Rangers. A forefather of American special operations, Rogers developed something known as the twenty-eight *Rules of Ranging*, a manual of practices that today's Rangers still learn. During the French and Indian War, Rogers and his men conducted deep raids into French and Indian territory. They hit French forts and ruthlessly annihilated an entire Abenaki Indian village. For his lightning raids, stealth, and ruthlessness, the Indians dubbed Rogers the *Wobomagonda* or "White Devil."

Other units called Rangers followed Rogers', including Captain Daniel Morgan's Ranger Battalion during the Revolutionary War, and later in the Civil War, the infamous Mosby's Rangers. Known as the "Gray Ghost," John S. Mosby terrorized the Union Army with his guerrilla tactics, blowing up rail lines and sabotaging Yankee camps.

During World War II, Lucian K. Truscott, then a colonel, encouraged General George Marshall to create a training program patterned along the lines of the British Commandos. Begrudgingly, General Marshall and Dwight D. Eisenhower approved the plan, but they advised Truscott, "I hope you will find some other name than 'Commando,' for the glamour of that name will always remain—and properly so—British." Truscott found his inspiration in Rogers and the colonial Rangers. He wrote in his memoirs, "I selected 'Rangers' because few words have a more glamorous connotation in American military history. In colonial days, men so designated had mastered the art of Indian warfare and were guardians of the frontier."

The man selected to lead the first American Ranger unit was Major William O. Darby, who formed the 1st Ranger Battalion out of two thousand recruits. Through rigorous training, he winnowed the group down to just 520 men. The Rangers then trained at the British Commando Training Depot in Achnacarry Castle, Scotland. The exploits of Darby's Rangers became legendary. They spearheaded the assaults in North Africa, Sicily, and Italy.

Although the unit was new, the men of the 2nd Ranger Battalion had to measure up to a prestigious legacy formed over hundreds of years.

The mainspring of Dog Company was Leonard G. Lomell, the twenty-three-year-old first sergeant. Born in Brooklyn, New York, Lomell was adopted by immigrant parents and grew up in Point Pleasant, New Jersey. After graduating from high school, he hoped to enter West Point; however, because of his adoption, issues arose regarding his birth certificate. Instead of West Point, Lomell entered Tennessee Wesleyan College and graduated in 1941. Over the summers, he worked at the Post Office and did manual labor for the Pennsylvania Railroad, for construction companies, and for a dredge company. After entering the military on June 13, 1942, Lomell became a rising star. His superiors quickly promoted him to platoon sergeant of a regimental intelligence and reconnaissance platoon within the 76th Infantry Division. Acknowledging his keen mind and leadership potential, the division soon sent Lomell through Ranger training. Built like a middleweight boxer, the good-looking young man with a generous soul made for an ideal first sergeant.

Hailing from Indiana, Lomell's commander, Harold K. "Duke" Slater, was only a year older. The Duke loved to win. With an amazing intensity, Dog's commanding officer always focused on the mission at hand. Good-looking and charismatic, The Duke had a softer side that he rarely showed: he had "a beautiful spirit and cherished every moment of life." His dry sense of humor often poked through his stern role as a commander. Like Lomell, Slater enjoyed a meteoric rise within the military and obtained the rank of captain in 1943.

Within several days, Lomell, Slater, and the core of D Company boarded a troop train and headed south to Nashville, Tennessee. Southeast of the city near the town of Tullahoma, the men arrived at Camp Nathan Bedford Forrest, named for the southern cavalry general. During World War II, Camp Forrest was largely a tent city nestled in the sandy hills and lush pines of southern Tennessee. Shoved in one corner of the facility, Dog Company had its own street of pyramidal U.S. government-issued tents. But the weather of April 1943 wasn't kind to the young volunteers. It rained nearly every day. Tents flooded, and the men trudged through oozy red mud to perform a regimented routine. Making matters even worse, the muggy spring weather brought with it swarms of biting horseflies. The nearest shower was a half a mile away in wooden barracks that housed another unit, so most men bathed in washbasins.

As they formed up in the sticky Tennessee clime, the 2nd Ranger Infantry Battalion* included six assault companies, designated A

*The full designation for a Ranger Battalion in World War II includes "Infantry" in its official title. For the remainder of the book, it will be referred to as "2nd Ranger Battalion."

through F, or Able, Baker, Charlie, Dog, Easy, and Fox. Only the core group of Dog Company arrived at Camp Forrest as a ready-made unit; the rest were assembled in Tennessee. Headquarters Company completed the 2nd Ranger Battalion. Each company consisted of sixty-five enlisted men and three officers. In all, the battalion totaled approximately five hundred officers and enlisted men. That brought the 2nd Rangers up to a little more than half the strength of the typical, nine-hundred-man infantry battalion.

Dog Company was divided into two rifle platoons, each commanded by a first lieutenant. The company headquarters section included the company commander, first sergeant, company clerk, and messenger. Each rifle platoon contained two Assault Sections and a Special Weapons Section with a 60 mm mortar. Each Assault Section contained an assault squad and a light machine gun squad.

The original core of Dog Company hailed from the Northeast. But on April 1, 1943, volunteers from all across the United States augmented the original men from Fort Meade. The new recruits came from all walks of life and had been recruited from units throughout the military, including cavalry, artillery, armor, and infantry—even a few castoffs from other units.

The nascent nature of the 2nd Ranger Battalion made it a dumping ground for undesirable men. *"What did I get into?"* one Ranger volunteer wondered. "When we had to retreat at night, each company would give their report, which included a lot of AWOLs. We had the dregs of the Army, actually. Division commanders sent their eight balls to the 2nd Rangers in order to get rid of those men. The Rangers were new then, and the Army really didn't know what to do with us."

In the early days of America's entry into World War II, special operations forces were in their infancy. The Office of Strategic Services (OSS), the Marine Corps Raiders, and the U.S. Army Rangers were developing some of the precursors to today's modern special operations units. The regular military brass disparagingly viewed the special units as "bleeding off" good men from regular combat units. As a result, the Rangers often faced internal challenges to their very existence. On the upside, these challenges gave the 2nd Battalion a bit of a *Dirty Dozen* feel, which filled the unit with tough men willing to do what was thought to be impossible, while the rigorous training eliminated the men who shouldn't have been there.

But the volunteer recruits of April 1943 weren't Rangers yet. Before they could earn that honor, they had to endure training meant to break most men. At Camp Forrest, the training exercises created for the men were even more difficult than combat itself. "What they really tried to do was destroy us. They wanted to see what the human body and the human mind [could handle. We were] psychologically young men, chosen young men, volunteers. All Ranger training was the toughest the armchair generals could make it. I felt that combat was a piece of cake as compared to the training," recalled Dog Company's first sergeant.

Vigorous competition allowed only the fittest to survive. Lomell remembered, "In those days, I saw all-American football players, the most magnificent specimens of men you ever saw, I saw them thrown right out of the Rangers, DQ'd, physically unqualified or psychologically unqualified. [And then] you'd find a little old farm boy that weighed one hundred to one hundred and ten pounds from Iowa that had it all, psychologically and otherwise. It was fascinating to me to see the process."

Lomell and Slater imbued in the men a gritty sense of competition that hardened like steel those who survived the training. It was about winning, being the best. Ranger officers like Slater led by example and weren't afraid to challenge their own men. Captain Slater's competitive streak even affected First Sergeant Lomell when Slater challenged his subordinate to a boxing match.

"You think you're pretty tough, huh?" asked Slater.

Lomell quickly realized the problems that would be created by fighting his company commander. He thought to himself, *"Jesus Christ, he's the company commander. I'm the first sergeant. I don't mind boxing an exhibition out here. One of us has got to go one of these times, and it isn't going to be me. It certainly isn't going to be me knocking him out."*

Slater was "one of those guys you couldn't box with because he was trying to knock you out with every blow," noted Lomell. "You couldn't have any fun boxing with somebody who was trying to kill you with every blow."

Lomell tried to kid his way around the issue, offering, "You know, Captain, maybe you ought to box with the officers, and us enlisted guys, we're a little reluctant to get too tough with you guys."

Slater's ultimate objective seemed obvious to the first sergeant *"He's never going to quit until he knocks me cold, and I don't want that in front of my whole company!"*

Slater persisted in his challenge, and eventually Lomell climbed in the ring with him. Surprisingly, Slater went down, not Lomell, "and that damn near killed him. Oh, he was quiet!"

Lomell later remarked, "Duke Slater was the roughest, toughest, bravest, most courageous officer we had." He added, "I loved the son of a bitch, but I hated him at times."

A typical day for a Ranger recruit in Dog Company went as follows:

0645 First Call
0700 Reveille
0715 Breakfast
0830 Drill Call
1130 Recall
1200 Lunch
1300 Drill Call
1530 Recall
1715 Retreat

Drill Call included calisthenics followed by the command "Assume position." Half a dozen Rangers would approach a giant twelve- or fourteen-foot-long telephone pole lying on the ground. Next, the commander barked, "Ready. Exercise!" The men lifted the log to their waists. The sergeant then hollered orders to place the log over their heads, on their shoulders, and in a variety of other positions. Muscles ached and throbbed as this torture went on for more than thirty minutes. "It made a man out of you," recalled Morris Webb, then a round-faced, prematurely balding recruit from Kentucky. Webb, who spoke with a characteristic Southern drawl, had a mind for numbers. He was pals with a northerner, Bud Potratz, who arrived at Camp Forrest at nearly the same time.

Throughout training, the men worked in pairs, and formed unbreakable bonds through this buddy system. They lived together, trained together, ate together, and shit together. They each had the other's back, and covered one another when negotiating certain training exercises. The Ranger training built friendships that lasted a lifetime. In battle, it reinforced a sense of brotherhood and, from a practical standpoint, allowed the mission to carry on despite casualties: if one buddy was hit, the other could carry on.

After training every day, the men were bone tired. Once they had dinner, they settled in for a tiny bit of downtime before the next day. One evening after training, a large crowd gathered around the tents. An ambulance arrived. The driver was furious. He was muttering something unintelligible while waving his hands. Webb, noticing the crowd of Rangers standing in a circle next to an OD tent, asked his buddy Potratz, "What's up?"

"Pat McCrone and Larry Johnson are at it again," Potratz chuckled. McCrone and Johnson were best friends who were well known for their practical jokes; but Potratz finished the sentence saying, "McCrone is dead."

It began when Johnson confronted McCrone for stealing his girlfriend. "You son of a bitch! If there's anything I hate, it's a double-crossing rat!"

Johnson pulled out a .45 and pointed it at McCrone, who promptly took off for the exit of the barracks and ran outside. Johnson fired several shots from the pistol, and McCrone fell to the ground. With the men in a panic, someone called an ambulance. When the ambulance arrived at the scene, McCrone was lying motionless on the ground. Suddenly, McCrone rose up and started laughing. McCrone and Johnson put their arms around each other, laughing their asses off. The ambulance driver wasn't laughing, however. The two best friends had played another joke—but nobody else thought it was funny. Luckily, Slater never found out about the incident; otherwise, both men likely would have been busted to private. A stern disciplinarian, The Duke didn't put up with bullshit.

In between the workouts —and the hijinks—the men got lessons in teambuilding. Drill call also included time in the "pit." The waist-deep sawdust pit measured eighteen-feet square with logs lining each side. Bill Hoffman explained, "They'd put a whole platoon in there with no shirts on. The other platoon was on the outside. The object was the guys on the outside needed to throw the guys on the inside out of the pit. On the side it was maybe two logs high, not very high. It was just high enough to keep the sawdust in."

"Go get 'em! Grab 'em by the neck," the bystanders would shout. "Throw 'em out! Throw 'em out!"

After a few times in the pit, Hoffman's group learned that the secret to surviving in the pit was to send two guys after each of the soldiers lining the pit. "Guys got hurt doing that," he recounted. "All our fatigues would start getting ripped up. We'd have torn fatigues. You'd turn it in to supply and get a new pair. The quartermaster got smart to it and then started to just sew up the uniforms rather than issue new ones." One of the smallest Rangers in the unit tried a different strategy, "I played it smart. I got in the corner. That would help the other guys throw people out." As soon as a platoon removed the opposing force from the pit, they had three minutes to prepare to defend against another assault.

D Company earned a formidable reputation when word leaked out that one of the company's platoons had cleaned out the pit in two minutes flat. "It was about competition. It was one platoon against the other," explained Hoffman. "It was just to see how much you could take."

To give the men a taste of combat, the commanders subjected Dog Company to a harrowing obstacle course. Machine guns fired over their heads as the Rangers slithered under barbed wire, swung on ropes, and crawled through mock shell holes. At the same time, the training officers detonated explosives to simulate shells and mortar rounds.

Near the end of the afternoon, the men sat and listened to demolitions experts who taught them the finer points of blowing up stuff. As the men of Dog watched intently during one session, Ranger Joe Camelo held on too long to a block of TNT. To everyone's horror, the blast nearly killed him as it vaporized his arm. Another Ranger had a block of TNT detonate between his legs. Fortunately, he survived the blast—but his family jewels did not.

One of the Ranger demolition instructors was prankster Larry Johnson, the one man who *shouldn't* have been allowed to play with explosives. Johnson lit a stick of dynamite during one demonstration. As the men watched, Johnson threw it into a crowd of seated Ranger recruits. "Terrified, everyone ran in opposite directions," recalled one Ranger. The "charge" was actually just an empty tube of cardboard.

Johnson achieved his greatest coup when he threw a *real* stick of lighted dynamite down the latrine and got away with it. Once again, everyone scattered. "Shit was flying everywhere," recalled one Ranger. Remarkably, even after a full investigation under the strict scrutiny of Duke Slater, Johnson managed to evade punishment.

Cocky tomfoolery aside, the training imbued the men with a winning spirit, a sense that they were better than any other combat soldiers in the world. The men were taught not only to be the best but also to fight dirty and outsmart their German and Japanese counterparts. Throughout the training, the men learned "Rangerism," which, an official training manual characterized as "the doctrine of a personal fight, a brain-and-brawn fight, a genius American fight, and a carefully thought out, dirtier fight that will top the instinctive, and naturally dirty fight of a blond, square-headed, self-appointed superman and the undersized, slant-eyed, yellow 'Nips' who wage war against us on two fronts today."

CHAPTER 2

"Rangers? Bullshit!"

Standing at attention, the men baked in the hot summer Tennessee sun as the square-jawed Ranger looked Dog Company up and down, snarling, "Rangers? Bullshit!" Disappointed by the entire battalion's progress, the veteran Ranger chewed them out for their lackluster performance. To hammer home his points, he attempted to inspire the trainees by recounting the exploits of Darby's Rangers, regaling them with tales about night raids in the African desert, where they slit the throats of enemy soldiers and made long perilous marches behind enemy lines. He finished by ordering the 2nd Rangers out on an arduous march of their own.

With Ranger training in its infancy, the 2nd Battalion had brought over several veterans of Darby's 1st Ranger Battalion. Among them was Dean H. "Blood-in-the-Boots" Knudson. Ranger Sheldon Bare from Altoona, Pennsylvania, recalled Knudson's parting line before sending the men on countless, multi-mile "speed marches": "There better be blood in your boots after the march!"

Geared up in full equipment, including gas masks, the Rangers tromped throughout the Tennessee countryside. One ball-busting speed march required them to traverse seventy miles in three days. Herman Stein remembered another occasion when Slater ordered Dog to march thirty-six miles in twelve hours with only one canteen of water each.

Born on Staten Island, "Herm" Stein grew up with a silver spoon in his mouth until his family lost everything in the Great Depression. Despite his family's difficulties, he retained his love of life and remained generous to a fault. These qualities followed Stein through the killing fields of WWII and beyond. He was destined to become a great Ranger and an even greater man.

On that particular speed march, Stein noted, "By midafternoon, the fellows were dropping like flies. Even The Duke fell ill—a victim of stomach cramps, which forced him to drop out of the march. That was a tipping point for Stein and several buddies, who thought, *"If these guys want to run themselves to exhaustion, go ahead, but we're going to do something about it."*

According to Stein, "On one extended break, we stopped by a swampy section, filled up our canteens, added a couple of iodine pills, and presto, instant revitalization. This was a civilian soldier's way of thinking. You take orders to a degree, but when it interferes with your rationalization, you start performing like a zombie." That attitude would later get Stein busted in rank. Yet ironically, this ability to think critically was one of the greatest assets the men of Dog Company possessed. It enabled them to act on their own, and even, in extreme cases, to disobey a direct order if it interfered with the mission. On countless occasions, this mindset gave them a decisive edge over their more regimented opponents.

Besides forced marches, Knudson also stressed hand-to-hand combat. Staff Sergeant Jack Kuhn, another Altoona native, helped to demonstrate fighting techniques. Once, as Kuhn deftly completed a judo move, Bare snickered in disbelief. "I thought judo was a bunch of nonsense," admitted Bare. Then he heard his name. "Bare, come up here and hit me with your hardest punch," ordered Kuhn. A five-foot-ten railroad worker, Bare weighed in at a muscular 185 pounds, making him one of the bigger members of the company.

"Come on, hit me," repeated Kuhn.

Not eager to show up his NCO, Bare said, "I don't want to do that, staff sergeant." Bare thought, *"I outweigh him by at least twenty-five pounds. I can flatten him."* But he did as he was ordered. Bare stepped back and put all of his weight in his punch, driving his knuckles toward Kuhn's torso. Kuhn grabbed Bare's arm and flipped him over, throwing his hips into Bare in a perfect judo hip toss. "I remember laying flat on my back looking at the bright Tennessee sun. I was a believer in judo after that."

Throughout the entire training process, men came and went. Tough guys were broken. Ironically, some of the quietest men survived, including Private Edward Secor, who "seemed to have [his] nerves snipped," Webb recalled. "He was fearless."

Unfortunately, the solid leadership in Dog did not translate to the battalion level. During the first few months of training at Camp Forrest, the 2nd Battalion went through a number of commanders. Forty-one-year-old Lieutenant Colonel William C. Saffrons originally commanded Ranger training school. Saffrons ate, breathed, and lived Rangerism. But after only a couple of months on the job, Saffrons received orders for another assignment, leaving the 2nd leaderless.

Major Rogers replaced Saffrons. As the men slogged through a grueling three-day march, Rogers merely rode up and down in a Jeep. That fell far short of the Ranger ideal. Rogers soon found himself replaced by Major Charles R. "Monk" Meyer.

An All-American West Point football player who could run, pass, kick, and play defense, the 150-pound Meyer was also known as "Mighty Mite." But Monk's football prowess didn't translate into Rangerism. The Army-trained halfback lasted only a few weeks before he, too, was sent packing.

The seemingly endless change of leadership, combined with squalid living conditions, caused the Rangers' morale to plummet. Eventually, Major L. E. McDonald assumed command of the battalion and introduced more members of Darby's Rangers to augment the training schedule. It was then that things began to turn around within the battalion. Though leaders credited him with improving Ranger morale, McDonald was soon replaced by Major James Earl Rudder.

CHAPTER 3

Big Jim

"I've been sent down here to restore order and get going with realistic training. Now let me tell you, I'm going to work your asses off. Before you know it, you're going to be the best trained fighting men in this man's army. Now with your cooperation, there will be passes from time to time when you have the time. I'll grant as many leaves and passes as I can. If I don't get your cooperation, we'll still get the job done, but it'll be a lot tougher on you. If such a program does not appeal to you, come to my office, and we'll transfer you out. It's so much better for you and us. Any questions?"

Sitting cross-legged on the ground, hundreds of men in the 2nd Ranger Battalion listened intently to Rudder. At 6 feet tall and 220 pounds, the gravitas of "Big Jim" captured the men's attention. He knew how to lead men, and he knew how to win. In 1932, Rudder graduated from Texas A&M, where he was a standout center on the football team. A year later, Rudder received his commission as second lieutenant in the U.S. Army Reserves and began a career as a high school football coach. Texans consider high school football a Friday night ritual akin to a religion. By 1938, Rudder became a football coach and teacher at Tarleton Agricultural College. But when the war broke out, he volunteered for active duty.

Big Jim had come to the 2nd Ranger Battalion to whip it into shape. One of his first orders involved ditching the tents and putting the men into wooden barracks. This appealed to the men, and morale soared. Like a Texas football coach attempting to get his team into the championships, Rudder cut his recruits no slack, putting them through brutal speed marches and other rigorous training exercises. Through the men were earning the right to be called Rangers, they were failing miserably on the parade ground.

In its first parade ground review, the 2nd Battalion looked like a "ragtag orphan mob, with no military bearing or discipline." Big Jim wasn't used to being humiliated. "Boiling mad and red-faced," Rudder vented and challenged any man in the battalion to step forward and fight him. Not a single man moved. The pace of change within the battalion accelerated. After improving their performance on the parade ground, Rudder coached and molded the men into true Rangers.

And as promised, he granted the men passes for R&R on rare occasions. A local dive bar known as The Wheel & The Hub became a favorite hangout. Equipped with a jukebox, the place served up cold beer along with its share of bar fights.

Under Rudder's leadership, Dog conducted other exercises designed to teach map reading, stealth, and other skills. On one such mission, Sergeant Herman Stein and a buddy received a map with orders to find a point ten miles away while circumventing all houses. "Nearing our destination, tired and hungry, we stumbled into the backyard of a small house. My buddy and I got a friendly greeting from an old lady and an offer for a cool drink and fresh buns. Who could refuse? Wouldn't you know, as we were coming out of the gate, Slater pops around the corner in his Jeep." Cracking the whip, The Duke immediately busted Stein to private.

Stein's closest friend and partner in crime was William "L-Rod" Petty, a private originally from the 30th Infantry Division in the Tennessee National Guard. Petty referred to his buddy Stein as his "pet ape" because of Stein's extraordinary climbing ability. An ex-paratrooper who had broken both legs on his Airborne qualification jump,

Petty moved around with a "sort of waddle like a duck." In time, Petty would become a brilliant Ranger, though he was a constant challenge to authority, and sometimes a "royal pain in the ass." Before he joined the Rangers, this characteristic regularly landed him in trouble—trouble that had him digging many a latrine ditch.

Petty's resentment towards authority began in his childhood. His father regularly beat him for the smallest infractions. "He would lash me, always beginning at the calves of my legs and continuing up my thighs, across my buttocks and to my shoulders. He would reverse it and cover the same area. . . . The pain was excruciating. It was only exceeded by my hatred. By the age of eight, I refused to cry. I just stood there and hated every blow." Petty saw the call for Ranger volunteers as his ticket out of trouble. However, because he was missing both front teeth, Petty had a dental implant, so he failed the Ranger medical screening.

"Sorry, son, you don't qualify. Next man!" barked the medical officer.

"Wait a minute now, sir! What do you mean I don't qualify? I'm in great shape."

"You've got false teeth. You can't be a Ranger with false teeth. There's no way you can get into the Rangers without your choppers, son."

Not one to take no for an answer, Petty had the balls to ask the officer, "Who's the top man here? I want to see him."

The doctor pointed to Rudder's office.

Petty wandered over to the office. "What can I do for you, soldier?" asked Rudder in a Texas drawl.

Petty related the story of being rejected for his teeth. After some back and forth with Rudder, Petty declared, "Hell, sir, I don't want to *eat* 'em—I want to *fight* 'em!"

Rudder then turned to Petty and handed him a slip of paper. "Here, take this back to the medics. You're in."

Both Slater and Rudder had tough standards. During the training, men washed out if they couldn't hack the tough marches and training. A steady stream of volunteer replacements arrived to fill the gaps.

One of those replacements was Sergeant Antonio J. Ruggiero, nicknamed "Ruggie" or "Rugg" by those who couldn't pronounce his name. A professional tap dancer from Plymouth, Massachusetts, the diminutive Ruggiero also had a stage name: Tommy Knight. Before volunteering for the Rangers, Ruggie was a messenger attached to a machine gun unit led by Second Lieutenant Morton McBride. "Big Mac," as the sandy-haired Scots-Irishman was known, was extremely streetwise and shrewd.

Following a seven-day furlough, Ruggiero returned to camp one day early because he wanted to make sure he got back in time. He wandered into the empty command post (CP) and asked, "Where the hell's everybody gone?"

Well, you're not supposed to be back until tomorrow. Why are you back one day sooner?" asked McBride.

Ruggiero answered, "Hey, I just wanted to get back so I wouldn't get into trouble."

"The few other men that are back like you, they're up at the parade field, and Major Rudder* is asking for volunteers to form the new 2nd Ranger Battalion."

Excited about the opportunity to join the special unit, Ruggiero asked, "He's at the parade field?"

"Yeah, he's been up there about a half an hour."

"Boy, I better run up there," Ruggiero said.

As he started running for the field, McBride called after him, "If you're interested...get an application from your first sergeant."

At that point, "the bottom fell right out" of Ruggiero, who thought, *"He'll never give me one. Hell, I'm gonna try anyway."*

Ruggiero was right. When he asked the first sergeant for the application, he growled, "Get out of here! They don't need you. You're too small. Besides, you're staying here until I'm ready to tell you what to do."

"I was so God damn mad. I started to walk back towards my barracks, where I was resigned to stay," remembered Ruggiero.

---

*Rudder would soon be promoted to lieutenant colonel.

Just then, McBride and another officer, Lieutenant Otto Masny, came walking by. Standing six feet and four inches tall, Masny looked like a football tackle. The men fondly called him "Big Stoop" after a then-popular comic book character who also possessed an imposing frame. A born leader, Big Stoop would later command Dog's sister company, Fox.

"Hey, Rugg, you gonna try for the Rangers?"

"Yeah, I'd like to."

"What do you mean you'd 'like' to?" McBride and Masny asked.

"I already went and asked the first sergeant for an application. He won't give it to me."

"Won't give it to you? What do you mean?" they asked, incredulous.

"He said I'm too small."

McBride made a decision. "Come on with us," he said, heading back to the building where the first sergeant was. McBride told Ruggiero to stay outside by the door while he and Masny "went in and chewed the living hell out of him," Ruggiero recalled, laughing.

"You don't have the right to stop anybody who wants to try for hazardous duty," McBride said.

"Oh, you're talking about that dago," retorted the first sergeant.

McBride shot him an icy stare with his steel-gray eyes. "You'll address him by his name. There's no name calling here."

The first sergeant then made the mistake of saying, "He's too damn small, anyways. What do you want, guys to get killed because of this guy?"

McBride looked him in the eye and asked threateningly, "Am *I* too small?"

"No, you're taller than he is."

McBride then said, "I'm not a big guy. I'm five-foot-seven."

As his final retort, the first sergeant added, "Well, I don't know where the hell he went."

Masny then opened the door and said, "Ruggie, get in here."

The first sergeant already had the application in hand. He said, "All right, I'll give him the application, but they'll never take him."

"Don't make a bet on it," warned McBride.

The very next day, Ruggie boarded a truck that took him to meet Rudder, who, along with two 1st Battalion Rangers, was interviewing the new recruits. While waiting for his turn, Ruggie could hear how the other volunteers were answering the questions. Then it was his turn.

"So, you want to be a Ranger, huh?" the interview began. "Do you like to fight with knives?"

"Sure, why not?" answered the tap dancer.

"If I asked you to go cut a guy's throat, would you do it?"

Ruggie knew some of the other men had answered, "Sure, why not?" But he had a better response. "No, why the hell should I?" he told them. "I'd just shoot the bastard."

Rudder and the other Rangers laughed.

"You're not very big, are you?" probed Rudder.

Ruggiero looked him in the eye and said, "You mean I'm not very tall."

"I can see that you aren't. Are you a pretty good shot?" Rudder followed up.

Ruggiero could see Rudder looking down at his service record, which indicated that at three hundred yards, he could hit the center of the bull's eye nine times in a row—an impressive feat.

Reading further down the application form, he noted, "You can dance? That might be useful." Then Rudder looked him in the eye. "You're in."

CHAPTER 4

Fort Pierce and Overseas

The rain pelted the men's faces as they made their way through a driving storm. Water soaked their uniforms while they slogged toward a train on a railroad siding. On board, Dog Company and the rest of the battalion rode all night to Fort Pierce, Florida, the site of the Scouts and Raiders School.

The school actually sat on a small island near the eastern Florida town of Fort Pierce. A heavy dose of Florida sunlight greeted the men, along with large quantities of flies and mosquitoes. "In the daytime, there were sand flies. They would just drive you crazy," recalled Bill Hoffman.

Once the men arrived, the first order of business was assembling several pyramidal tents for the company. Their work completed, the men looked longingly at the water surrounding the island. However, orders came down from the school: "No Swimming!"

After riding the rails for over twelve, hot hours and getting sweaty putting up company tents in the muggy Florida sun, a cool dip in the Atlantic seemed irresistible. So, of course, the men disregarded the order. Several sneaked out of their tents that night and waded into soothing ocean waves that gently lapped against their bodies.

"AAAUUUGGHH!"

Suddenly, the reason for the no-swimming order became abundantly clear. The calm blue water surrounding the island was teeming with jellyfish, including the lethal Portuguese man-of-war. The jellyfish's poisonous tentacles tore into the men's arms and legs, as they hastily exited the water. "They stung like a bastard," recalled Ruggiero.

The next morning, after leading calisthenics and a morning jog, Captain Slater decided that a refreshing swim would be just what the men needed to cool down. As he approached the water, he noticed that most of the company wasn't following him. The Duke soon understood why, when a large Portuguese man-of-war stung him. He quickly jumped out of the water with a painful sting across one of his legs. Everyone struggled to keep in his emotions; no one laughed.

Over the course of the next week, the men learned rubber boat-handling skills—how to maneuver the boats, and how to recover a capsized craft. "The first thing we had to do was learn how to use rubber boats," Ruggiero later remarked. "Held about nine guys. We had to run with those damn rubber boats quite a ways to get out to the water. The waves came in. That's why it was a tough job. We had one officer, and the boat got flipped over from a big wave. Damn near drowned."

They also practiced loading and unloading LCAs (Landing Craft, Assault). Putting their boat-handling skills to use, the men learned how to infiltrate an enemy beachhead, seize mock installations, and stealthily move past the watchful eyes of Navy and Coast Guard sentries posted around Fort Pierce. All up and down the eastern seaboard, American towns had blacked out their lights against a German invasion that never came. Culminating the week of training, the men loaded into LCAs and sailed to a point several miles offshore, where they clambered into the rubber boats. The final test for the Rangers would be to infiltrate the darkened city of Fort Pierce, which had its own civil defense system, including the United States Coast Guard and civilian guards. The exercise was nothing new to Fort

Pierce. Several units had gone through the school prior to the Rangers and the military had alerted the town to the mock exercise.

Smearing green and black camouflage paint on their faces, the battalion broke down into smaller assault groups, each tasked with a specific target, including the town's power station. Dog Company and the rest of the battalion landed on the outskirts of Fort Pierce to seize the town. They successfully took the town by surprise, earning accolades from the school's staff.

As a reward, Rudder issued liberty passes for the next day, allowing the men to visit Fort Pierce. The day ended in an alcohol-laced disaster—several massive fights broke out among the Rangers, "Coasties," and Navy sailors assigned to the town.

By September 17, the Navy sent the battalion packing to Fort Dix, New Jersey. On the long train ride to Fort Dix, some of the men heard the rumor that their commander planned to break up many of the companies. The discipline problems made evident by the carousing in Fort Pierce had encouraged Rudder to shake up his unit in the hopes of eventually generating greater cohesion.

When word of the plan filtered down to Bill Hoffman, he felt like he'd been hit by a hammer. Hoffman was quick to approach Slater.

"Sir, I don't want to leave D Company. This is the best company, and I want to stay with the best company. I really don't want to leave," he begged. Sergeant Hoffman didn't know if his commanders planned to move him to another company or not, but he wanted to pre-empt a move.

Slater smiled faintly before growling back, "Get back to your car."

Fortunately for Hoffman, he wasn't one of the men required to transfer to other companies. Years later, he explained, "Like anything else, you bond with these guys and you just don't want to leave."

Another member of Dog wasn't so lucky. Sergeant Augie Delasandros lived near Fort Dix, and while on the train, he wrote a short note to a couple of his buddies who lived near the fort. In it, he wrote, "Hey, Charlie, Tom, I'm going to be up there. Wait for me, and we'll have a ball." The sergeant gave the letter to the train porter to mail, but eventually, the letter found its way into the hands of the train commander, and then into Slater's.

Lomell and several other men from D were laughing and having a good time in one of the compartments when Slater walked in.

"Sergeant, I want you to go down and place Sergeant Delasandros under house arrest," the captain ordered Lomell.

Flabbergasted by being asked to arrest one of his finest sergeants, Lomell asked, "What do you mean, captain? What the hell did Augie do?"

"The stupid ass [tried to] mail a letter off the troop train by handing it to the porter, and I got it. Do what I tell you."

Stunned, Lomell thought to himself, *"Jesus Christ, this is one of my best friends."* Dutifully, he trudged down the train and approached Sergeant Delasandros. "Augie, I can't believe what I'm going to tell you, it kills me."

"What?" wondered Delasandros.

"You are under arrest, house arrest. You're not allowed to leave this compartment. I got two guards here to sit with you, and that's it. Because you were so stupid, you mailed a letter on a troop train," Lomell informed the stunned sergeant.

"Ah! For Christ's sakes, that's ridiculous!" he protested. "I was only telling a couple of guys up in Fort Dix, my hometown, that we're going to have a ball when we get there and to wait for me."

"Augie, that's not the rules. The rules told us we couldn't do this."

As a result of his court-martial, Sergeant Delasandros left the Rangers, but he went on to serve with an infantry division. "He was decorated two or three times and ultimately killed," recounted Lomell regretfully. "A great guy. He would have been the same great guy for the Rangers; that's the unfairness of it all."

Upon arrival at Fort Dix, the men received furlough and passes. Several of them never returned—AWOL. On October 18, Lomell wrote, "Private Drodouski moved [downgraded from AWOL to absent].

[In] the hands of military authorities as of the 17th. Men anxious to get their hands on him." A typical punishment was a reduction in rank, often down to private. As a private, Drodouski was already at rock bottom in rank, so that threat had no teeth.

Although Drodouski had been in the hands of military authorities in Linden, New Jersey, the clever private, a bit of a Houdini, escaped the local authorities. After his eventual recapture and return to Dog, Slater put Drodouski in the stockade. Lomell remembered, "The CO (commanding officer) was so fed up with this man that he was placed in the stockade for his safety. Upon arriving at the stockade, he pleaded insanity rather than face serious charges. Therefore, he was admitted to the hospital." The clever private's days as a member of Dog Company were over. He faced court-martial, as well as more time in the stockade.

At Fort Dix, men continued to join the unit, including one of the oldest men in the battalion: a forty-year-old pediatrician named Walter Block. Block had an adventurous streak and initially wanted to join the paratroopers. His wife talked him out of it, begging him not to go into the Airborne. After some fast talking, Block convinced her that "the Rangers had something to do with trees, and that was OK by her."

"Doc" Block headed the twelve-man medical section with aide men or medics attached to each assault company. One of those medics was Frank South, who had a brilliant mind. He would later become a tenured professor at the University of Delaware.

After completing their exercises at Dix, where they endured seemingly endless months of intense, rigorous training that broke even the strongest of men, Dog was awarded the blue-and-gold Ranger diamond—visual proof of their "rite of passage" and the right to be called Rangers.

On October 21, 1943, Dog Company and the rest of the battalion climbed into trucks on a blustery, chilly morning in the pre-dawn hours and drove more than two hundred miles to Camp Ritchie, Maryland. During World War II, Camp Ritchie housed an intelligence school and a training ground with mock buildings constructed and arranged to resemble French and German towns. Known as the "Ritchie Boys," the training personnel consisted largely of young Jewish men who had fled Nazi Germany. To strike back at the Nazis, many of the Ritchie Boys later dared to return overseas to serve as soldiers, interrogators, and psychological warfare specialists. For the training exercises, the Boys donned authentic German uniforms and transformed into menacing, German-speaking enemy forces. For added realism, they wielded captured German weapons and utilized maps printed in German.

After the men marched to the battalion bivouac area, they were thrown into the action. Part of the training exercise required Dog Company to infiltrate and capture the top of a mountain. Lomell wrote about what happened next: "We then moved out to the rendezvous point to get ready for the attack; A Company [was] on our left flank, and F Company on our right flank. We moved out for the attack at H hour, met slight resistance and were sent to the top of the ridge. Reports have it that we were the only company to get through the enemy installations. . . . It was a long and tiresome trek, [but] we accomplished our mission."

After completing the field exercise, Dog took intelligence courses and studied the finer points of German uniforms, insignia, and weaponry. They disabled Axis mines and booby traps. Most importantly, they learned how to utilize German rifles, MP-40 machine pistols, and the infamous MG-42 machine guns. Nicknamed the "Bonesaw" or "Hitler's Saw," the Maschinengewehr 42 was one of the most deadly machine guns ever made. With 1,500 rounds per minute sailing through its barrel, the gun sounded like a bed sheet being ripped in two. The bone saw had a rate of fire twice that of any Allied machine gun. Dog would encounter these weapons countless times, so frequently, in fact, that they lost track of the number. And in time, they would have the opportunity to turn the weapons against their makers.

After several intense days of training, the men returned to Fort Dix to conduct the usual camp activities. There, they viewed several propaganda films, including the classic film *Next of Kin*. The brass also force-fed them a campy training film about "sex morality," which the men took with a grain of salt.

The rigorous training schedule slowed as battalion headquarters prepared the men for overseas deployment—even though most of them had no idea where they would be going. Rudder subjected the men to countless inspections, checking and double-checking their gear. Days later, they moved to Camp Shanks, New York, and continued preparations for their overseas deployment. Amid constant warnings about security, they removed their coveted blue diamond Ranger patches from their uniforms.

On the blustery morning of November 20, 1943, the big day arrived. At 8 A.M., Dog Company and the rest of the battalion moved out of the camp by rail. After de-training, the battalion took a ferry to New York.

At the harbor, Pat McCrone remembers looking up at the largest ship he had ever seen in his life. He stared at the massive flat black hull of the RMS *Queen Elizabeth*. Before the war, she was one of the most powerful luxury liners of her day. When the war broke out, the Brits stripped the vessel of all gilt, glitter, and opulent furnishings and transformed the *Elizabeth* into a vessel of war, one of the fastest, biggest troop transports in the world. After the troops made their way up the enormous gangplank, Dog Company headed for their quarters in a passenger lounge on the aft side of the main deck. After they settled in, the battalion drew security detail as MPs (military police) for the voyage.

On November 23, the *Queen Elizabeth* pulled out of New York Harbor unnoticed. For many men in Dog, it was their first time on a large boat, and seasickness soon spread through the ranks like a pandemic. First Sergeant Lomell lost his voice from a "bad case of laryngitis." His best friend Kuhn recalled the moment fondly: "Oh, happy day; quiet at last!"

In between MP duty, the men spent time playing various games and reading, but inter-service rivalry seemed to be the main pastime.

Kuhn recalled that ribbing the Air Corps guys became a "full-time sport, calling them butterflies and USO (United Service Organization) soldiers."

Lucky for the men, the real USO was on the ship and entertained the troops on November 26. But the fun didn't last long for Dog Company. Much to their chagrin, the highly trained, skilled "spec ops" troops of Dog Company were also pulled for KP (kitchen police) duty. They took on the decidedly unglamorous, mundane task of peeling potatoes for the thousands of men on board the *Elizabeth*.

Four days into the voyage, the ship's PX (post exchange), which offered specialty food and other desirable goods, finally opened. The line "stretched for miles before you could even get a Pepsi-Cola or candy." The PX even catered to the more carnal desires of the Rangers; it sold American lipstick and face powder, giving the men the opportunity to "cement foreign relations with the English girls" on the other side of the pond.

The *Elizabeth* sailed without escort. The Navy claimed that she could outrun any U-boat and potentially a torpedo. Still, it was a risk. The troops drilled for an emergency, but as Lomell noted in his diary, "If we were hit, it would be impossible to get on deck due to the crowded conditions."

After nearly a week on the ship, the men were "fed up with the sea and ready to hike again on dry land." MP duty was also taking its toll on Dog Company, "proving to be plain hell." On the last day of November, the tedious trip finally ended when the *Queen Elizabeth* docked in Scotland.

Happy to be back on dry land, the men cheerfully boarded a train that whisked them through picturesque Scottish and English countryside. During the frequent stops along the route, the men had a chance to meet some of the local girls. Greatly impressed with the breathtaking scenery, the men of Dog Company also found themselves captivated by the beauty of the British women.

CHAPTER 5

Bude

In the bright light of early afternoon, the matte-black locomotive pulled into the brick station in the picturesque English coastal town of Bude, Cornwall. Steam hissed out of the train's pistons as its iron wheels slowed and then screeched to a stop.

Located along the southwest tip of England on the Atlantic Ocean, Bude boasts a charming, expansive waterfront, wide, sandy beaches, and many holiday cottages, making it popular with tourists. Farmers from the area used to collect sand from the beaches and spread it on their fields because it contained a natural fertilizer. In fact, farmers found the sand so beneficial that, in 1823, the town built a canal to transport the sand—as well as local limestone and coal—to other parts of England. The area's treacherous surf, which makes it popular with surfers today, contributed, however, to more than one hundred recorded shipwrecks between 1756 and 1969.

In Bude the men stayed in private residences, leaving behind the Spartan barracks of the military bases. "We all received good billets and were made to feel at home. We were treated swell by the English people," noted Lomell.

But the Rangers hadn't come to Bude for the fertile sand or legendary surf; they had come to conquer its towering cliffs. The sheer sandstone cliffs lining Bude's coast soar 75–100 feet in the air, making them perfect for the kind of climbing the Rangers needed to prepare for their D-Day mission, though at the time they didn't know the specifics of that mission.

On December 5, the Rangers started training for the mission that would change the course of the invasion. Without any safety equipment and carrying over thirty pounds of gear, the Rangers climbed the dangerously steep cliffs. Near certain death awaited the man who missed a foothold or unknowingly grabbed a loose rock. Dog spent several weeks scaling the cliffs of Bude, building up the muscles and calluses that would ultimately serve them well in what some would consider to be the toughest mission on D-Day: climbing the daunting cliffs of Pointe du Hoc.

Accompanied by several officers and noncoms, Captain Slater observed the progress of his men as he strolled with his characteristic swagger along the top edge of the cliffs, which jutted out into the Atlantic. None of his men were skilled climbers. They were learning "on the job" the difficult techniques that would enable them to successfully scale dangerous precipices, even while under enemy fire. Below Slater, the men of Dog toiled and sweated, hoisting themselves up the face of the cliff. The men quickly learned how to climb ropes using only their hands. Despite the extreme peril and challenges, over the next several weeks, the entire company "showed very well."

To break up the intensity of the dangerous training routine, Slater organized a football game between 1st and 2nd Platoon. Everyone came out a winner. To satisfy the competitive nature of the company and to "save argument, the score ended in a tie."

The men continued their climbing exercises in Bude, and "stress was placed on scrambling much faster." A few days into the training regimen, several large wooden crates arrived. After prying the tops off, each squad took delivery of two M1918 Browning Automatic Rifles, known as BARs. Capable of firing approximately 500-650 rounds per minute, these light machine guns were a remnant of World War I. The BARs greatly increased the firepower of Dog Company, whose rifle squads carried tommy guns and M1 Garand rifles.

At this point, British Commandos stepped in to augment the training of the 2nd Ranger Battalion for its mission on D-Day; however, at the time, none of the Rangers, including Rudder, knew what their mission would be. Veterans since the earliest days of the war, the Commandos had pioneered special operations tactics. Six-foot-four Lieutenant Colonel Thomas Trevor led the Commando cadre assigned to the Rangers. Detached from No. 1 Commando, Trevor carried a swagger stick and exuded the confidence of a man who'd been on countless combat missions. An expert on cliff climbing, the officer had formerly led No. 1 Commando in North Africa. A childhood spent reading about knights and castles shaped Trevor's views of war, leading him to develop some unorthodox survival tactics.

He demonstrated for the Rangers a strange move he believed would throw off a potential sniper's bullet: by taking a stutter-step, then a long step, and a short step, followed by a sidestep, Trevor had successfully thrown off the aim of many an enemy in North Africa. Even without the benefit of combat experience, the new Rangers had their doubts about the maneuver, and few of them adopted it. But Trevor wasn't there to teach them to avoid bullets; his job was to train them to climb cliffs.

Led by Trevor, with assistance from Rudder and several other officers, the men began getting ready for their mission. Later, the Rangers would be involved in planning the actual mission down to the minutest details. With time of the essence, Dog Company and the rest of the 2nd Ranger Battalion underwent some of the most intensive and difficult training of any Allied unit of the invasion: for the next six months, they would climb sheer 100- to 300-foot cliffs.

To give the Rangers combat experience, the Commandos started to integrate some of Dog Company into their operations, which involved conducting raids up and down the coast of occupied France. On December 17, McBride, the freckle-faced Scotch-Irishman, and Cruz, a smart, dark-complexioned Latino, detached from Dog Company to take part in a special mission with the British Commandos. Donning Commando uniforms, the pair embarked with the Commando unit for the French coast. After landing on a beach, the Commando team and the two Dog Company Rangers scaled a large cliff.

At the top, they cut through the barbed wire and slowly slithered through the opening with their hearts racing while twenty or thirty heavily armed German soldiers patrolled the area. As the bright December moon began to shine, it removed their cover. The Germans spotted Cruz, McBride, and the British Commandos. The men hastily aborted their mission and frantically scurried back down the cliff on their ropes. In the nick of time, a small boat picked them up and safely returned them to Bude.

Despite the less-than-spectacular results of the raid, the Commandos again tapped Dog for another mission. Lomell lined the men up in parade formation. The Duke sauntered out and addressed the men. "All right, you guys, listen up. The following named personnel will meet me in the air raid shelter behind company headquarters immediately after this formation: Lomell, Kuhn, McCrone, Johnson, Hoffman, Sparaco, Stevens . . ."

Several other men heard their names called and headed for the shelter.

"Men, you know how we stressed security and the importance of training. You all have been selected to undergo special training with the Fourth Commandos for a mission in the very near future. . . . You've been hoping to get in on the action, and it looks like you're going to get your wish. Get your gear packed."

The twelve men from Dog Company would become part of a reconnaissance raid on the island of Herm, one of the occupied Channel Islands. The Germans seized Herm and the other Channel Islands shortly after the fall of France, and the Allies wanted to know more about the German defenses. The men yearned for action after months of combat training. However, anti-climactically, command scrubbed the mission due to inclement weather and other factors.

Tomfoolery once again crept into the intense training schedule at Bude when Dog Company got into a scuffle with an English artillery unit. The two groups had exchanged words on several occasions, but

Dog was to have the last laugh. Sergeant Larry Johnson, an ex-artilleryman, led the Rangers on a midnight "raid" on the English artillery unit's guns. He showed them how to "take the breach mechanism down on the English artillery pieces. The men then removed the firing pins and brought them back to their billets." With their guns neutered, the Englishmen boiled in rage. Dog graciously returned the mechanisms on Christmas Day so their allies could "carry out their fire mission."

For many of the men, that day was their first Christmas overseas. To prevent the possibility of homesickness, The Duke thoughtfully scheduled another training exercise. "The company attacked a heavily held force of fellow Rangers holed up in a school. . . . A bridge was demolished without detection, and numerous recon raids were held with the loss of only two men being taken prisoner."

The day ended with a holiday feast of mashed potatoes, turkey, gravy, and peas. They washed it all down with some English ale, a special gift from the battalion. Dog Company had been together for nearly a year, and the men had become a family.

On January 4, 1944, Dog headed over to the amphibious base used by Commandos on the doomed Dieppe Raid of 1942, during which the Germans slaughtered many Commandos on the beach at Dieppe, France. While there, the Rangers learned about the different types of amphibious craft. They made several trial runs and landings. The Rangers experienced "the feeling when one gets wet in the month of January in the cold sea," but the cold water of the Atlantic didn't douse the men's desire for combat. As Kuhn wrote, "The vision of a possible raid and combat is imminent in each and every one's mind. We were raring to go."

CHAPTER 6

The Needles

The five-foot-six Ranger hugged the massive thirty-story cliff. Sweat poured down his face as he peered up at the side of the 300-foot sandstone precipice. Looking up, he reckoned he needed to climb another 150 feet reach the top. Climbing the thick hemp rope, he gingerly maneuvered his foot into a crack in the brittle precipice he used as a toehold. But as T/5 (Technician Fifth Class) Raymond J. Riendeau moved his foot, the cliff crumbled. He was in free fall. Time seemed to stand still as his body rushed to meet the ground. The medics ran over to what they thought was a dead man. But somehow, the black-haired, lanky Ranger miraculously managed to rise up on his own, earning him the nickname "Tough Guy." Just a few hours after being admitted to the hospital, Tough Guy was again climbing the treacherous cliffs.

A few days earlier, on January 17, Dog Company had boarded LCAs and set off for the Isle of Wight. The small island town of Freshwater was near The Needles, imposing, chalky cliffs that soared above the beach. For Dog Company, it represented the ultimate challenge: 300-foot cliffs composed of brittle, crumbling sandstone that made for perilous climbing.

Riendeau was not the only Ranger to defy death while climbing. About a week earlier, Dog spent a day at Alum Bay, scaling more cliffs while carrying heavy equipment without safety harnesses. Lieutenant

McBride fell from a 120-foot cliff—the equivalent of a twelve-story building—and somehow survived. After "bouncing against the cliffs," he landed in a pile of soft dirt. Another Ranger experienced a similar twist of fate. But "both men were fortunate in that the cliff face was composed of soft sand. Neither man was injured, miraculously."

Amazingly, Riendeau himself only suffered slight bruises, minor lacerations, and a sprained back. But Doc Block admitted him to the hospital for further evaluation. As Riendeau entered the hospital, he saw Ruggiero who was just leaving. "What the hell happened to you?" asked Ruggiero. Matter-of-factly, Riendeau responded, "I fell off the cliff."

"I'm leaving and you're coming in," responded Ruggiero, who had nearly bled to death in the hospital several days earlier.

Ruggie was hospitalized for a different reason that also nearly cost him his life. His family, Ruggie later explained, "didn't believe in circumcision. I kept getting urinary infections." To remedy the problem, Ruggiero checked into a British hospital for the procedure. "They didn't do a very good job, though," he commented. The only American in the hospital, Ruggie almost became one of the unit's first casualties. The first operation was a disaster and extremely painful. Awake for the circumcision, Ruggiero said, "It felt like the doctor was using a 'horse needle' to perform the procedure." While he was lying in bed after the surgery, blood began pooling in front of him. Alarmed, one of the Commandoes sharing a room with the recovering Dog soldier yelled, "The Yankee is going to bleed to death!"

The second time around, the doctors put the tap dancer to sleep. Afterwards, to prevent infection, they gave him sanitary pads—the kind women use during menstrual cycles. Embarrassed, Ruggiero managed to hide the pads from the men—all except First Lieutenant McBride. McBride taunted, "I'm going to tell everybody what you're wearing!" Fortunately for Ruggie, Big Mac never followed through on his playful threat.

Once the Rangers completed their training at The Needles, they moved to Shanklin on the other side of the island, where they climbed more cliffs and honed their demolition skills.

Before they left, the men of Dog also found themselves in a little bit of trouble in the island town. As Lomell recorded in his diary:

"January 31, Blue Monday—SNAFU. To cheer the men up after this bitter disappointment, Captain Slater . . . arranged a farewell party. Invitations were graciously accepted by the WRENS [the Women's Royal Navy Service]. Due to the curfew regulations regarding the WRENS, the party came to an end at 2300 hours. Everyone enjoyed themselves immensely." That is when the evening ended for the WRENs. But true to traditional Ranger habits, after escorting the girls home, the men returned to continue to party on into the early morning hours.

"As dawn drew closer, the men became more intoxicated. Along about 3:00 in the morning, a small group of 'blind' Rangers, comprised of Captain Slater, First Lieutenant McBride, First Sgt. Lomell, Staff Sgts. Kuhn and McCrone, and Private First Class Fruhling, planned what would prove to be the most embarrassing moment to date of Sgt. Corona's life. To make a long story short and keep comments at a minority, let's just say that Sgt. Corona was spending the night with the belle of the village, cementing Allied relationships. The abovementioned group [the 'blind' Rangers, sans Slater and Fruhling, who went on their own little 'side mission'] proceeded to the young lady's apartment and by use of their tactical knowledge and stealth made entry. Lt. McBride entered the bedroom imitating an intoxicated Scotsman looking for his own room. In a few short moments, the entire group was stumbling around the apartment searching for Sgt. Corona's clothes. Upon securing the clothing, the group made a hasty withdrawal. Corona and the belle were never awakened through the commotion.

"It is said that Sgt. Corona made quite a spectacle of himself walking through town clad only in an overcoat and GI shoes. During the above escapade, Capt. Slater and Private First Class Fruhling were absent, but we understand that they had quite an experience with a brunette named Doris."

CHAPTER 7

The Mission

Lieutenant Colonel James Earl Rudder and his executive officer, Major Max F. Schneider, passed windows draped with black-out curtains in the long hallway as they made their way towards General Omar Bradley's office. The duo had recently come off the train at London's Paddington Station and walked about a mile to Bryanston Square. A fashionable apartment building there had become headquarters for the First Army, which would eventually lead the American portion of the Allied invasion into France. Accompanied by an armed escort, Rudder and Schneider entered an office on the second floor occupied by Colonel Truman Thorson, General Bradley's operations officer. They noticed numerous maps marked "TOP SECRET" lining the walls of the office. Black-and-white aerial reconnaissance photographs and additional maps covered several tables.

For a little over two weeks, the Rangers had been in England, scaling cliffs every day, training for an unknown mission. In the office that day in London, Rudder learned what it was all about.

Thorson called the men's attention to a rocky peninsula labeled "Pointe Du Hoe."* Considered the most dangerous German coastal

*World War II maps and even later publications would misspell Pointe du Hoc as "Pointe Du Hoe."

battery, the D-Day planners singled out the Pointe as the number one priority on the invasion target list.

Bradley's operations officer pointed towards the photographs, which revealed a massive German fortress atop the rocky peninsula. The Germans considered the position largely impregnable from a seaborne attack thanks to the ninety-foot cliffs. Nevertheless, they had placed artillery shells suspended by a wire—precursors to today's IEDs (improvised explosive devices)—along the cliff faces as an added defense against a seaport assault. German machine guns and anti-aircraft guns could also hit the beach at the base of the cliffs, where any attacking craft would be forced to land. German fortifications had made land-borne and parachute attacks similarly difficult: heavy minefields, machine gun nests, bunkers, and barbed wire made an overland attack without armor practically impossible.

The German defenses guarded six 155 mm, long-range artillery pieces. With a potential range of 25,000 yards (14 miles),* the guns could reach both Omaha and Utah Beaches and even a portion of the landing beaches in the British zone. The German battery also threatened the Allied naval armada carrying the invasion forces. Of the twenty-two guns the Germans had at their disposal within the First Army's landing zone at Normandy, those at Pointe du Hoc were "the most formidable." Destroying them would be "the most dangerous mission of D-Day." Learning of the German defenses, Rudder thought to himself, "*You've got to be kidding. This is just to scare me.*" But the presentation was not a joke; taking out the guns at Pointe du Hoc was critical to the success of D-Day.

During Thorson's dramatic presentation, Rudder observed his executive officer nervously whistling through his teeth. A veteran of Darby's Rangers, Schneider had previously made three assault landings with the legendary unit. A metal plate protected a portion of his skull—a souvenir from a traumatic air accident in the 1930s. While in combat with Darby's unit in Italy, a detonated grenade may have ag-

*The actual range for the guns was more likely approximately 17,400 yards. By modifying the carriage and using modern ammunition, a greater range could theoretically be achieved.

gravated the metal plate in his head. He also experienced painful, recurring "festering sores as the internal shell fragments worked their way through the skin."

Unfortunately, Schneider also suffered from Post Traumatic Stress Disorder (PTSD). In WWII, doctors often misdiagnosed PTSD as "shellshock" and did not widely understand symptoms or treatment. Three days after the presentation, Schneider experienced an "episode," and Doctor Block concluded that he "suffered from a neurasthenic condition brought on by overwork and mental fatigue." He added, "Unless a radical measure is resorted to, he may suffer a mental crackup."

Alarmed by the doctor's diagnosis, Rudder hastily requested Schneider's transfer out of his battalion. However, General Eisenhower personally "interceded in order to utilize [Schneider's] services in the initial invasion of the continent." Schneider later brilliantly commanded the 5th Ranger Battalion, which would serve as part of Rudder's Provisional Ranger Force.

The Allied plans called for Dog and most of the Provisional Ranger Force to land on a small beach, scale a cliff ten stories high under a torrent of enemy fire, and destroy the most lethal gun battery of the invasion—a suicide mission. Headquarters projected casualties would top seventy percent. One intelligence officer remarked, "It can't be done. Three old women with brooms could keep the Rangers from climbing that cliff."

Although Bradley and Thorson had described the mission to Rudder and Schneider, he hadn't told them *how* to accomplish it. The final planning rested entirely on their shoulders. Later, General Bradley met with Rudder about the mission. Rudder looked at Bradley and said confidently, "Sir, my Rangers can do the job for you." Bradley would later recount in his memoir, "No soldier in my command has ever been wished a more difficult task than that which befell the thirty-four-year-old commander of this Provisional Ranger Force."

At the strategic level, the Allies planned to hit five beaches in Normandy. The Americans would storm Omaha and Utah Beaches while the British and Canadians would assault Sword, Juno, and Gold

Beaches. Together, these forces would land more than 160,000 troops along approximately fifty miles of the northern French coastline. In addition to the ground troops, more than 5,000 ships would support invasion, and over 20,000 British and American airborne troops would parachute or glide behind German lines.

British and American commanders worked together to plan the landing operations of the Allied invasion of Normandy, code named Operation Neptune, which would be the largest amphibious invasion in history. America's General Dwight D. Eisenhower served as supreme commander of the Allied expeditionary forces, with Britain's General Bernard Montgomery commanding the ground forces.

Facing the Allied attack were four divisions of German infantry plus three more divisions in the surrounding area. For the last three years, the Germans had been building the Atlantic Wall, a series of defensive fortifications that stretched along the coasts of France, Belgium, Denmark and Norway. But the German commanders disagreed about the appropriate strategy for defending against the inevitable invasion.

Field Marshal Erwin Rommel believed Germany would inevitably lose the war unless they could halt the Allied forces on the beaches, and he argued that German armor should be moved closer to the coast. However, Field Marshal Gerd von Rundstedt believed the Germans could successfully counterattack even if the Allies gained a beachhead, and he argued for keeping the German tanks closer to Paris and Rouen. Hitler made a fateful decision to split the difference between the two, sending fewer tanks than Rommel requested to the coast, while keeping the majority clustered near the cities.

Attached to the 29th Infantry Division that would hit Omaha Beach, Rudder initially considered landing on Omaha and assaulting Pointe du Hoc overland. But that approach seemed nearly impossible. The Germans had prepared for land-borne attack by flooding low areas with water and creating a kill zone with minefields, machine guns, and bunkers. It would take too much time for the Rangers to breach the defenses and destroy the guns of Pointe du Hoc before the rest of the invasion forces could cross the beaches.

It became obvious the only feasible approach would be a frontal assault. But how do you get two hundred men up sheer cliffs lined with IEDs, Hitler's MG-42 bone saws, and anti-aircraft guns firing at the assault group? Rudder had just been handed a nearly impossible mission, sure to cost the lives of many of his men and decimate Dog Company.

To accomplish the mission, Rudder formed the Provisional Ranger Force and took command. It included not only the 2nd Ranger Battalion, but also its sister unit, the 5th Ranger Battalion. Big Jim and his planners went to work, first by dividing the Provisional Ranger Force into three groups. The companies of assault Force A—Dog, Easy and Fox—would breach Pointe du Hoc's initial defenses. Force A would form the first wave. After initial shore bombardment, Easy and Fox would land on the eastern side of Pointe du Hoc, while Dog Company would land on the west. If the men made it up the cliffs, they would send the message, "Praise the Lord." If they failed, they would signal "Tilt," the vernacular used for a failed play on a pinball machine.

If Force A accomplished their objective, Force C—which included Able and Baker and Headquarters Companies of the 2nd Ranger Battalion and the entire 5th Ranger Battalion—would follow up the initial assault force and help take out the guns. If Force A failed and the guns were not eliminated by thirty minutes after landing (H+30 minutes), Force C would land on their secondary objective: Omaha's Dog Green Beach. The force would then fight through the German defenses overland and try to destroy the guns.

Force B—Charlie Company—would undertake Rudder's secondary objective: taking out mortar and machine gun positions at Pointe et Raz de la Percée, which overlooked Omaha Beach. Rudder and his staff spent the next several months developing and fine-tuning the plan, while Dog Company trained relentlessly.

CHAPTER 8

Final Preparations

"Fire in the hole!"

Larry Johnson hurled a five-foot, thirteen-pound metal tube known as a Bangalore torpedo at the target. BOOM! The stick of TNT obliterated a large swath of heavy barbed wire fencing at Braunton Camp. Introduced in 1912, the Bangalore, invented by a British Army Engineer, is so effective that soldiers still use it in modern warfare, including the war in Iraq.

In mid-March, Dog Company moved to Braunton Camp, a British assault training school in North Devon. Taking a break from climbing cliffs, the Rangers focused on strengthening their combat skills. Building on their experience at Camp Ritchie, Dog and the rest of the battalion fired bazookas, scorched targets with flamethrowers, detonated Bangalore torpedoes, and deployed antitank grenades. They learned how to take down German pillboxes and fortifications, clear minefields, and disarm booby traps. Lomell recalled, "We learned how to handle flamethrowers. We learned a lot about house-to-house combat, fighting in villages. . . . It was something different than we had before."

What *hadn't* changed was Dog Company's penchant for mixing it up with other units. "Fights were an everyday affair with us, if anyone dared challenge us," noted Lomell. The Rangers wore coveted paratrooper boots that laced up high along the ankle. During one of the countless nights out on the town, Lomell and the other men remembered hearing, "You didn't earn those boots!"

"The next thing you know, there'd be a fistfight," Lomell remembered. Dog Company acquitted itself well. Months of cliff climbing and assault course training had given the Rangers a mental toughness and the belief that they could do anything. "We were so proud, so sure of ourselves, so competent, so completely in charge that we didn't worry about anything."

After the assault training, the men returned once again to the cliffs. As Dog climbed, Staff Sergeant Jack Kuhn traveled to London. There he learned that Merryweathers Ltd., which specialized in firefighting equipment, had outfitted a six-wheeled, amphibious truck called a DUKW or "Duck," with a 100-foot-long extension ladder used by firefighters. After Kuhn returned to camp, Lieutenant Colonel Thomas H. Trevor, now actively involved in the planning for the assault on Pointe du Hoc, put the Duck through its paces. He mounted .30-caliber, twin Vickers light machine guns on the top of the extension ladder. With the daring of a circus high-wire performer, a Ranger would have to climb the 100-foot ladder and provide covering fire for the Rangers who were scaling the cliffs. When fully extended, the ladder would reach slightly higher than the cliff tops, allowing the Ranger to pour deadly fire from the twin Vickers down upon the Germans. The task of manning the tricked-out DUKW went to men outside of Dog Company.

The assault companies would also need other specialized equipment to scale the cliffs at Pointe du Hoc. The Department of Miscellaneous Development of the Admiralty, known informally as the "Wheezers and Dodgers," created a variety of specialized devices for the invasion, including rocket-propelled grapnel hooks. High tech at the time, the grapnels, each with multiple ropes attached, could fire 200 feet in the air and easily hit the top of Pointe du Hoc. Once the hooks were in place, the men could scale the cliffs using the ropes.

On April 1, 1944, Slater, Kuhn, and a couple of other men from the company tested the grapnels and other experimental devices. They found "that it could be successfully done from LCAs." After some further tweaking, they fired the rockets on cliffs as high as 175 feet.

Once the serious business of testing was completed, the men organized a comedy show. Ruggiero took on his former stage moniker, Tommy Knight, and burned up the floor, treating the men to an over-the-top tap dancing routine that had everyone cheering and jumping out of their seats. Hoffman and Fruhling, with Private First Class Dominic Sparaco, a feisty, acid-tongued northerner, took turns acting out funny incidents from training. In the process, they even roasted The Duke, who took it in stride. After the show, the men gorged on chicken and "all the beer they could drink." They held a battalion dance attended by beautiful local women. Kuhn later remembered, "A good time was had by all."

But the party soon ended, and the men went back to climbing. Slater started to achieve near-mythic status for his prowess on the ropes. "Company D's commander has displayed a case of sheer guts and daring so far above that of any other man that he is now a legend in the battalion." The men of the company sometimes referred to him as "Batman" of comic strip fame. Kuhn, his sidekick, "was affectionately known as Robin."

Working the buddy system, the two men would assist each other up the cliff, as would other two-man teams within Dog Company. The men of D Company frequently heard Slater say, "Foot me, Jack." The response would be "Yes, sir!" as the two men made their way up the cliff. For added realism, Slater and other Rangers shot live rounds at the men as they scaled the precipice. "They fired at any men who exposed themselves. It was very helpful training," recalled Lomell.

During the continual climbing, more life-threatening accidents took place. One near fatality involved twenty-six-year-old Second Lieutenant George Kerchner, a recent Ranger recruit from Baltimore, Maryland, where, as a hard-working "soda jerk," he had developed a knack for management and business. Kerchner joined Dog Company in England with no experience in cliff climbing but soon made a "habit of trying the hardest cliffs." Kerchner pushed himself and quickly became one of the top climbers. He would ultimately command Dog Company's First Platoon. One day, Kerchner's helmet came undone and fell to the bottom of the cliff. Unfortunately, at that moment, a heavy piece of chalk fell off the cliff and struck him in the head. Bleeding badly from a massive gash, Kerchner somehow managed to cling to the rope and lower himself to the ground.

On a separate occasion, another dangerous piece of chalk from the top of one of the cliffs hit Lomell squarely on the right knee as he was climbing. Amazingly, Lomell kept hold of the rope despite the severe pain and worked his way to the top of the cliff.

During the climbing exercises, one Dog Company man who was coming into his own was Sergeant Sigurd Sundby. "Sigurd Sundby was about five-seven" and a "thinly built, quiet guy. He never had much to say. To get him to talk you had to really dig. He mainly kept to himself," one Ranger related.

Toward the end of April, Dog Company and the rest of the battalion made their way to the channel fort at Weymouth in Dorset, England. The Rangers loaded onto LSIs (Landing Ship, Infantry), old seagoing tubs that had been converted from British and Belgian passenger liners. Command had assigned Dog Company to the HMS *Amsterdam*, which carried about two hundred fully equipped combat troops. The upper decks of the craft housed eight LCAs for a simulated assault landing. From the decks of the "mother ship," the men conducted several realistic training exercises in which they boarded LCAs for a simulated assault landing. During one "big show," hundreds of landing craft hit the beach amidst the tumult of naval and aerial bombardment. "If one looked seaward, he would have seen huge geysers spouting skyward."* The men charged out of their landing

*As depicted in the front jacket photograph of this book.

craft and crossed the beach under naval fire as Lieutenant George Kerchner reveals, "it was a full-scale dress rehearsal . . . a firing exercise in which the Navy shelled the area and [we] went in using the same time schedule that we were planning to have on D-Day."

Upon landing, D Company scaled a steep cliff at the end of the beach. Leading by example, Lieutenant McBride cut his way through barbed wire as the company made it to the top and seized their objective. But not everyone was happy about the outcome. "Above the roar of the bombardment, Sergeant Corona could be heard cussing at the top of his lungs." Sergeant Harry Fate had unintentionally kicked a loaded ammo bag off the cliff. This incident likely contributed to Slater's busting Fate down to private. Lomell was given the unceremonious task of delivering the news and removing Fate's stripes. Devastated, Fate lashed out at the messenger, issuing a veiled threat to Lomell: "That's all right. All first sergeants get their due in combat. I'll see you in combat."

CHAPTER 9

A Tough Spot for a Landing

Major Max Schneider called Dr. Block into the operations room to brief him about the battalion's D-Day mission and pointed to a map. "That's It! Doc, that's the spot where we're going to operate—Pointe du Hoe [sic]."

"Now take a look at this," Schneider continued. He slowly rolled up a thick cloth that covered photographs hanging in the room. "This is a series of photographs taken at every possible angle from airplanes and the coastline."

Block noticed the sheer cliff and a distinctive spear-like precipice. "That's going to be a pretty hard climb, Major. Why such a tough spot to make an assault landing?"

"Good question, Doc. Come over here, and I'll show you some more pictures." Schneider, characteristically whistling between his teeth, directed the medical doctor to another set of reconnaissance photos. The grainy images revealed the top of the cliffs, with "several houses, hedgerows, paths, and roads." But most menacing of all was a "square, whitish-gray outline. On each side there were three whitish-gray masses approximately thirty-five feet in diameter." Schneider looked at Block and explained they were six 155 mm gun emplacements. The tip of Pointe du Hoc was capped by a concrete observation post.

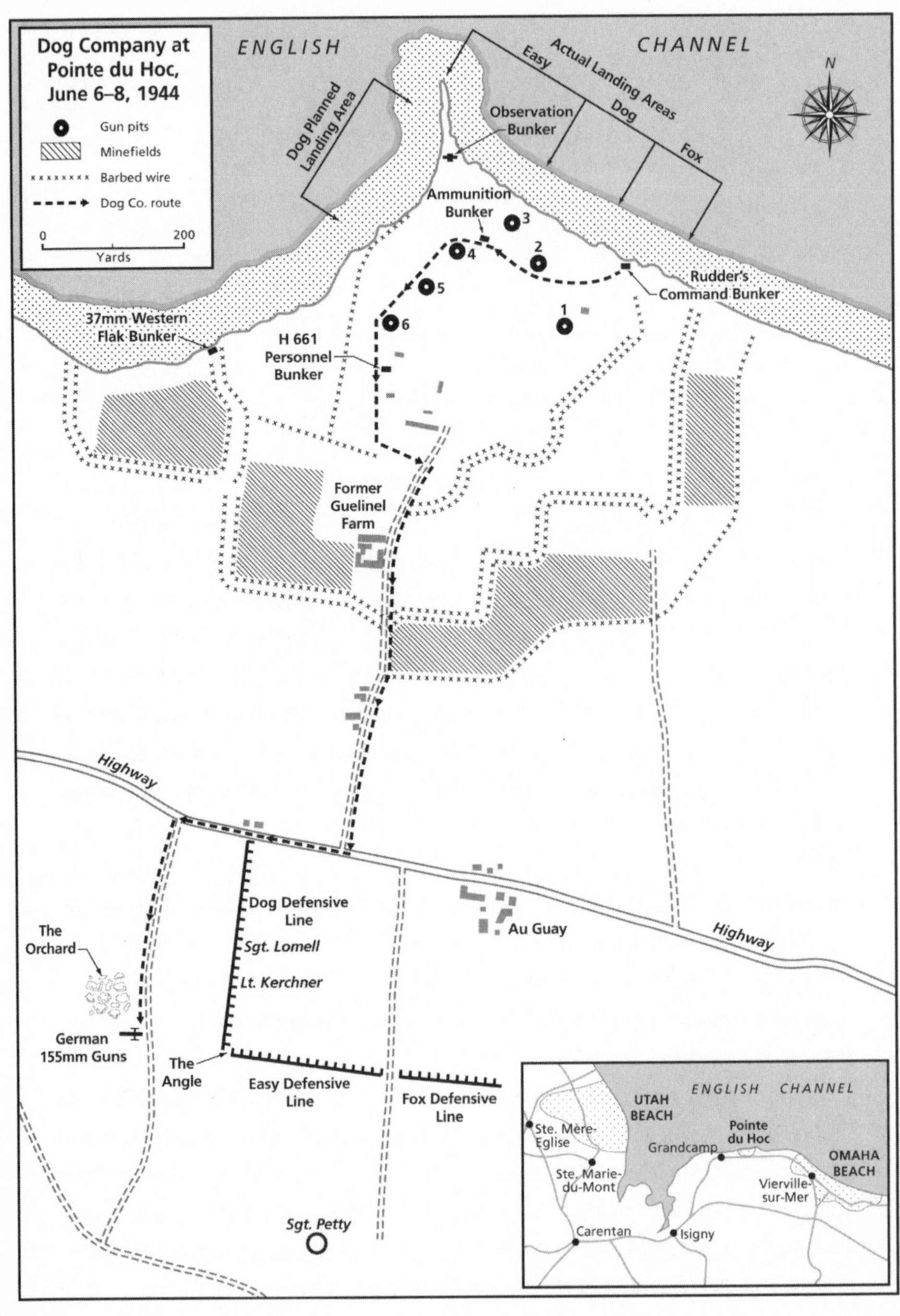

Dog Company at Pointe du Hoc, June 6–8, 1944
Gun pits
Minefields
Barbed wire
Dog Co. route
0
200
Yards
ENGLISH
CHANNEL
N
Dog Planned Landing Area
Easy
Actual Landing Areas
Dog
Fox
Observation Bunker
Ammunition Bunker
Rudder's Command Bunker
1
2
3
4
5
6
37mm Western Flak Bunker
H 661 Personnel Bunker
Former Guelinel Farm
Highway
Highway
Au Guay
Dog Defensive Line
Sgt. Lomell
Lt. Kerchner
The Orchard
German 155mm Guns
The Angle
Easy Defensive Line
Fox Defensive Line
Sgt. Petty
ENGLISH CHANNEL
UTAH BEACH
Ste. Mère-Eglise
Ste. Marie-du-Mont
Grandcamp
Pointe du Hoc
OMAHA BEACH
Vierville-sur-Mer
Carentan
Isigny

Schneider then went on: "Each of these emplacements was linked to the others by a series of camouflaged paths and underground tunnels. Such gun emplacements were protected by coverage varying anywhere from six to ten feet of solid concrete. Most of it had been poured in the past year, but some of it was at least three years old and had become harder with each succeeding month. Extending back from the cliff and encompassing all six guns was row upon row of wire, single- and multiple-apron. Our G-2 information revealed that the space between the protective wire and on both sides of the protected position were extensive minefields. Truly a formidable setup! And that was not all! Extending along the cliffs on both sides of the point were open and closed machine gun positions. There were four that could easily be seen on the left flank of the point and three on the right flank. These were the ones that were visible; how many more [they had] that were well camouflaged was anyone's guess."

Reminiscing about the meeting, Block later wrote, "This bastion could not be permitted to stand by any invading army because these guns could command and control a vast area to each flank and out to the sea. If the main assault on the continent were to be made anywhere near this area, the guns must be silent. There was one way to do it—an audacious and bold plan to attack the position from the rear, that is, the seaside."

Schneider repeated his dramatic presentation at the battalion level. According to Sheldon Bare, the executive officer put most of the men in parade formation and bluntly stated that their D-Day mission was nearly suicidal, informing them that "casualties will be high; we already filled out 517 death certificates."

On May 6, 1944, with the invasion only weeks away, Dog Company moved to Swanage, Dorset, where the relentless climbing continued along with other rigorous, special training exercises. The exercises became even more fraught with peril. One night, German E-boats approachd Slapton Sands in the dead of night. The E-boats sank two fully laden LSIs (Landing Ship, Infantry) and severely damaged a third with American troops, drowning nearly eight hundred GIs. For security purposes, the United States Government hushed up the incident, which wouldn't fully surface for decades.

With training finally over on May 19, the battalion moved to D-5, a staging area in Dorchester, England. Cordoned off from the outside world, they remained isolated as they made final preparations for D-Day, the most important amphibious landing of the war.

CHAPTER 10

"Into the Valley of Death"

Late evening on board the *Amsterdam*, June 5, 1944

A waft of blue-gray cigarette smoke lifted from the table. "*I have a hell of a hot hand*," Lomell thought as he looked into the eyes of his opponents. Normally not a poker player, Lomell stood on the verge of winning, and he knew it. His concentration shattered abruptly when a Ranger blurted out, "Father Lacy is aboard!"

Lomell was Protestant, but as first sergeant, he was instrumental in getting his men, including the "Jewish boys, Protestant boys, and Catholic boys," to attend Lacy's masses. Several of the Catholic players at the table stood up. One of them stated flatly, "We gotta go and do a little praying. Maybe we'll get some protection for tomorrow."

Lomell looked up at the man. "Hell, no. I got a good hand here. I'm sweating out this hand. If I don't deserve protection by now, it's just too damn late for me to ask for it." The first sergeant would remember this incident for the rest of his life.

Lomell and three others from Dog Company continued playing while the more pious Rangers sauntered into another area of the ship to see the priest. Father Joe Lacy, the Rangers' chaplain, visited all of the Ranger mother ships that night. The fearless, "fat little Irishman" would later receive a Distinguished Service Cross for his bravery on Omaha Beach. That night, he provided spiritual comfort to the men. George Kerchner remembers Lacy saying, "When you land on the beach and get in there, I don't want to see anybody kneeling down and praying. If I do, I'm gonna come up and boot you in the tail. You leave the praying to me, and you do the fighting."

Unbeknownst to all that night, every man who left Lomell's game to pray would die the next day within an hour of landing at Pointe du Hoc.

Several hours earlier, another type of gathering—which changed the mission—took place on the troop ship *Ben Machree.* Rudder had previously assigned Major Cleveland A. Lytle to lead Force A, which included Dog, Easy, and Fox companies—all of them designated to assault Pointe du Hoc. A graduate of Clemson University, Lytle was one of the few Army officers who had been with the battalion since day one. Courageous and brave, Lytle put his men first. A few months earlier, he addressed his men after a training exercise: "You fellas have broken about every rule and law there are in the Army regulations. Not only that, but when you ran out of rules, you made up your own, and then broke them. You are a bunch of characters, but characters I can't help but admire. Your manner, your cleverness, willingness, your fighting spirit . . . I am so proud to be amongst you and be one of you."

Prior to D-Day, Lytle and several of his fellow officers threw a party to celebrate Joe Rafferty's promotion to captain. When Lytle assumed command of Force A, Rafferty replaced Lytle as Able Company's commanding officer. Whiskey flowed freely at the party and spirits ran high, until the tone turned sinister when an inebriated Lytle told the entire group that the mission was suicide and in vain. Rumors swirled that the French Resistance had reported that the guns had been moved and were no longer on Pointe du Hoc. Somehow word had reached Lytle (likely a G-2 report) that the guns were not in their emplacements atop the Pointe.

In the cabin next to Lytle, medic Frank South overheard the drunken rant from Force A's commanding officer. Several more words were exchanged. As South put it, "our newly appointed commander, Major Lytle, had become drunk and was convinced that all the Rangers were being sent on a suicide mission. He was complaining loudly about it."

Someone informed Rudder about Lytle's tirade. Rudder took action swiftly, relieving Lytle. Several Rangers escorted Lytle out of the room. Along the way, he punched the battalion surgeon, Doc Block.

South witnessed Lytle being dragged off, kicking and screaming: "The process of arresting and leading off the former commander of the operation was a noisy one. I opened the door to find out what was going on, only to see a group of struggling and shouting [men in] uniforms."*

Lytle's arrest left Big Jim in a lurch. Rudder, who commanded the Provisional Ranger Force, which included the 2nd and 5th Ranger Battalions, planned to direct the force from the command ship like an orchestra conductor. Staying on ship would put him in a position to command groups from both battalions: Force A and C as they assaulted Omaha Beach and Pointe du Hoc and Force B as it attacked Pointe et Raz de la Percée. With Lytle relieved, however, Rudder could think of no one else qualified to take his place. So Rudder quickly informed the 1st Division's commander, Major General Clarence Huebner, that Rudder himself was taking Lytle's position.

Shocked, Huebner objected, "We're not going to risk you getting knocked out on the first round." Leading the assault on Pointe du Hoc would also greatly diminish Rudder's ability to direct the entire Provisional Ranger Force.

Firmly and respectfully, Rudder responded, "I'm sorry to have to disobey you, sir, but if I don't take it, it may not go."

Lieutenant Colonel James Rudder would now participate directly in the assault on Pointe du Hoc.

Although Major Lytle wasn't able to dance his way out of his insubordination charge, five-foot-three Ranger Tom Ruggiero was literally tap dancing away the evening. In an effort to cut the tension, the

---

*Lytle later become a battlefield hero and received the Distinguished Service Cross (DSC) for single-handedly rescuing two non-swimmers from the enemy side of the Moselle River. Years later, South's best friend and fellow Ranger Willy Clark ran into Lytle, who bitterly claimed that he "never wanted to hear anything about Rangers or the name 'Ranger' again."

diminutive Ranger gave what he thought might be the last performance of his life. One of the Rangers had smuggled a ukulele on board, and the man sang and played the instrument as Ruggie entertained the men. Meanwhile, Kuhn cracked jokes like a professional stand-up comedian.

On the same ship, Lomell, Hoffman, and the other men who had remained at the poker table finally called it a night. Lying in their bunks, no one could sleep. Their nervous anticipation of what would be the most audacious invasion in history kept them awake. Kuhn, not far from Lomell, sheepishly murmured, "You know, I'm worried about tomorrow. What the hell am I going to do if I turn chicken and my platoon goes crazy?"

"We spent the next half hour reassuring each other," explained Lomell.

"Oh, no, no, Jack, you won't go chicken," he told his close friend.

Kuhn reassured Lomell, "Oh, no, Lomell, you won't go. You know, Len, you'll be there."

"And every one of them was worried about whether or not he could carry it off the next day and be out in front of their men, to inspire them and so forth. We were all bolstering each other's morale and all reassuring one another," remembered Lomell.

On another ship in a secluded area between two large crates and the railing, two men stood in silence as the rough channel seas crashed against the hull. Private First Class Garness Colden then "let it all come out" to Sergeant L-Rod Petty. Colden told him about the close, loving relationship he had with his father "for all of his life." He shared with Petty his premonition of dying in combat and how much that would hurt his father. Petty, listening intently to "Garney," couldn't help but think about how much he hated his own violent, abusive father—thoughts he would never reveal to the earnest young Swede. Colden continued to press, "L-Rod, if I don't make it, would you mind writing to my daddy and tell him what I've told you tonight? I always meant to after I came into the Army, but I never got around to doing it. I would want him to know how I felt about him—it might make him feel better."

Petty reassured Colden, "Hey, you dumb little Swede, you're gonna make it. You are too sly to get killed." The two men shook hands, making "a silent oath," with L-Rod giving Garney his word that he would deliver the letter to Garney' father should anything happen to the private. Petty's prediction proved true. Colden survived Pointe du Hoc, but Petty ultimately found himself fulfilling his promise to the Swede, who died in battle only six months later.

Despite L-Rod's bravado in front of Garney, he had his own private doubts. When he heard about the mission, the first thing that passed through his mind was the Battle of Balaclava in the Crimean War. Outnumbered, the British Calvary troops charged the enemy on a sure suicide mission immortalized in Alfred Lord Tennyson's poem *"The Charge of the Light Brigade."* Petty recited a line in his head: *"Onward, onward rode the six hundred into the Valley of Death." "Yeah,"* he thought, *"it was indeed a Balaclavic mission all right. . . It would not be 'onward, onward,' but upward, upward climbed the two hundred [Rangers] into the Valley [of Death].'"*

At 4:05 A.M., a voice on the ship's PA system barked, "Rangers, man your craft."

Earlier, before Ruggiero headed towards the boats, he noticed that one of the prongs on his lifebelt was bent, rendering it useless. If the landing craft capsized, Ruggiero would sink like a rock because he was loaded down with over sixty pounds of ammunition, equipment, and his rifle. The nimble Ranger went over to Len Lomell and told his first sergeant that the belt was defective.

"We'll get you another one," responded Lomell.

Lomell was gone for a few minutes. "OK, try this one," he offered.

The belt fit snugly on Ruggiero's slender waist. Lomell looked on approvingly. "There you go, Rugg. You're all set."

Ruggiero didn't want to be accused of theft, so he asked, "What do you want me to do with this one?"

"Just throw it overboard."

"Where?"

"Just go open a porthole and throw the damn thing away!" Lomell exclaimed.

As Ruggiero made his way down to the porthole, he ran into "Tough Guy" Riendeau. "What are you doing with two life belts?" asked the dark-haired Ranger, who had miraculously survived a 150-foot fall from a cliff.

"I gotta throw one away."

"What do you mean you gotta throw it away?"

Ruggiero looked at him. "It's defective. It's no good. Won't work."

Riendeau was by far the best swimmer in the battalion. He "swam like a fish," but he was panicking. "Don't do that. I can't find mine," he confessed.

"What happened to it?" asked Ruggiero.

"I dropped it as I was coming on the boat and somebody took it," Riendeau explained.

"Just ask Lomell for another one," suggested Ruggiero.

"Jesus, if I go to Lomell and tell him I lost it, he's going to skin me."

"No he won't. Here, just take this one; go back to Lomell and say it was yours."

"I didn't think of that. That's a good idea," said Riendeau.

Sensing that Riendeau might not go back to Lomell and get a new lifebelt, Ruggiero pressed the other Ranger. "Promise me you'll do that," he said, looking into his eyes.

"OK, I'll do that, Rugg," agreed Riendeau.

Perhaps Riendeau thought he was bulletproof after surviving his near-fatal fall from the steep precipice of the Needles. More likely, he feared possible demotion and punishment for losing his equipment. Either way, he continued to wear the useless lifebelt that Lomell had ordered Ruggiero to throw in the water.

CHAPTER 11

"The Sky Was Burning"

Early morning hours, Pointe du Hoc, France, June 6, 1944

"Alles kaputt! Alles kaputt!" Bleeding from his head, with blood pouring down his dust-covered uniform, a German soldier suddenly burst into the home of nineteen-year-old French civilian Gerette Le Normand, who lived on a farm near Pointe du Hoc. While the young man and his grandmother held each other tightly and cowered in the corner, the German soldier shouted that all was lost on the Pointe.

"It seemed like the sky was burning. All the houses in the vicinity shook," recalled Le Normand. Meanwhile, the distraught German continued shouting. "Because of what he was saying, I deduced that everything at Pointe du Hoc was destroyed—the commandant and all the soldiers killed," the Frenchman remembered.

Beginning around 4:50 A.M. on June 6, 108 heavy Royal Air Force (RAF) bombers saturated Pointe du Hoc, dropping approximately 635 tons of ordnance as part of Operation Flashlamp. While the intensity of the barrage was a dramatic increase from earlier attacks, this was hardly the first raid to hit the area. Prior to D-Day, the U.S. Ninth Air Force and the RAF bombed Pointe du Hoc more heavily than any other target on its bombing list. Leading up to the massive June 6 attack, the Allies dropped 380 tons of bombs on the site—more than ten tons per acre. However, to prevent the Germans from determining the exact location of the Normandy invasion, the Allies flew three missions against other targets for every mission executed against the D-Day landing sites.

The first raid occurred in mid-April when thirty-five A-20 bombers dropped more than thirty-three tons of bombs, damaging some of the guns at the Pointe. The Germans wisely moved the artillery pieces out of their emplacements and into an apple orchard about a thousand yards away. They draped heavy camouflage nets over the twenty-foot-long guns and placed telephone poles in the casements to deceive Allied photo reconnaissance.

The movement of the guns did not go unnoticed by French Resistance cells working in the area. Although accounts vary, the French partisans apparently did attempt to alert the Allies of the guns' movements. According to one person on the scene, the French attempted to use carrier pigeons to relay the crucial information; but the German 352nd Infantry Division defending the area had established anti-pigeon patrols. Based on German records, the 352nd shot down twenty-seven birds from March 20 to May 27.

One French civilian who knew of the guns' new location was Guillaume Mercader, a famous French cyclist who became an active member of the resistance in Normandy. During the war, Germans used his shop to repair and maintain their bicycles. Following "the first Allied bombardment," Mercader explained, "I was visited by Jean Marion who informed me that the cannons on the site had been moved." Mercader then told "Eugène Meslin, alias 'Morvin,' who, like me, thought the information should be communicated as quickly as possible. It was transmitted to London by radio, and on April 26 was decoded by Raymond Berthier, encoding attaché for London."

Meanwhile, the Germans continued beefing up their defenses on the Pointe. Along with approximately 120 artillerists from 2./HKAA 1260 assigned to man the six big guns at Pointe du Hoc, they also deployed over a hundred more men—all from an infantry unit—to the west of the Pointe. Most of the German positions were located further inland to fend off a land-based attack. The first line of the inland defense comprised fifteen men from an artillery unit that employed six-barrel rocket launchers known as Nebelwerfers. They were moved to augment the interior defenses about two weeks before the landing. Converted into machine gunners, the former artillerymen hunkered down in foxholes along the eastern and western sides of the cliff top.

One of those gunners, nineteen-year-old German Wilhelm Kirchhoff, arrived at Pointe du Hoc two weeks before D-Day and described the massive Allied attack the night of June 5–6. "When the bombers arrived, we the fifteen men of the Werfer unit crouched down in our little earth bunkers. There were so many bombers that we couldn't count them. They were coming from the northeast direction, and the raid was heavy. We could see red flares and bursts from the explosions and everything shook. I didn't know it then but my ears would be permanently damaged during this attack. The bombardment lasted for well over half an hour."

Louis Le Devin, then a thirteen-year-old French civilian from Criqueville, recalls the terrifying attack that preceded the Allied invasion. "The bombing during the night... was the most violent of all. Our house was shaking, and we were all frightened. When the bombs began falling, we all ran outside. The sky was on fire." Louis's family waited out the bombing in a trench-type air-raid shelter covered with logs and earth in their garden. Other villagers were not so prepared and had to hide in the ditches. At least one bomb hit the village church, blowing out all the windows with the intense pressure.

The overwhelming onslaught became too much for some of the German soldiers. Karl Jäger, one of the artillery sergeants, admitted to a fellow German veteran after the war that he and several of his men deserted their position. "They can go to fucking hell!" Jäger shouted as he left.

About the same time, the Germans received word that American paratroopers had landed. A German detachment stationed on the Pointe set off to look for the airborne troops.*

*Several C-47s carrying the 3rd Battalion of the 506 Parachute Infantry Regiment landed in the Pointe du Hoc area. Paratroopers Leonard Goodgall, Raymond Crouch, and Bob Dunning landed near Pointe du Hoc's rocky beach and would later fight alongside Rudder's Rangers.

When the Allies' carpet bombing finally ceased, the Germans took stock of the damage done. "My unit was untouched in the bombing, but all the camouflage net fixings were torn loose and the trenches were filled with earth," recalled Kirchhoff. "In darkness we repaired what we could so we could move about once again. Then we had something to eat and we asked ourselves what else would happen to us that day?"

The answer came at 5 A.M. in the pre-dawn light. With a light fog hovering over the sea, German soldiers at Pointe du Hoc remained on alert. Suddenly, they saw the silhouettes of hundreds of ships approaching their cliff-top position. "After the fog lifted, we couldn't see the water any more—only vessels," remembered twenty-five-year-old Rudolf Karl an *Unter-offizier* (NCO) in 2./HKAA 1260.

Kirchhoff noted, "There were so many landing craft that I couldn't count them all. Then suddenly the enemy navy started to fire at the coast, and everyone was shouting anxiously, *'Sie kommen! Sie kommen!'* ['They come!'] This was at exactly 5:55 A.M.

"We could still see the flashes of naval guns in the distance," Kirchhoff continued. "As a soldier, I never really felt worried, but because of the violent bombardment I hunkered into the ground as low as I could and sat behind my machine gun. Again the shells mostly passed overhead, but a few hit the cliff edge and caused masses of earth to fall. Suddenly on the horizon we saw the ships so precisely we could identify them by exact type. They were large vessels and in large numbers. I had never seen anything like that before… I panicked and shivers went down my back. I asked myself what was going to become of us because something was about to start right now."

CHAPTER 12

The Landing

In the early morning, LCA 668, carrying Len Lomell, Jack Kuhn, and most of the 2nd Platoon, cut through the choppy, green waters of the English Channel. As the men poked their helmets out of the top of the boat, they were looking at what would be center stage of one of the greatest amphibious landings in history. They saw, heard, and felt the intense bombardment on the shore, demonstrating the full might of the American and British battleships, destroyers, and bombers. The sight mesmerized the twenty-two young Rangers. Through the smoke and fire, the men watched as scores of rockets from a naval barge ignited and streaked through the air.

Not far behind Lomell, LCA 858 carried Lieutenant George Kerchner and his 1st Platoon. Massive shells from the battleship passed directly over their heads. "We were close enough to hear and feel some of the muzzle blasts," Kerchner later remarked. "One of the rocket-firing crafts that was near Omaha Beach fired their rockets. This was also a terrifying thing; I think there were a thousand or more rockets on these landing craft, and they fired in salvos of maybe ten or fifteen at a time. It was just one continuous sheet of fire."

"How can anybody live through that?" thought Kerchner.

As the small flotilla of British-crewed craft carrying the Rangers of Force A plowed through waves of the channel, something seemed off. In LCA 668, Lomell knew it. Through the mist and spray, the dark, rocky cliffs of what appeared to be Pointe et Raz de la Percée came into view. Len Lomell turned to his close friend Jack Kuhn.

"Hey, Jack! Look at this. That's not the Pointe. That's C Company's target."

Kuhn nodded.

Lomell moved across the crowded landing craft towards the British coxswain who was piloting the craft and asked him if they were headed in the right direction. The coxswain nodded affirmatively.

Lomell pressed the issue. "Are you sure you are right about this?"

From the photos that Lomell looked at during the training exercise, he was sure the ten landing craft, three DUKWs, and other small boats in Force A were at least two miles off course from Pointe du Hoc and heading in the wrong direction.

In the dense smoke and haze, guiding the flotilla in ML-304 (Motor Launch), Lt. Colin Beever of the Royal Navy Volunteer Reserve, was in fact, dangerously off course. In Beever's defense, the new 970 Radar equipment was at fault. Introduced a month earlier, the equipment tested well in controlled settings but failed on D-Day. Dog and the rest of Force A were mistakenly heading toward Pointe et Raz de la Percée, Force B's objective. The error in navigation would change the course of history by putting Force A nearly forty minutes behind schedule in reaching their target. About one hundred yards from what was clearly Pointe et Raz de la Percée, Rudder realized the error and ordered Beever to change course and turn west toward Pointe du Hoc.

The operation's entire timetable was now blown. The follow-on force known as Force C—which included Able and Baker companies and some elements of Headquarters Company of the 2nd Ranger Battalion and Schneider's Fifth Ranger Battalion—would not be heading to Pointe du Hoc because they never received the appropriate radio signal from Force A. Hence, Force C headed to its second objective, Omaha Beach. Dog Company, along with the rest of Force A, was now on its own and outgunned, heading straight for Pointe du Hoc with no follow-on reinforcements.

★ ★ ★

Late, but back on course, the DUKWs and assault craft of Ranger Force A raced towards Pointe du Hoc. With the flotilla just a few hundred yards from the Norman coast, the Germans peppered the landing craft with machine gun fire, hitting several men. As bullets flew by, fierce waves pounded the incoming landing craft, and the icy froth of the churning channel waters soaked the men, who frantically bailed water to avoid sinking. Most of the men became seasick. The Army had issued them paper bags, but no one had time to use them. "We were taking on water. Men were throwing up as we were bailing seawater out of the landing craft. I know I did," Bill Hoffman noted.

The turbulent channel waves relentlessly lashed LCA 860, nearly capsizing the craft carrying Duke Slater, McBride, Ruggiero, Riendeau, and seventeen other men from Dog Company. With his boat a mere twenty yards in front of them, an anxious Lomell stared back at The Duke. The roar of the waves crashing into the boats drowned out the dull hum of the craft's motor. Inside the British-made boat, Slater and his men feverishly bailed water with their helmets to keep from drowning. Waves from the channel cascaded over the sides of the craft, filling the boat, and drenching everyone inside. They were sinking, and Force A's supply boat was also taking on water.

Remarkably, despite the swirling seas and incoming German fire, the men were focused on a standing bet they had made about who would reach shore first. One hundred dollars would go to the winners. Spawned at Camp Forrest, the Ranger's highly competitive ethos and winning spirit permeated their every bone and fiber. Lomell and the men of LCA 668 were determined to win. Focused on being the first boat to land on shore and not realizing the deadly force of the channel's currents, several men on board Lomell's boat and Kerchner's landing craft cheered and applauded when they saw Duke Slater's craft going down. Lomell remembers some of the men saying, "That's one less group we have to compete with. We've only got Kerchner now."

Over a half an hour late, Rudder's flotilla, minus The Duke's foundering LCA and the Rangers' supply boat, headed for the eastern side of Pointe du Hoc. The original plan called for Dog Company to land on the western side of the Pointe, but Rudder, in an effort to keep everyone together, ordered all craft to land on the eastern side of the 500-yard rocky peninsula, landing at approximately 7:08 A.M., nearly forty minutes behind schedule.

Shortly after landing, communications officer Lieutenant James Eikner signaled "Tilt," indicating that Force A was behind schedule and Schneider's Force C should pursue their secondary objective, Omaha Beach. Mysteriously, the radios were not operating properly. Acknowledgement was "receipted," according to Eikner, but Schneider's records show that they never got his message; the only message received by the 5th was a word that "sounded like Charlie." Even the guide-crafts' radios were inoperable, and unable to send the same message.

These two bizarre circumstances—Beever's navigation error and the inoperable radios—created an auspicious chain of events that resulted in Force C landing on Omaha Beach, instead of their primary objective, Pointe du Hoc. After waiting an extra ten minutes, with still no message from Rudder affirming his landing on Pointe du Hoc, Schneider redirected his boats to their secondary target, Omaha Beach. This alteration in Schneider's plans changed the outcome of the invasion by putting his men exactly where they were needed, though the initial wave sustained heavy casualties. The first elements of Force C to reach their objective, "Dog Green" beach, were craft bearing A, B, and Headquarters Companies of the 2nd Ranger Battalion, which landed on a shoulder of the Vierville Draw, where the Germans constructed a deadly *Widerstandsnest* or "Resistance Nest." In a bloody scene immortalized in the movie *Saving Private Ryan,* waves of men from the 2nd Ranger Battalion were cut down in a kill zone containing numerous bunkers with enfilading machine gun fire. German antitank guns and mortars mercilessly fired upon the incoming Rangers, who later dubbed the area "The Devil's Garden."

Seeing Dog Green was shut down, and the enormous losses A, B, and Headquarters Companies were taking and being waved off by landing control on the beach, Schneider, a veteran of Ranger landings in Africa, Sicily and Italy, ordered the 5th to land on a quieter beach known as Dog White, located next to Dog Green beach.* The extra battalion landing in the right place at exactly the right time proved crucial to the American breakout on Omaha. Near the seawall on the beach, men of Schneider's battalion ran into Brigadier General Norman Cota, assistant division commander of the 29th Division, who uttered the famous command to the men of the 5th: "Rangers, lead the way!" With that, the 5th broke out of the beachhead and flanked the German defenses.

Force B's attack on Pointe et Raz de la Percée would also prove critical. Using "bayonets and their bare hands," the men of Charlie Company scaled the cliffs and took out numerous German mortar positions that were zeroed in on Omaha Beach.

At Pointe du Hoc, the delay of Rudder's Force A had given the Germans precious time to recover from the initial shore bombardment and contest the landing. The original Allied plan called for the shore bombardment to cease at 6:30 A.M.** only minutes before the Rangers were supposed to begin assaulting the cliffs. But now, the Germans were ready and waiting for Dog Company's frontal assault, due to the extra thirty minutes afforded by Force A's late arrival.

Nineteen-year-old German Private Wilhelm Kirchhoff of 2./Werfer-Regiment 84 vividly described the scene: "The American landing craft were coming from the [east] and were fully loaded with men and material. When they arrived, the waves were very high and the little boats

*Elements of Force C landed on the boundary between Green and White beaches. Captain Arnold's B Company landed on Dog Green and the 5th's A Company and the HQ boat on Dog White. Other portions of the 5th landed to the east on Dog Red.

**Beever's navigation error likely saved the lives of many of Rudder's men. Their delay in landing on Pointe du Hoc prevented them from being hit by B-26 bombers, which bombarded the Pointe 20 minutes late (between 6:25 A.M. and 6:45 A.M.) the exact time when Force A was scheduled to land.

were thrown about violently. Once they hit the beach, the ramps dropped and the men charged out. We received no orders to fire, but the enemy was there below us so we fired! At that moment we were nervous but active. We fired from the edge with our machine guns.... We targeted the Americans as they exited the landing craft. They were firing up [at us] but were out in the open."

Kirchhoff and the other members of his regiment were dug in near a bunker on the eastern edge of the Pointe. All told, about 120 of them, including fifteen men from the Werfer Regiment, took full advantage of their superior position and firepower to resist the Rangers' landing.

"From the Pointe we started throwing grenades until we couldn't see them anymore... For the Americans down on the beach, the effect would have been devastating. They had no protection there at all," recalled Rudolf Karl, an artillerist NCO atop the Pointe.

Machine gun bullets slapped the water in front of the Rangers' incoming boats. The Germans also hurled potato masher grenades down on them. According to Kirchhoff, even "radio and telephone operators in the trenches... fired with their weapons. I continued firing my machine gun but also witnessed grenades being thrown. There were also mortars ahead of me [that] fired onto the beach below. I stood up from my trench, picked up my weapon, and kept firing, uncertain how many times I fired."

One Ranger recalled the fury of the German defense: "As we approached these cliffs, all hell broke loose. We could hear the zing of the bullets, and a few artillery shells being lobbed in... [We] heard the splatter of the machine guns and the German riflemen up on the edge of this cliff shooting down at us. There was a Ranger sitting across from me who was shot in the chest. A *Stars and Stripes* photographer vomited on me."

Fittingly, Rudder's craft hit the thirty-yard strip of rocky beach first. Bombs and artillery shells from the Allied ships had blasted away part of the cliff face where it met the narrow beach, creating massive underwater craters near the base of the peninsula. As Jack Kuhn's landing craft approached Rudder's boat near the rocky shore, Kuhn looked up at the ominous precipice. Momentarily stunned by what he saw, his Thompson slipped out of his hand and into the several inches of seawater and floating vomit that filled the bottom of the craft.

Inside the cramped boat, Kuhn turned to Sheldon Bare and snapped, "Bare, I lost my Thompson!"

Bare reached down into the filthy, brackish water and fished out Kuhn's weapon. "Here you go, Jack," he said as the boat neared the shore.

From his position on LCA 668, Lomell ordered the grapnel rockets fired at the cliff. Ironically, "the grapnels seemed like a lifeline, but were just as likely to lead the men to death as to life. Climbing the ropes would take the men out of the frying pan of German machine gun bullets and potato mashers landing on the beach and into the fire of the battle on top of the cliff."

Several yards away from Lomell, Fox Company Commander Otto Masny tensely estimated when to fire the grapnels from his boat. He noticed several craft had fired too soon, causing the rockets to fall short and miss the cliff. Masny barked at the British coxswain guiding his craft to the Pointe, "Don't fire those things until I give the word! We've got plenty of time."

To hammer home Masny's order, Lieutenant Richard A. Wintz pulled out his .45. "You drop those gates or let those charges go before I give the order, and I'll put a bullet in your head."

On board LCA 668, the loud explosion caused by the coxswain's firing the grapnel rockets jarred Lomell, as he stared at the cliffs of Pointe du Hoc looming in front of him.

SPLASH!

The ramp dropped, and the coxswain barked, "All right, everybody out!"

Lomell's boat had stopped several yards short of the shoreline. "We had amphibious DUKWs but [there were] so many underwater craters they couldn't get in too close to the cliff."

Lomell led the group. As he stepped off the ramp, he completely disappeared from view. A massive underwater bomb crater had swallowed up the first sergeant. The icy water, just forty-two degrees, rushed around him. He quickly submerged eight feet below the surface. Bullets pierced the silence underwater, as he swam out of the crater and joined the other men, who had avoided the hazard.

"Ow!" Lomell felt a sudden sting of pain through his right side. A German machine gun bullet barely missed his ribs and went through the fleshy portion of his torso. Not realizing where it came from, Lomell spun around and came face to face with Private Harry Fate.

"Harry, you son of a bitch. You shot me!"

Fate pleaded his innocence. "I didn't do it! I didn't try to kill you!"

"I was about to kill him for doin' it," Lomell admitted later.

After all, Lomell had busted Fate from sergeant to private just a few weeks prior. After losing his stripes, Fate had made a veiled threat to Lomell: "That's all right. You know all first sergeants get their due in combat. I'll see you in combat."

Breaking the standoff, Bill Geitz, Lomell's medic, socked the first sergeant in the jaw and knocked him down, yelling, "Len, he didn't do it! He didn't do it!"

The altercation lasted only a few seconds before Lomell snapped out of his rage and focused on assaulting the cliff towering in front of his men.

Minutes later, George Kerchner's LCA 858 touched down next to Lomell's boat. Before the craft landed, Kerchner thought about the half-hour delay and felt an overwhelming sense of foreboding. *"Holy hell, someone made a hell of big mistake sending us in here. We'll never get up there."*

Kerchner looked in front of him. Twenty feet of murky water stained with a reddish mixture of Ranger blood and clay from cliffs lay between him and the shore. Kerchner looked back at his men, "OK, let's go!"

As he turned back around, the green lieutenant slipped and found himself submerged in eight feet of water in the same shell hole Lomell had fallen into minutes earlier.

"Oh, hell, here we go!" he thought angrily as he "doggy paddled" to keep his head above the water. The men of 1st Platoon saw what happened and moved around the crater. "I remember being angry because I was soaked… wringing wet. I turned around and wanted to find someone to help me cuss out the British Navy for dumping me in this eight feet of water," remembered Kerchner.

But the ripping sound of a German bonesaw machine gun as it zeroed in on 1st Platoon silenced any cussing Kerchner intended to unload on the British coxswain. From the top of the cliff, the German soldiers relentlessly fired on the incoming Americans. As German machine gunner Kirchhoff related, "Until that moment, I had probably fired 10,000 rounds. I had switched barrels several times but the flash hider still sometimes got red hot."

On the beach, a bullet ripped into Sergeant Francis Pacyga's arm. The same bullet blew out the kneecap of Private First Class Lester Harris, causing him to drop his weapon. Kerchner, armed with just his .45, grabbed Harris's discarded M1 and led his men to the side of the cliff. Running about twenty-five yards down the beach, Kerchner found Rudder. Kerchner informed him that Duke Slater's boat was missing and "presumed capsized," so Kerchner now commanded Dog Company. Under heavy fire, Rudder turned to Kerchner and yelled, "Get the hell out of here and get up and climb that rope!"

CHAPTER 13

The Climb

As the men of Dog dashed toward the cliff, MG-42 machine-gun bullets kicked up the gravel around them. "I thought I was kicking up pebbles and dirt. But they were actually bullets that were hitting the sand and kicking up the dirt around me," one Ranger explained.

Months of training kicked into gear. The men ran like rabbits towards the base and began to climb. Several Rangers returned fire as they rushed to the ropes, but the German defenders took their toll as more and more Rangers went down.

When Dog started climbing, Sheldon Bare fired at the Germans; but as the men neared the top, he ceased fire. "I stopped firing because I didn't want to hit our men on top of the cliff," recalled Bare.

Then it was Bare's turn to make the hazardous climb. "The ropes were slippery, and the Germans were cutting them.* Some dropped grenades," he remembered.

"Further to my left, I saw the grappling hooks that the Americans fired to the top of the cliff. But one of the artilleryman crawled forward and cut the rope," recalled Kirchhoff, the German Werfer-Regiment private. "The Americans were unable to climb up. They remained on the beach but kept trying."

---

*Some of the grapnels contained burning fuses, which deterred the Germans from cutting the ropes because they mistook them for explosives.

Some of the men, like Sigurd Sundby from Dog Company, struggled with the ascent. "The rope was wet and kind of muddy; my hands just couldn't hold. They were like grease, and I came sliding back down. I wrapped my foot around the rope and slowed myself up as much as I could, but my hands still burned."

As Sundby slid back down the rope, he landed near another Ranger. "What's the matter, Sundby, you chicken? Let me—I'll show you how to climb."

Bill Hoffman described the confusion, "I was assigned a specific rope [and] to a specific gun. I was supposed to do some specific damage. I had a big stick of C-2 in my pocket. I just grabbed a rope, and somebody yelled 'Hey, Hey, that's mine.' They were firing down at us and throwing down potato masher grenades, and they also cut some ropes. I don't really know how we got up the cliff."

As the 225 Rangers from Assault Force A crowded the tiny beach, machine guns, grenades, and small arms fire peppered the men. Making the climb even more perilous, the Germans had also booby-trapped the cliff face with "roller mines."* Precursors to the IEDs of today, roller mines were old French artillery shells suspended on wires. Cutting the wires would detonate the shells. Accounts suggest that the Germans detonated one shell, causing a landslide near Easy Company climbers.

Lomell soon realized the ropes his boat had fired at the cliff weren't allowing the men to climb fast enough. He ordered the Rangers to assemble the four-foot metal sections of ladder they carried to assist with the climb. With the ladders in place, Lomell concentrated all of his energies on climbing. Adrenaline coursed through his body, allowing him to ignore the searing pain from the gunshot wound in his side. Exhausted, Lomell's muscles strained to carry him upward.

Climbing next to the first sergeant was 2nd Platoon's radio operator, Sergeant Robert Fruhling. Interspersed with the din of battle, Lomell could hear the ominous sound of crumbling rock as the face of

---

*According to interviews with French civilians living in the area, the Germans had suspended numerous shells in intervals along the cliff face.

the cliff gave way with each foothold. Running out of strength from making the treacherous hand-over-hand ascent while avoiding enemy fire, the wounded Lomell clung to the wet rope. Straining to lift his body the last few feet, he finally crested Pointe du Hoc.

RRRRRRRRRRR!

The incessant fire from the MG-42s rained down on the men. From the top of the cliff, Lomell looked down and spotted Fruhling, who was now near the summit, but barely hanging on. Fruhling cried out for help.

Unable to reach the radioman, Lomell provided covering fire from his Thompson and shouted, "Hold on. I can't help you!" Lomell then spotted Sergeant Leonard Rubin, an "excellent athlete with a powerful build," and called out, asking him to help the struggling Ranger. Just as Fruhling was slipping down the rope, Rubin grabbed him by the nape of his neck and, with a mighty swing, hoisted him over the top of the Pointe.

★ ★ ★

"Medic! Medic!"

Cries of dying and wounded men sounded up and down the beach. Ranger medic Frank South struggled to answer each call. South carried on his back what amounted to an aid station, complete with plasma, bandages, and other first aid supplies.

A machine gun nest on top of the cliff had a "superb enfilading position," South noted, "We were caught in its field of fire."

South scrambled to assist his fellow Rangers. Dodging the machine gun fire from the cliff, he reached one Ranger with a sucking chest wound and dragged him towards an indentation in the cliff face where it met the beach. There he began to treat the man. Moving as quickly as he could, the medic was soon joined by the battalion surgeon Doc Block.

As Block looked up from treating one of the wounded Rangers, he saw one of Fox Company's strongest climbers, Sergeant L-Rod Petty, scaling the cliff above him. Each boat had two or three excellent climbers or "top monkeys." But at that moment, the waterlogged rope was getting the best of Petty. As he slid back down, a nearby Ranger joked, "Hey, L-Rod, you're going the wrong way!"

Petty landed a few feet from Doc Block. As Petty looked over towards Block, the surgeon ordered, "Soldier, get up that rope to the top of that cliff! It's *up* you're supposed to go."

"Pissed off" Petty acidly snorted, "Go to hell, Captain! What's it look like I'm trying to do?"

Petty scrambled back up the rope. Nearby, his close friend and "pet ape" from F Company, Herm Stein, struggled to make his way up the slick line. Suddenly, Stein felt as if the rock itself was pushing him away from the rope. Stein looked down and realized that his "Mae West," or life vest, had inflated. Tearing it off, he continued to hoist himself up the slimy rope.

THUD! Small arms fire had just hit the Ranger in front of him. Yelling down, Stein barked, "Cole's been hit! Hit the dirt!" so the men climbing below him would stay low when they reached the top of the cliff.

★ ★ ★

Throughout the carnage, they stayed focused on the mission and most of the men in Force A made it to the top. When one man fell, another took his place. By 7:20 A.M., nearly all of the twenty-two men in Lomell's boat successfully scaled the cliff. Sniper, machine gun, and 37 mm antiaircraft fire ripped through the air. Lomell thought to himself, *"God damn it, we made it this far; we will beat them! We're in their land. We're gonna regroup here."*

As they had been trained to do, small groups of men now set out to complete their mission: find the guns of Pointe du Hoc and destroy them.

CHAPTER 14

Atop the Fortress

Somehow, Sheldon Bare survived the onslaught of machine gun fire and potato masher grenades that rained down while he slowly hauled his 185-pound frame over the top of Pointe du Hoc. But his ordeal wasn't over. More small arms and artillery fire greeted him and the other men of Dog Company like a swarm of angry bees.

Finding unknown reserves of energy, the young Ranger dove into a shell hole occupied by Captain Sammy Baugh, E Company's commander. "A sniper got me," Baugh told Bare. A bullet had gone through the back of Baugh's hand, piercing the grip of his .45-caliber pistol and exploding the magazine. "His hand was a bloody mess, so I gave him white sulfa powder and bandaged his hand," recalled Bare. It was Bare's first taste of combat. With the bravado and naiveté that comes with "being only twenty-one years of age," the green Ranger turned to the severely wounded officer and said, "I'll get that son of a bitch."

Reflecting on the incident sixty-five years later, Bare said, "I don't know how he knew it was a sniper. . . . I got out of the crater hole and started in the direction Baugh told me. I don't know how far away the German was from me, but I got out of the crater hole about fifteen feet and got shot."

The German bullet seared into Bare's right shoulder and burrowed into his back. It felt like it "almost took my arm off," he recalled.

"Mother fucker! Son of a bitch!" Bare blurted at the German sniper, dropping his rifle and diving back into the hole with Baugh.

After the Allied air forces and war ships bombarded Pointe du Hoc with hundreds of tons of bombs, the pockmarked top of the cliff resembled the surface of the moon. The men of Dog Company dashed from one shell hole or bomb crater to another. The deadly fire of a 37 mm antiaircraft gun zipped by. Zigzagging across the landscape, Lomell momentarily leaped into the shell hole shared by the groggy and badly wounded Captain Gilbert Baugh and Sheldon Bare. Lomell noticed Baugh's wound right away. "It blew his hand off, or most of it." Concerned, Lomell asked him if he was OK. Lomell knew the mission came first but compassionately told both men, "We'll send back a medic." Leaving the wounded Rangers in the relative safety of the crater, he and a small group of Dog Company men made their way to gun position number four.

When they got there, they stared at the empty emplacement in shock. To deceive Allied aerial reconnaissance, a telephone pole had replaced the 155 mm gun that was supposed to be there. Ranger Sigurd Sundby looked inside the emplacement, which held a tangled bunch of wires. Unsure what the wires were for, he thought to himself, *"Well, I better cut them, just in case."*

Terrified by the battle going on around him, at that moment Sundby fell victim to the call of nature. "I must have gotten scared, because I had to take a crap, so I pulled my pants down. I took a crap," he explained.

In a textbook example of Ranger tactics, the men, acting on their own initiative, broke up into small groups to achieve their objectives. Sundby separated from Lomell and his small group and emerged from the gun emplacement, bumping into Sergeant Richard J. Spleen. A strong, silent type who "kept to himself," Spleen spotted two Germans firing upon them.

"I see two of them," Spleen said to Sundby. Spleen leveled his M1 Garand at the Germans and "shot up the two Jerries." But they managed to flee into the labyrinth of tunnels connecting the bunkers atop Pointe du Hoc, disappearing into the moonscape.

Another officer then shouted at the two men to go after several snipers who were picking off Rangers on the face of the Pointe. Spleen pointed in the direction of one sniper and the two men split up. Sundby attempted to flank the German by moving around a small knoll. As he did so, he saw two men from Fox Company behind their machine gun. Sundby approached the weapon, but the gunner had been shot right between the eyes. The other man had been killed too. *"He must have put his head up, and they got him,"* thought Sundby. At that moment, Sundby realized that he was standing, making himself an easy target for the snipers. A bullet snapped by his ear as he lunged to the ground.

He landed in a depression that provided cover from the sniper's bullets. Moving forward, he found that he had crawled right into a morass of manure. "You know what it was? It was the darn settling pond where they must drain out the manure for the liquid to fertilize their fields," Sundby remembered. Coated in the cow dung, Sundby ran for better cover.

Someone hollered, "Get down!"

Another bullet passed close to his ear. "And this time I saw it come through a little tree right in front of me, and I saw the bark snap out. Then I dove down after that. I crawled away, and I got up on the hedgerow again. And I had kind of an idea where the bullet, what direction it was coming from, so I got up there and put my rifle in there, and got behind some brush—it was kind of a bush there. And I was just looking out there, and I couldn't spot that sniper. But I figured, I saw a tree out there, and I thought maybe he's up in that tree. So I kept my eye on that. I didn't fire any shots right then because I thought he would move or something, so I could see him. Then I couldn't shoot. So I waited there."

★ ★ ★

While Sundby was pinned down, Lomell's small group moved towards gun emplacements five and six. Again, the 155 mm guns, the focus of their entire mission, were not in their emplacements. Here, too, Lomell noticed the Germans had replaced the steel barrels of the actual guns with telephone poles. At first glance, it seemed the Rangers had undertaken the mission for naught. Where were the guns?

At this point, Lomell had gone through three emplacements without finding any guns. He thought to himself, *"Jesus Christ, there's no guns here. They gotta be somewhere."*

Avoiding the insistent 37 mm fire, Lomell dashed for another shell hole. In the crater crouched about a dozen men from Dog Company, including men from George Kerchner's 1st Platoon. Germans in nearby bunkered positions and farm buildings were giving the Dog Company men hell. Several men fixed bayonets on their M1 Garands, planning to make an over-the-top, World War I-like charge. Lomell remembered, "We were gonna charge across. We were gonna come out the shell crater as fast as we could and hit those encasements and see what the hell was there."

Staff Sergeant Morris Webb was one of the first out of the hole. "Webb jumped the gun," remembered Lomell. After ducking rifle and machine gun fire, Webb dove back into the crater—and directly onto the scalpel-like steel of another Ranger's ten-inch bayonet. It impaled Webb's thigh, digging deep into the muscle. Lomell treated Webb, sprinkling sulfa powder on the fresh wound and throwing a bandage on it.

"Webb, you stay here," barked Lomell.

The charge across Pointe du Hoc had been costly. In the process of moving from one shell hole to another and avoiding German fire, Lomell had lost half of his men—some only wounded and some dead.

Despite the losses, Lomell knew he must complete the mission. "Our mission and the mission of the 2nd Ranger Battalion, D, E, and F Company, was to get up on those cliffs and destroy those guns. The next part of our mission was to establish a roadblock and prevent any vehicles coming from the east with Germans toward Omaha Beach.

The third part was to cut off any communications that we could and hold the line."

The men separated into small groups, each trying to accomplish their primary objective of destroying the guns. Their search for the guns developed along three axes. About a dozen men from Dog Company, led by Len Lomell, moved from gun position number six toward the coastal highway. Fox Company paralleled them on the eastern side of Pointe du Hoc. Another pocket of men, led by Sergeant Frank Rupinski of Easy Company, advanced down the middle between the other two groups.

CHAPTER 15

Bunkers and Farms

En route to the coastal highway, First Sergeant Lomell and his men knew they had to overcome several bunkered buildings that served as German crew quarters. From his training and his memory of photographs presented at various briefings, Lomell remembered that the Germans had mined the entire area. The Rangers would have to traverse these dense minefields. In addition, the 37 mm antiaircraft gun on their right flank was tearing up the area around them, putting up a lot of fire.

As the Rangers advanced upon the bunkered position, Lieutenant Ted Lapres and a couple of E Company men approached Lomell. "What are you doing, Len?" Lapres asked.

"What I'm gonna do is move up and throw a bazooka into them and blow the whole God damn thing up." Lomell moved the bazooka into position. Unfortunately, the loader forgot to pull the pin on the bazooka round, and it failed to detonate.

Meanwhile, the antiaircraft gun bore down on Dog Company. "The son of a bitch was giving us a really hard time," recalled Lomell. Lieutenant Lapres and several men moved off to the right flank to try to take out the AA gun.

From the shell hole, Lomell and his men studied the crew quarters. "We're gonna hit 'em hard," Lomell told his men. The Rangers charged. "We were hooting and hollering, yelling 'EEAAGGHH!!' We wanted to scare the shit out of them," recalled Lomell.

The Americans attacked the quarters, firing their Thompsons and M1s into the buildings. Many of the Germans were unarmed, dashing for their weapons as they were putting on their shirts and uniforms. While some of the enemy fought back tenaciously, others ducked into underground tunnels.

As the Rangers pushed inland in pursuit of the enemy, a creeping artillery barrage exploded behind them.

Lomell's men charged forward to the coastal road with a deadly rain of steel at their backs. The first sergeant's small group included his best friend, Staff Sergeant Jack Kuhn. The two best friends each led a column of men, one on either side of the sunken road. The men soon came across a centuries-old stone barn.

Suddenly, Lomell grabbed Kuhn's arm, threw him into the doorway of the Norman barn, and rushed inside himself. Kuhn was startled. "Why'd you do that?"

"Didn't you see that Jerry kneeling on the road, aiming at us?" Lomell asked in amazement.

Kuhn peeked around the doorway. Two German rounds barely missed the Ranger sergeant.

Lomell poked his tommy gun through a window of the barn and fired at the Germans. He missed. Kuhn went to fire his tommy gun, but a bullet had struck the ammunition clip where it inserted into the weapon, rendering it useless.

Meanwhile, elements of George Kerchner's 1st Platoon came up the side of Pointe du Hoc with Rudder's command group. The 37 mm gun continued taking its bloody toll, while small bands of Rangers made their way toward the projected gun positions.

The Germans counterattacked, emerging from the rubble of Pointe du Hoc. They seemed to pop up all around the maze of ruined trenches and underground shelters and bunkers. For the Rangers, the pockmarked surface of the Pointe made it difficult to distinguish friend from foe. Similar to a game of whack-a-mole, Germans emerged from craters and trenches. Kerchner rounded up most of his 1st Platoon along with other members of Dog Company. The German AA gun continued to fire at his group while 1st Platoon tried to take it out with rifle fire. Pinned down, they had difficulty even getting a shot off.

In an attempt to flank the gun, Kerchner jumped into the communication trench. "I was by myself at this time, and I have never felt so lonesome before or since in my life because every time I came to a corner in this communications trench, where I had to make a turn to see what was in the next twenty-five-yard section, I didn't know whether I was going to come face-to-face with a German or not."

Kerchner stooped low as he darted through the trench. His loneliness gave way to sadness when he caught sight of Bill Vaughan, one of Lomell's climbing "monkeys." The Ranger officer related, "I realized as soon as I saw him that he was dying. He had been practically stitched across with a machine gun. He wasn't in any pain because he was hit too bad. I knew he was dying."

The lieutenant from Baltimore approached the mortally wounded Ranger and compassionately told him, "Bill, we'll send a medic to look after you."

Kerchner continued skulking cautiously through the trench, eventually meeting up with the rest of his men, much to his relief. Together, they found their way through the labyrinth until it emptied out near the ruins of a farmhouse. Finally out in the open, 1st Platoon pushed on toward the coastal road, their secondary objective.

When Dog Company sergeants Bill Cruz and William Robertson reached the top of Pointe du Hoc, they ran into Lieutenant Colonel Rudder. Despite being wounded, Rudder's charismatic presence inspired the men around him. Cruz had been hit in the arm on the beach before scaling the cliffs, but, like many of the Rangers, he carried on in spite of the pain. The men were told to guard the area that

Rudder had designated as his new command post, but the persistent crack of deadly sniper fire filled the air around them.

Sergeant Cruz and another Ranger fired at the sniper, but missed. Suddenly, machine gun and antiaircraft fire from the 37 mm opened up. Rudder looked at both men and said, "Go after it."

Whenever the Rangers opened fire, artillery rained down on their heads. As they crawled forward through the countless shell craters, they came upon approximately ten men pinned down near gun position number six, including Richard J. Spleen of D Company and Harold D. Main of E Company. Together, the Rangers held their fire "for fear of drawing 88 fire."

The small group crawled west in an attempt to get a better position on the German machine gun nest and the AA gun. Cruz spotted a German soldier waving a helmet on a rifle, attempting to draw the Rangers' fire and expose their positions. "Somebody [in our group] came up from behind and unwisely fired on this decoy. Right away, 88 fire and mortar fire hit."

Because the men were bunched up in the craters, they took off in different directions to avoid being hit in one group. When the men separated, Cruz found himself alone in the maze of tunnels and craters. He yelled out, "Is anybody there? Is everybody alright?"

Sergeant Main responded, "[We're] OK."

Cruz waited for fifteen minutes. Small arms fire crackled in the distance. The Ranger NCO started crawling back across a crater and took fire from snipers. He reached a trench near gun position six, where he spotted Spleen, who was recently separated from Sundby, and two other men in a trench right nearby. "All the sudden, [a]lot of firing, machine guns and machine pistols… [began hitting] close to the west. He saw Spleen's men throw down their guns out of the trench they were in, surrendering." Cruz kept quiet, hugging the ground.

"The firing died down and after the first few seconds, he saw no one. Later, crawling out back toward the command post he passed a pile of weapons, lying on the ground near gun position number six—eight or nine rifles, some pistols, and four Thompsons." Later, the

Rangers found some of the packs from the captured group. Cruz was the sole survivor.

Another Ranger also found himself alone. Bill Hoffman was the only Ranger in an underground bunker atop Pointe du Hoc. "I managed to get over to a bunker, not the one I was supposed to be in, but I got in there. They were shelling us pretty good. Inside the bunker things got quiet." Hoffman ended up in a room full of German bicycles, where he considered his next course of action. "I was sitting there trying to make up my mind when I heard this God awful explosion in the corridor between the rooms. It scared the hell out of me."

"What is that? What am I gonna do?" Hoffman thought to himself.

After a second explosion, Hoffman threw one of the bicycles out into the hallway. Seeing fins from a bazooka round nearby, he thought, *"Oh, my God, they have our equipment!"* Suddenly, a voice barked out, "Come out with your hands up!"

"Geez, they speak really good English," Hoffman thought to himself. After sticking his hand out into the hallway to make sure they weren't planning to shoot, he slowly emerged. In front of him stood a lieutenant and a sergeant, who was holding a grenade.

"Hey, Sarge! What are you going to do with that?" asked Hoffman.

"I'm going to roll it right down that hallway," replied the sergeant.

"What are you doing in here?" the lieutenant asked Hoffman.

He answered, "I'm getting out of the artillery fire."

"We got word there were Germans in here," said the lieutenant.

"There are no Germans here, just me," Hoffman replied.

★ ★ ★

Bleeding and exhausted from climbing and fighting through the trenches, Lomell looked at his remaining men and said, "Follow me."

The firefight in the farm buildings had taken its toll. Still, Lomell led the most sizable force on top of Pointe du Hoc. The small band headed along a dirt road that led to the blacktop coastal road.* The

*In 1944, the coastal road was called GC32. Now, it's known as D-514.

men made their way towards the intersection. Abruptly, a wall of small arms fire enveloped the Ranger patrol. Jack Conaboy, one of Lomell's platoon sergeants, was flattened in the middle of the intersection. "Len! Len! I'm hit!"

"Where're ya hit?"

"In the ass," responded Conaboy.

"Well, get the hell over here," said Lomell.

With a burst of adrenaline, Conaboy jumped up and ran towards the ditch where Lomell and the others had taken cover.

Conaboy dropped his pants, and Lomell inspected the wound. The bullet didn't go all the way through.

"You're lucky; you've got a souvenir here." Lomell pulled out the bullet and packed the wound with sulfa powder.

After taking care of Conaboy, Lomell's group cautiously made their way down the coastal road. Suddenly, Lomell and Kuhn spotted a platoon of about thirty-five heavily armed Germans. They knew engaging them would be suicide. The men flattened themselves in the ditch as the Germans marched past. "Three men against thirty-five was stupid, and it would ruin our mission," recounted Lomell. "So we let them pass."

A stone fence paralleled the road. Suddenly, a German soldier appeared in an opening in the fence and looked down the highway. Not detecting the Americans, he ran across the road and right up to where Jack Kuhn was hiding. Kuhn jumped up and fired point blank with his tommy gun, hitting the German in his chest.

"My slugs must have cut the strap on his weapon, for it fell to the ground about three feet in front of me. The German ran a few steps and dropped."

Johnson asked Kuhn to retrieve the dead German's MP-40 submachine gun. As Kuhn attempted to grab the machine pistol, he saw another German soldier aiming at him. "I had no way to protect myself and felt I was about to be shot."

Just then, machine gun bullets from Lomell's Thompson ripped into the German, killing him, but not before one of the enemy's bullets struck the road next to Kuhn, barely missing him. At this point, Lomell and Kuhn decided to have the men pair up and keep searching for the missing guns: "There's a minefield on our left full of mines. 'Well,' we decided, 'there's nobody but us, so let's split up into twos.'"

Lomell and Kuhn set off together and soon discovered tire tracks in the lane. Lomell realized that the grooves couldn't have been made by a simple farm wagon—the impressions were far too deep. Something massive had crossed the earth. "We figured we ought to take a look."

CHAPTER 16

The Guns of Pointe du Hoc

Lomell and Kuhn moved down the sunken road, which cut through several pastures and high hedgerows. "You could have hid a column of tanks in it, that's how deep it was," recalled the first sergeant.

The two Rangers carefully traversed the road, moving about one hundred yards down the country lane. Lomell scouted out the position while Kuhn covered him, then the two men switched off, or "leapfrogged," as they made their way deeper and deeper into German territory. Suddenly, Lomell and Kuhn came upon a picturesque, lush apple orchard.

"My God, there they are!" Lomell said to himself.

Lomell turned to Kuhn. "My God. Look at them. They're ready to go." The long, 155 mm barrels of the guns of Pointe du Hoc loomed directly in front of them.

Five of the K418 guns—the German designation for the former French artillery pieces—had been towed inland and pointed at Utah Beach. They could easily have been turned around and used to fire upon Omaha Beach as well. Netting covered in fake leaves was draped over the five guns. But the sixth gun was mysteriously missing.

Amazingly, not a soul stood guard near the artillery.* However, they could see about seventy-five to one hundred Germans assembling several hundred feet away in the corner of an adjoining field. "The Germans were in various states of undress. They were putting jackets and shirts on; they were being rallied. They were being talked to by some officer standing in his vehicle. This is now about eight in the morning," noted Lomell.

It appeared to Lomell that the group included the thirty-five heavily armed Germans who narrowly missed discovering him and Kuhn just minutes earlier.

Lomell asked Kuhn for his incendiary grenade, adding it to his own. With Kuhn covering him, Lomell climbed over towards the guns. Armed with only a submachine gun, his .45, and two thermite grenades, he moved into position near the artillery. He placed a thermite grenade on two of the guns. "The thermite grenade was special for this type of action because we were going to lay them on the moving parts of the artillery and destroy the movable gears in the guns."

Lomell pulled the pins. POP! A molten, metal-like substance flowed over the parts, seeping into the crevices and welding them together so that they were inoperable. Remarkably, the nearby Germans didn't detect the first sergeant. He wrapped his field jacket around the butt of his tommy gun, using it to smash the sights of all five artillery pieces. "I didn't know if I was going to get back, so I wanted to do as much damage as possible."

---

*For over sixty-five years, historians have debated why the Germans failed to man the guns. The most plausible theory is that when the Rangers took out the German forward observation posts, they took out the German eyes on Pointe du Hoc, severing communication with the gun crews. As *Small Unit Actions* notes, "All that can be stated with assurance is that the Germans were put off balance and disorganized by the combined efforts of the bombardment and assault, to such an extent that they never used the most dangerous battery near the assault beach but left it in position to be destroyed by weak patrols." The Germans could clearly see Utah Beach. It's a mystery why they didn't fire directly on that sector, even without official orders.

Lomell and Kuhn's actions—the actions of two men who were willing to risk their lives for the mission—had a profound impact on the entire invasion.

Not thinking about anything other than the mission, Lomell scurried back over to Kuhn and whispered to him, "We've got to get more grenades."

Kuhn and Lomell dashed back a hundred yards or so down the road, where they met other men in their platoon and asked for their incendiary grenades. With his field jacket full of incendiaries, Lomell ran back towards the guns with Kuhn at his side.

When they reached the guns, Kuhn trained his Thompson on the Germans in the field. The first sergeant placed thermite grenades on the three remaining guns. As Lomell finished rigging the last field piece, Jack said, "Hurry up! Hurry up!"

After pulling their pins, Lomell scrambled over a nine-foot-tall hedgerow, where Kuhn was standing.

Then "the whole world blew up," as Lomell and Kuhn flew off the hedgerow and onto the sunken road. "Dust and the stones and the brush came out of the sky. Ramrods and all kinds of things fell around us."

"What the hell just happened?" asked Lomell. Unbeknownst to the two men, Sergeant Frank Rupinski from Easy Company had detonated an ammunition store near the guns, causing a massive explosion.*

It was now approximately 8:30 A.M. Two Dog Company Rangers, Leonard Lomell and Jack Kuhn, had achieved what scores of bombers dropping hundreds of tons of bombs, and the massive fourteen-inch guns of the battleship Texas, as well as a constant bombardment from off-shore destroyers had failed to achieve. Thanks to them, five of the six guns of Pointe du Hoc would never fire again.

*Sergeant Rupinski led a patrol from E Company and advanced on the guns from the east. Accounts differ, but besides blowing the ammunition store, his group may have placed grenades in the barrels of the guns after Lomell had already disabled them.

After locating the sixth gun nearby, a patrol from Easy Company soon eliminated it.

Rejoining the other men, Lomell dispatched two volunteers to relay the news that they had accomplished the mission. Ironically, he chose Private Harry Fate, the man he accused earlier of shooting him in the side. Sergeant Gordon Lunning accompanied Fate.

Going back through the country roads, traversing the moonscaped surface of Pointe du Hoc, Lunning and Fate fought their way back to the German bunker that Rudder had converted into a command post. The runners from D Company arrived at the command post at approximately 9 A.M. Lunning encountered Lieutenant James Eikner and told him the news. Eikner then informed Rudder. "Should I send a message, sir?" Eikner asked.

"Yes," Rudder answered.

Most of the Rangers' radios had been waterlogged or damaged in the landing. Astutely planning for such a contingency, Eikner had brought along a signal lamp. Luckily for the Rangers, Eikner was trained in Morse code and sent off the pre-designated signal to confirm destruction of the guns: "Blow 6." The lieutenant also requested re-supply and reinforcements.

As the final contingency, in case all the technology failed, Eikner relied on the wings of a carrier pigeon to relay the message. Slipping a small note inside a tube attached to the bird, Eikner released it. Initially, the winged messenger failed its duty miserably, repeatedly circling the command post. Eikner threw pebbles at the bird until, finally, it flew towards the Allied fleet.

An hour later, the destroyer USS *Satterlee* responded: "No reinforcements available—all Rangers have landed on Omaha."

Like Lomell and the rest of the men on top Pointe du Hoc, Rudder and the others in his command post were on their own, and tragically, the guns of their comrades would pose the greatest danger.

Several forward artillery observers, including Private Henry Genther and Navy Lieutenant Kenneth "Rocky" Norton, had accompanied the Rangers. Using Eikner's signal lamp, the men now called in artillery from the nearby Allied warships. They also called in a strafing run from P-47 fighter-bombers. The Thunderbolts arrived first, and the lead plane mistakenly began a deadly dive-bombing raid directed toward Rudder's command post.

Quickly, Eikner spread out an American flag along the side of the cliff. Spotting Old Glory, the American pilot waggled his wings and flew off toward the German positions across Pointe du Hoc.

The shore-fire control party then used Eikner's lamp to call in naval fire upon the German machine gun nests and the 37 mm AA gun that was wreaking so much havoc on them. But an artillery shell from the battleship *Texas*'s 14-inch guns landed short, detonating near Rudder's command bunker. The shell killed Captain Harwood and Private Genther, also wounding Lieutenant Colonel Rudder and Lieutenant Norton. The fatal round was like an armor piercing shell containing yellow pigment known as "Explosive D" or Dunnite. "The men were turned completely yellow. It was as though they had been stricken with jaundice. It wasn't only their faces and hands, but the skin beneath their clothes and their clothes which were yellow from that shell."

Bill Hoffman recalled seeing one of the men killed by the shell. "He had no head and no blood. He was covered with yellow dye. The shrapnel just took his head off, nice and clean. He was all yellow. I said to myself, *What the hell is that?* It was my first introduction to death in the war."

Already wounded in the leg, Rudder was wounded again by the yellow marker shell. Despite his wounds, he refused to relinquish command and continued leading his men.

After Eikner sent out "Praise the Lord," indicating success, Rudder instructed Lunning and Fate to take a message back to Lomell's group, which had set up a roadblock—the second part of their mission. Rudder's orders were simple: "Hold 'til duly relieved." The pair of Dog Company men set out across the maze to find the roadblock.

CHAPTER 17

Swimmers

"Keep moving your legs!"

Hypothermia was setting in and the strong current of the English Channel was pulling their exhausted bodies downward. Several had drowned already as Ruggiero, Slater, and McBride encouraged fellow Rangers to keep their legs moving to keep the icy water from claiming more lives from The Duke's sinking landing craft.

Earlier, when Lomell's boat had pulled ahead, things began to go horribly wrong for Slater and the others on LCA 860. While the majority of Dog Company was engaged in scaling the cliffs and searching for the missing guns, Slater and the other Rangers aboard LCA 860 were fighting a very different kind of battle. Still out in the channel, the men riding in the captain's boat struggled to avoid capsizing in the turbulent, freezing seas.

Sometime around 7 A.M., when Lomell's LCA 668 took the lead, LCA 860 was already in trouble. Shells whizzed by, nearly hitting the boat several times. "We were bailing water. We were all seasick and throwing up—I know I was," recalled Tom Ruggiero. In an attempt to get some fresh air and see how far they were from the objective, Ruggiero stood up in the boat. "How far is it until we land?" he murmured.

Dominick Sparaco, who was behind Ruggiero, reached up, yanked the five-foot-three Italian down, and yelled, "You damn fool! There's things flying all over. They hit you, they're going to blow the whole boat up."

Ruggiero was carrying C-2 plastic explosives intended to destroy the guns on top of Pointe du Hoc. He had placed the C-2 in a belt around his waist. Like most of the Rangers in the boat, he was carrying about sixty pounds of equipment, which included several bandoliers of ammunition, six fragmentation grenades, a thermite grenade, a trenching tool, and a .45 he had attached to his belt with a rawhide lanyard.

In the channel, the *Texas*, a stalwart battlewagon from World War I, continued to shell Pointe du Hoc with its large guns. But German ordnance persisted in firing at Slater's landing craft as well as the bigger ship. Several near misses brushed by LCA 860. "You could feel it. Every time a shell came down, it was like it was knocking you in the guts," recalled Ruggie.

From one of the shells splashing down, Ruggiero caught a mouthful of saltwater, which "made things even worse. Stuff was coming in pretty close," he recounted.

Then a shell came in and hit near the front of the boat. "The front went up and the boat tipped over sideways. That's when we knew we were going to flood. Before we entered the boats, they told us they wouldn't sink. 'Don't leave the boat.' I never saw a boat go down so fast in my life," declared Ruggiero.

As LCA 860 was going down, The Duke stood up and dramatically yelled, "Abandon ship!"

The men started shedding their extra equipment and gear, tossing it all over the side of the boat. Johnny Corona had his girlfriend's picture in his helmet. "Baby, it's either you or me," he said, tossing the picture and his helmet just before he hit the cold water.

Around them, geysers of water from landing shells engulfed the men. The concussion blast of a shell killed one Ranger instantly. Life or death boiled down to a matter of reflexes, a handful of seconds, and a lot of luck. Besides scrambling to remove their sixty pounds of equipment, the men also rushed to press the buttons that would inflate their lifebelts. "I squeezed it as soon as I hit the water, and it self-inflated," Ruggiero explained.

All were not so fortunate, though. Tough Guy's fingers anxiously worked on the defective lifebelt he wore, as he struggled in vain to activate his lifebelt. But as Ruggiero had warned him, it didn't work. And so Riendeau, the best swimmer in Dog Company, the miracle man who had survived a fall from the steep precipice of the Needles, went down in the channel waters "like a rock." Several other men soon shared his fate, including Army photographer, Private First Class Kegham Nigohosian, who had been attached to the outfit only days earlier.

The rest of the men continued scrambling to remove the heavy equipment that was pulling them into the dark, cold waters. Ruggiero's .45 pistol was tapping his knee. With all his "brute strength," he broke the rawhide lanyard and freed the gun. He looked over at the men, including Slater and McBride, who were bobbing in the water.

"Keep it going! Keep it going!" Ruggiero and the officers yelled to the men.

Sparaco turned to Ruggiero, "Oh, God, I'm tired. I can't feel my legs anymore."

Ruggiero could sense that his friend was starting to slip into the water and drown. "I was a dancer; my legs were strong. I told the men, keep your legs going like pedaling a bicycle."

A similar fate had befallen another landing craft, LCA 914, the Rangers' supply boat. It went down, drowning most of those on board; the lone survivor was Private First Class John Riley of Dog Company.

While the men from the capsized boat were battling the frigid waters of the channel, they could see their fellow Rangers assailing Pointe du Hoc. Hypothermia began setting in, dragging more men to the bottom. Duke Slater and his Rangers were dying a slow, cold, watery death.

As they desperately fought to survive in the ice-cold water, help arrived, surprisingly in the form of a gunboat that had initially gone to the wrong beach. After having gone to Utah Beach, it had been directed back to Omaha Beach. It was there that the boat intersected the path of Slater, McBride, Ruggiero, Secor, and other Dog Company men still clinging to life

At that point, Ruggiero noticed that one of his fellow Rangers was about to go under. He pointed at the man, yelling for the crew to save him first. The gunboat crew cast a donut-shaped life preserver to the man. "He got one arm in it and lost it." As the crew pulled the donut towards the boat, they hoisted the freezing Ranger on board. "He was dead when they pulled him up," recalled Ruggiero.

The gunboat started retrieving the other men of LCA 860. A weighted rope "nearly hit me in the face," remembered Ruggiero. As he grabbed it, the crew pulled him through the water "like a torpedo." Once he reached the boat, friendly arms tried to pull him aboard. "That's OK, I can climb," Ruggiero told the crew. "As soon as I hit the cold air, I went right back down like a rock," he later admitted.

Several men never came out of the water alive. Ruggiero, Slater, McBride, and the other survivors were separated from one another, given blankets, and taken into the warm, inner part of the ship. Ruggiero ended up in the powder magazine. Shells still splashed in the water near the boat, some of them coming in pretty hot. A crew member snidely remarked to Ruggiero, "Since we're in the magazine, we won't even know what happened when it hits."

In addition to receiving blankets, the men were given shots of medicinal brandy to warm them up. Still suffering from the hypothermia, the Rangers then transferred to the *Texas*, where the ship's surgeon examined them. Gung ho, eager to join the fight and help his fellow Rangers, Slater begged to be allowed to go back to Pointe du Hoc. Realizing they lacked weapons and equipment and were barely alive, the ship's surgeon looked at Slater and said flatly, "You're not going anywhere right now." It would be nearly two and a half weeks before Slater, McBride, Ruggiero, and the other "swimmers" of LCA 860 would rejoin the rest of Dog Company.

CHAPTER 18

The First Counterattack

"Hold 'til duly relieved,"

Gordon Lunning and Harry Fate fought their way across the battered landscape of Pointe du Hoc and stumbled upon George Kerchner. The two men relayed Rudder's command.

THUD! THUD! THUD!

The 37 mm antiaircraft gun peppered the small group as the words of Rudder's order trailed out of Fate's lips. Kerchner determined to do something about it. Forming up, they moved through the trenches and fired at the cannon. It was useless. The men couldn't get close enough to the German AA gun that had stymied a large part of the assault group. Kerchner's M1 even failed to fire because it was clogged with dirt. Pinned down, he broke off the attack, and they linked up with Lomell and what remained of Dog Company. They counted twenty heads.

In preparation for the inevitable German counterattack, the men dug in near the blacktop road. The Rangers consolidated their roadblock position, forming a position that resembled the letter *L*. Each company held a line extending about three hundred yards. Dog Company was on the west; they linked up with Easy Company, forming a right angle, which then met up with Fox Company. All told, the Rangers had approximately eighty-five men among the three companies. "The twenty men [of Dog Company] were drawn in to form the knight position on a hedgerow from the highway up to E Company. Lieutenant Kerchner was at the hedgerow intersection [a right angle] where E and D joined: Sergeant Lomell was near the center of the line. One BAR-man [T/5 Harry Stecki] was in an angle with Kerchner; another was about one hundred yards to the north. The two men were out west of Kerchner's post about halfway to the lane on that flank. Another outpost of two men (one with a BAR) was on the angle made by that lane with the highway. The rest were strung out along three hundred yards of hedgerow in a ditch at the foot of the embankment."

As the Rangers were attempting to consolidate their position near the blacktop road, the Germans were planning a counterattack. The moment the Rangers landed on the beach below, the watchful eyes in the observation bunker atop Pointe du Hoc immediately alerted German command. After about an hour passed with "no messages from Pointe du Hoc," the Germans began assembling a platoon from Saint-Pierre-du-Mont to attack what they believed was a weak Allied commando force. Hours passed before the Germans realized this was *not* a small-scale raid.

A German first lieutenant ordered a grenadier regiment to send as many troops as possible to Pointe du Hoc. The Germans had their hands full with Omaha Beach; nevertheless, one of the German regiment's battalions was able to muster several hundred men from its 9th and 12th heavy weapons companies. The first major German attack fell on the line held by F Company, commanded by Lieutenant Richard Wintz and Sergeant L-Rod Petty.

That afternoon, two listening outposts along the line received the brunt of the action, particularly the one manned by Petty and several other Rangers. Ensconced beside a stone wall at the foot of a wheat field, the Fox Company sergeant and his squad hid behind a piece of farm machinery. "From this area, during that day, Petty's group delivered effective surprise fire on many German parties across the stream valley. The ground sloped steeply to the stream just in front of his position, and observation had been excellent." Petty's position was about three hundred yards in front of E Company's hedgerow.

Petty peered out across the stream valley, and he noticed a group of Germans riding bicycles close together. Petty depressed the trigger on his BAR. Several bursts sent the Germans tumbling. A French farmer then attempted to move a wagon across Petty's field of fire. Seeing the way the animals were lashed together, Petty thought, *"[They look] just like the chariot race from* Ben Hur."

"Hold your fire!" Petty barked.

Petty's assistant BAR gunner, Private First Class Carl Winsch, blurted out, "Hold your fire, hell! That wagon's loaded with Germans lying down."

At that, Winsch and Petty, along with the other Rangers in the outpost, opened up with their BARs, blasting the wagon. The Germans concealed under the hay bailed out of the wagon, but Winsch and Petty cut them down with their BARs. Petty later mused, "During this day, me and my BAR became familiar and inseparable friends."

The Germans began to assemble and hit the Ranger lines. Len Lomell peeked over a wall near the blacktop highway. "Looking over the five-foot wall edging the highway, he saw a German force of about fifty to sixty men coming from the Pointe toward the road through the orchard. The enemy was moving in an organized fashion with scouts ahead. Lomell could see two machine gun sections and a mortar. There was no time to make preparations or even pass word down the line. Lomell could only hope the enemy would pass by and that his own men would have the sense to hold their fire."

An attack of this strength with the German's fire superiority could easily have wiped out the twenty men. But the Germans did not attack as they slowed their course, and they did not detect the men's position. About thirty feet from the wall where the Rangers waited, poised to defend themselves, the enemy turned westward. They paralleled the highway, stealthily moving through the farm fields westward of Lomell's outpost, and then marched south across the blacktop. To a man, the Rangers, demonstrating their finely honed combat skills learned from months of intense training, made no move to betray their position.

★ ★ ★

While many men of Dog, Easy, and Fox manned the L-shaped position, Rudder worked to secure Pointe du Hoc, which still crawled with enemy troops. German artillery fire and, on occasion, American friendly fire continued to rain down on the Rangers.

Rudder tasked Big Stoop of F Company with establishing a defensive perimeter around the command post and cleaning out the Pointe. The antiaircraft gun represented the most serious danger to the perimeter. As Masny was organizing his defense, he barely avoided being hit by several shells from the AA gun. Furious, Masny quickly gathered a small band of men—as many as he could round up—to attack and destroy the gun. The group included several stragglers from Dog Company—Sigurd Sundby, Robert Fruhling, and George Schneller.*

British Commando Lieutenant Colonel Thomas Trevor, with a bandage covering his head wound, joined the F Company commander and his band. Trevor—the towering, six-foot-four officer who helped plan the mission—had participated in the assault as an observer. At Bude, he had famously taught the men his bizarre way of avoiding bullets: telling the men that if they used a stutter step first, then a long step, then a short step, followed by a sidestep, they could throw off the Germans who had them in their sights. Earlier that morning, with a swagger stick tucked under his arm, he had calmly walked the beach at Pointe du Hoc using his special technique. The tactic had worked beautifully for Trevor in North Africa, but that fateful morning in France, as he did his little dance, a German sniper drilled a bullet into his helmet, grazing the top of his skull. When the bullet knocked him off his feet, Trevor rose and waved his fist in the direction of the Germans, yelling, "Is that the best you can do?"

*One of the wealthiest men in Dog Company, Schneller, a socialite from New York, had ditched the silver spoon and volunteered for the Rangers.

Moving around the deep craters, Big Stoop and the men advanced the length of a football field across the top of Pointe du Hoc. Heavy shelling from the antiaircraft and machine gun fire challenged their advance. As the group crept across the Pointe, they came to a farm road with a hedgerow alongside. Sundby recalled, "They started shelling us with mortars in that position. When I was laying there up on that hedgerow, a mortar landed just between my legs, and it never went off. I looked over my shoulder, and I could see those fins sticking up between my legs. So I crawled away from there." Then Sundby looked over and saw George Schneller. "He got hit with shrapnel right in his back, so I went up there, and I dressed his wound and gave him some morphine," he recounted. After that, he went back along the hedgerow, "looking for that sniper."

Machine gun and rifle fire and rounds from the antiaircraft gun lit up the group. Diving into shell holes, Big Stoop and his men fired back. A barrage of German mortar and artillery blanketed the men. The first rounds went over their heads. Succeeding rounds then crept down the road towards them.

Death moved closer as the projectiles landed right next to Masny, who bizarrely commented, "It was the prettiest firing I ever saw." Suddenly, deadly shrapnel tore through Big Stoop's muscular right arm. The devastating fusillade killed several men and wounded nearly the entire group.

Unexpectedly, the German fire died down, and a white flag appeared near the antiaircraft gun. Two of the Rangers rose to accept the surrender. Big Stoop sensed something was wrong. "Stay down! You guys get down!" he barked.

It was too late. German bullets ripped right through their bodies. The two men were killed.

"Withdraw! Every man for himself!" shouted Masny.

What was left of the group stumbled back towards the command post. German snipers killed two more of Masny's men. Making the journey ever more difficult, the Rangers had to navigate a minefield. Under fire, the remaining men carefully retraced their steps for fear of losing a limb.

The group made its way back to gun position number six. There, what was left of the group dove into a shell crater to avoid a German sniper who had a bead on some of them. In the shell hole, Big Stoop bumped into Fruhling, who had a large radio strapped to his back. German shells continued to fall. The entire area was hot with small arms fire. Masny looked at the men and suggested they make a run for the next shell crater. Nodding their heads, the men agreed.

Bullets whizzed and cracked by their ears as Masny dove head-first into the crater. With the bulky radio on his back, Fruhling was a giant target. The sniper drilled a bullet through his helmet. As blood ran down his face, he ripped his helmet off and realized the round had just grazed his skull. Masny ordered him to take the radio off and destroy it. Still several hundred yards away from the command post, the bloodied private pulled out his .45 and blasted the radio with two bullets.

Still in the hole, Sigurd Sundby went up to George Schneller and grabbed him, saying, "Come on, George, I'm going to carry you back."

"You know what Captain Slater said—nobody helps anybody," responded Schneller. "You fend for yourself. You don't stop to help somebody."

"Come on, I can carry you," insisted Sundby.

But Schneller, with an enormous, gaping wound in his back, refused to let Sundby move him. "I'll be all right," he repeated. Eventually, the rest of the men had left, leaving Sundby alone with Schneller. Reluctantly, Sundby also pulled back, leaving his friend alone. Unfortunately, the time spent pleading with Schneller meant Sundby could no longer see where his fellow Rangers had gone. He took off towards the road. "There, I saw one of our BAR men. We used to call him Kelley. He was dead."

Separated from Masny and Trevor, Sundby thought, *"Well, I'll go back towards the cliffs."* Dodging from crater to crater to avoid any potential snipers, Sundby worked his way back towards the Pointe. "I'd run from one shell hole, then zigzag up and down and come up," he later explained, because, "well, if anybody was watching me or shooting, you didn't want to come up straight ahead. You'd shoot up one side and down the other one."

Seeking cover, Masny's battered group (minus Sunby) dove into a shell hole occupied by a Ranger with his legs casually crossed and hands behind his head. Mystified and glaring at the relaxing Ranger, Masny asked Fox Company Staff Sergeant James E. Fulton, "Are you hit?"

"Hell, no, Cap'n! Am just restin'. This is the third load of ammo I've hauled around this mornin'. I'm tired."

Pissed off, Masny looked at the man, "Well, get that damn BAR workin'. Get that kraut sniper that's chasin' us, will ya?"

To draw the sniper's fire, Big Stoop pulled the helmet off his head, placed it on his tommy gun, and raised it over the top of the crater. The sniper fired upon the helmet, exposing his position. Fulton emptied his entire BAR on the sniper. Twenty rounds ripped through his body, killing him instantly. With the sniper gone, Big Stoop, Trevor, and the rest of the group limped their way back to the command post.

CHAPTER 19

Nighttime Attacks

Around 7 P.M., Kerchner and his fellow officers manning the *L*-shape line welcomed twenty-three members of the 5th Ranger Battalion. Captain Ace Parker, commanding officer of A Company, had led most of that company's 2nd Platoon as they spent all day fighting their way off Omaha Beach and through German defenses to the Pointe. The newly arrived men from the 5th were organized into small bands taking up positions between E and F Companies.

Weapons and supplies soon became an issue of critical importance, and ammunition was running low. "Very few U.S. grenades were left, but a plentiful supply of German 'potato mashers' had been found. . . . A few Rangers had lost their rifles and were using German weapons, for which there was plenty of ammunition. E Company had three German machine guns." The men had not eaten since 3 A.M., and all they had then were the bitter-tasting, chocolate D-Bars, "plus a captured loaf of bread and one can of chicken." Yet the men's adrenaline continued to pump, keeping food off their minds.

To increase the amount of daylight for the operation, the men were on what the English called "Double Summer Time." Darkness wouldn't fall until after 11 P.M. As they waited for darkness, things became unusually quiet. George Kerchner was lulled into feeling a false sense of security: "We were beginning to relax and feel that the war was almost over for us, and anyway, very shortly the friendly troops were going to come up. We were going to go back to England. We had accomplished our D-Day mission."

Minutes after darkness fell around 11:30 P.M., a yellow flare streaked into the inky blackness, shattering the silence. The flare destroyed Kerchner's thoughts of being relieved as the field-gray silhouettes of a large German force loomed in front of Dog. Scores of enemy soldiers descended on the Ranger lines at near point-blank range. The cries of men, the shrill sound of whistles, the staccato of automatic fire, the violent explosions from German potato mashers, and acrid smoke all permeated the air. "This was the most frightening moment of my entire life—from being completely quiet and solemn . . . to this tremendous firing . . . going on. Grenades bursting, flares, men yelling, whistles blowing, and it just seemed like there were hundreds and hundreds of Germans running toward us," remembered Kerchner.

The attack focused on the angle between Dog and Easy Companies. The huge tide of German soldiers nearly swept over the two-man listening positions of Dog Company's Sergeant Branley and Private First Class Carty.

"Carty, we gotta get the hell outta here!"

BOOM! A grenade detonated near Carty, killing him instantly. A machine gun bullet tore into Branley's shoulder as he limped back to D Company's line. He jabbed his thigh with a morphine syrette to block the unbearable, throbbing pain.

Another outpost almost suffered the same fate. A group of Germans suddenly came around a corner in the hedgerow and nearly walked over Thompson and Hornhardt. Thompson saw their distinctive German helmets outlined across his field of vision, "close enough to shake hands with." The Rangers fired first and immediately knocked down three of the enemy. The others hugged the ground to avoid the deadly German fire and started chucking grenades at them. A potato masher blasted Thompson's face, closing his left eye for three days. "He gave his BAR to Hornhardt, and they started for the corner."

In the chaos of battle, American and German lines became fluid. The captured MG-42s in the hands of the Rangers put fear in the hearts of some Germans. Karl Wegner, a private from Grenadier Regiment 1.914, later recalled: "Once we heard the familiar rattle of one of our MG-42s off to our right and I thought one of our groups had broken through their lines. I looked over the edge of our hole but [someone] pulled me back. He yelled at me 'Wegner, the Amis are using MGs they captured from us, so keep your foolish head down.'... During the night the Rangers would attack and infiltrate our lines, even though we vastly outnumbered them. [We] were too jumpy to try and sleep with these men against us. When we attacked we learned that they were good fighters all around.... We were opposing the Americans' famous Rangers. They were far better soldiers than us."

George Kerchner surveyed the impending onslaught and turned to Harry Fate, "Look, this is what we're gonna do. We're gonna get all the men together, and we're gonna pull out of our line and go around and make an attack on the rear of the Germans."

Kerchner shouted to his men, "I want you to follow me." Fate and Kerchner attempted to gather men for the counterattack, but during the "firing and confusion, the men didn't hear them." Only Kuhn and Lomell heard.

As the young lieutenant moved toward the German flank, he stumbled into Lomell's foxhole. Lomell could see that Kerchner was nervous. "George, what do you expect to accomplish by this? First of all, you don't know how many they are. You don't know where they are. Let's talk this thing over." Lomell shouted, trying to calm Kerchner down. It was sound advice. Lomell convinced Kerchner to break off the ill-advised counterattack and hold their position.

About two minutes after the German assault started, the Rangers saw "an immense sheet of flame over to the west, near the position of the German 155s." The Rangers' guess was that more German powder charges had somehow been set off. The explosion illuminated the entire area, silhouetting the Germans in the orchard. After about a minute, the white glow of the flare died down and the firing ceased.

★ ★ ★

Over seventeen hours after reaching the shore below Pointe due Hoc, the whistles and flares started again at about 1 A.M.: the Germans were practically on top of the Rangers, with their attack focused on the angle. Then, perhaps as a form of psychological warfare or maybe just to locate their men, the Germans, who outnumbered the Rangers, began shouting out their names in the form of a roll call.

"Hans!"

"Johan!"

"Klaus!"

Heavy machine gun fire and bursts from machine pistols swallowed up the German voices. "Much of the fire was [from] tracers, high and inaccurate, designed for moral effect. Ball ammunition was spraying the hedgerow from the angle east." Sporadic mortar fire also peppered the Rangers' position. Potato-masher grenades sailed into the Ranger lines. And, according to one report, "some mortar shells were thrown in by hand."

The German attack overwhelmed the Rangers manning the angle. Some survivors of the night's attacks were about twenty-five yards to the east. "Branley, wounded, had gone out about thirty yards north of the angle on Dog's front. Branley reports hearing Stecki's BAR open up from the corner and fire almost steadily for about two minutes. He heard grenades explode near the angle. Then came a lull."

A Ranger then yelled, *"Kamerad!"* More grenades sailed into the Ranger position. Dog heard German voices and realized the enemy had captured the angle—the line had been breached.

"Nobody north or east of the threatened angle knew after the attack just what had happened at the corner. North of it, the bulk of Dog Company's men, who, [largely] had not been involved in the firefight, lay quiet. Twenty-five yards east of the corner, Sergeant Rupinski and Barnett didn't go over and see what the situation was." After the attack, the Rangers were unclear about how far the Germans had penetrated. Communication had ceased with D Company.

At the makeshift command post behind the *L*-shaped line, Lieutenants Lapres and Arman were laying plans for a withdrawal. Ominously, the Ranger officers failed to communicate their plan to Dog.

★ ★ ★

Rudder's command bunker, early morning hours, June 7, 1944

Doctor Block moved from one wounded patient to another. Rudder's command bunker doubled as an aid station and resembled a Civil War field hospital, complete with the sights, sounds, and smells of dying and wounded men. It was "pitch black," with the darkness pierced by flickering candlelight, which eerily illuminated the cavernous, subterranean pillbox, casting shadows on the rusted steel ceiling. Ranger casualties from the German night attack poured into Rudder's bunker. The adjoining room doubled as a mortuary and a "spare ammunition room." The bodies of the fallen were positioned tightly, side by side.

"At times there were so many patients, the men had to lie in the command post until maybe one of the other patients would die or be patched up well enough to go back out, maybe to fight," noted medic Frank South.

Every Ranger on the Pointe strained to stay awake. Under constant attack, most men hadn't slept for two days. The Army had issued stimulants in pill form, which Block dispensed to the sleep-deprived men. As he described in his medical report: "We carried stimulant drugs, but suggest that drugs, such as epinephrine [adrenaline], caffeine sodium benzoate, and digitalis, be put in syrette form such as the morphine syrette packet."

In the dimly lit cavern with the din of battle erupting outside the command bunker, Corporal Louis Lisko attempted to provide succor to Doc Block's patients. As Lisko approached Captain Jonathan Harwood, the artillery fire control officer, he saw Harwood's bandaged and bloodied body lying on a stretcher. Lisko tried to put a spoon up to the captain's mouth. Fighting back tears, Block looked at Lisko and said, "He is not going to need it. He's going to be dead in a couple of hours." Both residents of Chicago, Block and Harwood were boyhood friends tragically reunited at Pointe du Hoc. Within hours, Block's prediction came true when Harwood succumbed to his wounds.

Lieutenant Colonel Trevor was also in the command bunker. Rudder approached the rugged Commando and asked, "What do you think will happen next?"

Trevor lit his pipe and replied, "Never have I been so convinced of anything in my life as that I will either be a prisoner of war or a casualty by morning."

That night, the bunker was under constant sniper fire. Lisko, a member of James Eikner's radio team, recalled one incident: "We motioned for a young, freckle-faced German soldier to come walking out of the command post... He started to walk up, and the other German followed him." The Germans put their hands on their heads as the Rangers trained their carbines on the backs of their enemies. When the young German emerged above the lip of the crater, the Rangers "heard a burst of fire." Having seen the young man emerge from the command post, a German sniper had assumed he was an American: "And when this freckle faced boy stood up and the bullets hit him, he fell forward. . . . A second German . . . had his hands clasped in a prayer-like motion, begging us not to send him up. He thought we were sending them up to have them killed."

Behind the *L*-shaped line, early morning hours, June 7, 1944

"I think we've been overrun!" Lapres told Arman.

"Yeah, I know, and the krauts are yelling behind us. I think maybe they broke through and have cut us off!"

At Arman and Lapres's makeshift command post, panic set it. Initially, the German voices they heard were the German prisoners they captured earlier in the afternoon. In the confusion, the officers mistook those German voices for an attack that had enveloped the Ranger line.

But minutes later, an actual German attack began. The shriek of the whistles blew, and a steady roll call of names pierced the night air once again. Several German MG-42s and machine pistols sprayed the Ranger line with fire. Pushing out from the angle, the German attack fell on the middle of E Company's positions and "rolled up the Ranger line from there westward."

A great deal of machine gun fire and mortars slammed into the Ranger position. "The western half of E Company's position was overrun a short time after the attack opened." Ranger participants noted:

> One foxhole east of Lieutenant Leaggins's E-Company command post near the middle of E Company portion of the line, Maine heard the Germans come up close in the wheat field just in front of him. After the pause following the heavy opening fire, they rushed the command post area [and] Crook's BAR went silent. In a few moments, Maine could hear the Germans talking on his side of the hedgerow and knew what had happened. Wounded by a grenade, he crawled under the thick tangle of briars and vines into the hedgerow. Hidden there, he saw Simmons, ten feet away, surrender. But the Germans came no further east. Burnett, about twenty-five yards east of the corner, where E and D joined, confirmed the impression that the decisive action was over toward Lieutenant Leaggins' command post. Near his position, the Germans had come close through the orchard; heavy fire from automatic weapons sprayed the hedgerow, keeping the Rangers from delivering much return fire. However, they used their plentiful stock of German grenades in a close-range exchange. Burnett had a box of twenty-four. After a fight which seemed in Burnett's memory to have lasted an hour (but by the weight of much other testimony could have only been a few minutes), Begetto's BAR near Lieutenant Leaggins had gone silent. The fire began to come along the hedgerow from due east, insulating the Ranger positions. Burnett and Palmer (nearby) were wounded.

The Germans had broken the center of the Ranger line. "They started attacking, and we were shooting at the enemy tracers," remembered Salva Maimone. "Every time we'd shoot, and every time we would fire, they'd come back with another [round of] fire. They could see the bullet tracers, ammunition, and somehow, they'd know where to shoot. They had lots of mortar shells going in the position where they thought we were, but we weren't in there. We took about another twenty-five or thirty yards in front of their position, and the mortar shell was going over us. So we fought for about a couple of hours on top of that—up there, and machine guns on each side, and the more fire we put out, the more fire we'd get. Then we'd started slacking up a little bit and tried to feel our way—which way to shoot."

The Germans had rolled up E Company. As dawn began to break, a sergeant near Maimone asked how many Rangers were left. According to Maimone, only a handful of E Company remained in the fight. "I was working on a boy, my buddy, who was shot right through the shoulder, and the bullet ran all the way through his right shoulder and left a hole about as big as my fist. I had a kit there with a needle, and I gave him a shot and pushed the sulfa inside of this hole."

As Maimone was patching up his Ranger buddy, Germans suddenly appeared. A Ranger "sergeant turned up the flag to surrender. They were right on top of us with bayonets." The Germans then barked, "Anyone alive, stand up!"

According to Maimone, the Germans threatened to stick bayonets in them if the Americans didn't stand up. "So that's what we did. We all got up, and I picked [the wounded man] up and got him on his feet," Maimone remembered.*

*Maimone and the other Rangers with him began a long odyssey after their capture by the Germans. They were placed in a truck along with a farmer and his daughters who had been taken prisoner. "We were going down the road, and then this English Spitfire comes and attacks the truck. When they made the first pass, one or two guards got out and held a gun on us to keep us in the truck. . . . At the attack, this little girl gets out of the truck and stood right in the middle of the road, and the Spitfire bullet hit her and just killed her instantly. Also, the

There was a brief scuffle, when Rupinski and other Rangers discussed whether or not to surrender. Suddenly, Rupinski shouted, "*Kamerad! Kamerad!*"

The Germans then rounded up Rupinski, Burnett, about twenty men from Easy Company, and several men from Dog Company. Lieutenant Leaggins was dead. "Then they marched us on out to the road and finally we walked through that night to the next morning."

Enemy fire came from a field north of the angle. A Ranger from Easy Company burst into the command post and frantically shouted, "The Germans have broken through. We couldn't hold them, lieutenant! My God, there's guys getting killed everywhere!"

It was the final nail in the coffin, precipitating Arman's decision to withdraw. A Ranger even came across the field from the D Company position, "reporting that [Dog] had been wiped out."

About ten minutes earlier, someone had informed Sergeant Petty of Lieutenant Arman's plan to withdraw. Several of the officers had a hasty council of war. "The message was that, if attacked, the outpost was to withdraw to the main line of defense immediately [back to Rudder's perimeter]." Grudgingly, Petty inquired, "What do you mean immediately? Do you mean not even try to fight them off? Some Ranger outfit we are!"

---

guard that held us with a rifle was killed. . . . As the [German] sergeant was coming out [of the truck] a .50 hit his head and took the top of his head off. So I went up and dove out of the back of the truck and went to the right, and you could feel the bullets right down by my leg where they were coming by.

"We later kept on walking instead of getting on trucks. We told them, 'If they're going to put us in a truck, we'd like to be in an open truck and hold a white flag up showing that we're prisoners of war. We don't have a chance in a closed truck, because they're going to bomb everything that moved.'"

Maimone and the other Rangers were then transported to a prisoner of war camp. Maimone spent the rest of the war there and barely survived—his weight down to less than 100 pounds. When he was hospitalized and receiving vitamin treatment after the war ended, several nurses asked, "Can we take pictures?" The nurses snapped a picture "that was just all bones."

Sarcastically, the lieutenant replied, "You've had a couple of years of college, so you should know what 'immediately' means; I mean just that—no heroics; withdraw the moment that they hit."

L-Rod retorted, "But lieutenant, I have eight good men out there, a German machine gun, and my BAR, plus the fact we are at the top of a steep bluff behind a stone wall. Christ, we can kick their ass, or at least hold them off until you get ready back there. Give us a shot at it."

The lieutenant acidly responded, "No more lip. You're getting too big for your britches! Get on back there and prepare your men for withdrawal when the time comes."

Petty, a classic pain in authority's ass, responded, "How does one prepare for withdrawal? *That* wasn't included in Ranger training."

The officer's face turned "choleric" as he sternly raised his voice. "You're the self-appointed leader out there. Figure it out for yourself, damn it!"

L-Rod turned his back on the officer and let off a final salvo: "Not 'self-appointed'—you put me in charge; but what's going to happen to our Rangers' fighting spirit if we run every time we're attacked?" Petty walked away with a "spring in his step." He thought to himself, *"God, how I like to break officers' chops, especially this swaggering loudmouth."*

Petty wondered to himself if he was up to the challenge. "Rather than fear, I discovered that I was ready and willing to close with the enemy whenever the opportunity arose. Somewhere in me, there has always been a sort of instinctive energy that emerged when there was [an] unknown or danger [that] alerted me for whatever action was needed. I knew from my farm background that when a startled sheep broke away from the herd, the entire flock followed regardless of the clear path. Was there a hidden sheep syndrome working in the hearts of frightened soldiers?"

Petty tackled problems head-on. "If it was really tough or dangerous, I seemed to be removed from my body. I was L-Rod watching some stranger functioning." The sergeant didn't learn this tactic at Ranger training—he most likely developed these finely tuned survival mechanisms, defending himself against a violent father. Little did Petty know how well these skills would serve him now.

Petty remembers when the full force of the German attack finally hit his position. "It had to be fate. Seconds later, a machine gun opened up with a vengeance from the right flank." The bullets pounded the metal farm roller in front of Petty "like a hailstorm." Petty thought to himself, *"Where the hell is Easy Company?"* He soon found out. "The German attack had opened with a fury—whistles were blowing, burp guns coughing, flares bursting overhead, and Easy Company men screaming, *'Kamerad!'*"

"Piss on the lieutenant's stupid orders," Petty thought to himself. *"That son of a bitch is trying to kill me."* When there was a lull in the fighting and a flare silhouetted a German machine gunner, Petty rose to his feet, charged and shot from the hip, "emptying a full magazine" as he ran.

After his charge, Petty dove into a nearby ditch, which held several other Rangers, a platoon leader, and an American paratrooper who had "mis-dropped." "Tracer bullets from across the field began to enfilade our position, strangely, at three or four feet above the ground." The men began to make wise cracks about the Germans' marksmanship. Everyone in Petty's group was "too stupid until it was too late," to realize the elevation of the tracers had a purpose: the enemy was crawling under the stream of gleaming, white tracer bullets. Someone yelled, "They're crawling in on us under the tracers!" Petty and the men opened fire, but not the platoon leader, who "ducked to the bottom of the ditch." Petty thought to himself, *"The yellow bastard!"* He later recalled, "I wanted very much to empty my gun into the cowering leader."

Suddenly, six to eight Germans jumped into the ditch with Petty and the other men. Petty shouted, "Everyone hit the dirt!" Somehow, the paratrooper became separated from the group.

Only the Germans were standing. "I fired a full burst of twenty rounds into them." Several of the Germans were still alive. At that point, Winsch, Petty's assistant BAR gunner, yelled out, "Hey, there's a German crawling this way from the other end!"

Winsch rolled a grenade right under the wounded man's body; the pineapple grenade detonated, hurling the figure several feet in the air.

Petty then asked the platoon leader, "Lieutenant, what about a rear guard?" The officer responded, "What about a rear guard? Do you want to do it?"

"No, but I will," answered Petty. "I'd hate to see Rangers get shot in the ass, running."

"OK, you're the rear guard," the lieutenant scoffed.

Meanwhile, with the center of the Ranger defense line punctured, Arman, Lapres, and Ace Parker of the 5th Rangers had withdrawn, unbeknownst to Dog Company.

As the rear guard, Petty and another Ranger "lay in the lane and enfiladed the other side of the field with fire," and then moved back towards the ditch that they had recently evacuated. Suddenly, Petty spotted an American helmet still buckled on a man's head. Riddled with shrapnel, the corpse wore a paratrooper patch on his shoulder. To Petty's horror, he realized that the "German" whom Winsch had blown up with a grenade was actually the American paratrooper.

"Damn! Damn!" Petty swore.

"I became so filled with guilt that I wanted to vomit." He suppressed his emotions as scores of Germans crossed the field, heading straight for his position. Petty decided to keep the tragic news of the paratrooper's fratricide to himself. "I could not tell Winsch of my discovery. There was no point in him carrying the guilt too." The Germans were coming in full force, and Petty thought to himself, *"To hell with being the rear guard!"* He bolted down the country lane toward Rudder's perimeter.

As he ran for his life, he encountered two "Dog Company men" crossing the lane. Petty began pushing them aside, shouting, "We're retreating back to the Pointe!"

They resisted his shove, and the shadowy figures began cussing at him in German. To his horror, he realized the men he thought were from D Company were actually the enemy. Petty managed to escape from the two men and ducked into a hedgerow.

Before the landing, Petty had decided he would never surrender. "No German would ever hear a cry of *'Kamerad!'* coming from my throat! . . . To me, it was not about being brave—that I was not—it was a combination of common sense and fear. I knew that when a man lay down his weapon before an armed enemy, his fate rested with the amount of feral that still dwelled in that man's breast. To some, the battlefield was a place where the thrill of [a] kill could be savored without being concerned about the hangman's noose. It had always been thus, proving that civilization is only skin-deep for some."

Petty made a quick decision. Adrenaline surged as he continued to run, firing his BAR from the hip. Scattering the Germans, he dove into the next hedgerow, "out of breath but with a feeling of exhilaration."

Darting in and out of hedgerows, Petty made his way back to the Pointe. Along the way, he recognized another Ranger. Suddenly, a German burp gun coughed. Four Germans emerged from the shadows. Petty yelled at the other Ranger, "Hit the dirt! I can blow them away. When I open up, run!"

The first burst missed the Germans. The Ranger stood with his hands raised over his head. Petty shouted, "Run, you damn fool!"

Suddenly, the Germans began returning fire. Rescuing the other Ranger was now out of the question. If Petty stayed, they would surely kill both men. So he continued pushing back towards the Pointe alone.

As Petty worked his way back to the cliffs, he remembered that minefields ringed the area. Rather than risk life and limb negotiating his way through the deadly mines at night, he found a large bomb crater and "soon fell asleep in deep exhaustion."

When Petty, the rest of Fox Company, and Easy Company withdrew from the defense line near the apple orchard, they did not inform Dog Company of their plans. As the men of Fox and Easy ran towards Pointe du Hoc, they split into two groups. One group went down the exit road to the Pointe; the other went to the small Norman village of

Auguay, which was near the Pointe. A German prisoner, a captain familiar with the area, led the group from Auguay to the Pointe, where the men reassembled in gun positions five and three.

Back in the hedgerow defensive line, Dog Company was now completely on its own, but continued to man their positions, carrying out Rudder's order to hold until relieved. "We didn't know they were pulling out. . . . E and F had gone. They didn't know we were in this hedgerow that was heavily overgrown, in the brush and deep holes," noted Kerchner. Reduced to little more than a dozen men, Dog Company held their line and blocked the coastal highway. As Lomell explained, "Dog Company didn't even move. We didn't move an inch, and the reason for that was simple. We knew we had a roadblock here; we had an outpost here. . . . We just stayed in this area around this roadblock, and we held it. . . . These men knew, as we all knew in Dog Company, this is our mission. . . . These [men] were dedicated and would give their life for this roadblock if it needed it. My wife gives me hell for saying this. I've been quiet for forty-some years. What am I going to do, go to my grave for all the guys that died with me? Seven guys died with me here, and not tell the truth? We didn't retreat. We didn't withdraw. We all did what we were told to do."

Completely surrounded and cut off nearly a mile behind German lines, Dog was now alone. Obeying his orders from Rudder, Kerchner was determined to remain in position until "duly relieved." Outnumbered, with hundreds of Germans between them and Rudder's command post nearly a mile away, the men dug in for a long wait. Unable to leave their holes, the men were forced to use their helmets as toilets.

True to their mission, they waited to see what the dawn would bring.

CHAPTER 20

June 7

With the sun well over the horizon, its blinding rays reached Petty's position deep in the shell crater, awakening him. Groggy and disoriented, L-Rod heard the murmur of voices coming from a nearby house. Glancing down at his watch, he noticed "it was well past eight" and thought that American forces would soon be advancing off Omaha Beach towards Pointe du Hoc. *"Surely they will be arriving soon,"* he reasoned. *"Or maybe the invasion did not go well?"*

He considered waiting until they arrived. Had the invasion been successful? Or had the Germans overrun the Pointe? Suddenly, to his horror, he realized that the voices coming from the house were German. Petty was lying dangerously close to a group of Germans who were forming a skirmish line to advance towards Pointe du Hoc.

As the Germans lined up for battle, he realized his Ranger brothers on the Pointe must be still alive. The urge to be with the other Rangers "was strong." Casting caution aside "without hesitation," Petty decided to risk running through the minefield. But as he advanced toward the Pointe, he spotted several more Germans soldiers forming up for the assault. "I hit the Germans from the rear. I ran through them, hip firing at random. They scattered and hit the dirt, but they were too startled to shoot back."

As Petty neared Rudder's perimeter, he felt the crack of bullets whizzing past him and realized his own men were firing at him. In the nick of time, he heard Winsch yell, "Stop shooting! It's L-Rod!"

"When I reached the Ranger line, I slid into a bomb crater. It was as though I scored a winning touchdown, with much backslapping and handshakes." One Ranger gave Petty a "rib-cracking hug" and blurted out, "I told those dumb shits you were too ornery to get killed. And besides, I knew with your balls you would make it."

Just then, Petty came face to face with Big Stoop.

"My God, am I looking at a ghost?" Captain Masny asked. "Everybody thought you were dead or captured. I thought I was finally rid of my main chops-breaker."

"No such luck for you," the sergeant responded dryly.

Concerned, Big Stoop looked back at Petty. "L-Rod you look terrible. You're shaking like a leaf!"

Masny then gave Petty half a chocolate bar. He said, "I hear you were great out there across the road. I knew from the beginning you would be. You surprised your lieutenant. You shook him a little too."

Still trembling from the shock of his experience, Petty caught Big Stoop's eye and said. "Tell that yellow son of a bitch to go fuck himself. I'll tell him face to face if I get the chance. I know it will cost me my stripes, but it will be worth it."

Reassuringly, Big Stoop told him, "Not while *I'm* the CO will you revert to private. We'll handle that later. Right now, you're a sick man, and I'm taking you to Doc Block."

Petty said, "Yeah, thanks, but I don't think Doc will be happy to see me. I threw a few cusswords at him at the foot of the cliffs."

"That wouldn't stop Doc from helping you. He's a man of integrity and a fine doctor."

Petty reported to Doc Block, who joked with him, "I see you finally did get up the cliffs, and I heard a few men speak of what you did when you *did* get to the top."

Petty attempted to apologize to him, but Doc brushed it off. Describing his symptoms, L-Rod told him, "I feel as tight as a drum, and crazy as it sounds, I feel frightened and I don't [know] of what. I didn't feel frightened yesterday or last night when I guess I should have." Doc diagnosed him with nervous exhaustion. Petty recalled, "[South] gave me a pill that I guess was relaxing. He then told me to lie down on one of the bunk beds for a while." The pill worked quickly, and in a couple of hours, Petty was calm and his "tremors had ceased."

★ ★ ★

In the early morning hours of June 7, the German's attack ground to a halt after naval gunfire hit them as they were assembling to assault Rudder's command post and perimeter. Meanwhile, what was left of E Company and F Company formed a hasty defensive line around gun emplacements three and five. With the German and American lines more or less solidified, skirmishing continued. For the time being, though, naval bombardment kept the Germans from wiping out Rudder's men.

With ammunition running low, the Rangers scavenged the area for German weapons and pressed the walking wounded back into their line. Even medic Frank South joined his brothers on the line: "After taking care of a few men in the morning, I took off my Red Cross armband, and arming myself with a captured German Schmeisser machine pistol, volunteered to go out on perimeter defense. After about four hours, it was apparent I was no longer needed, and I returned to the aid station with a wounded man."

The Rangers' situation looked grim. Ammunition was running out. There were no reinforcements. And the Germans had just broken all the lines by the coastal road except the one held by Kerchner, Lomell, and Dog Company.

Through his communications officer, Lieutenant Eikner, Rudder was able to keep a steady stream of communications with the Navy. However, communication with Ranger Force B and Force C on Omaha Beach, as well as the Army's 116th Infantry of the 29th Division, was non-existent. Rudder partially created this problem when he failed to appoint a liaison officer after he relieved Major Lytle and assumed command of Force A.

The Army also had problems of its own, as it held on to Omaha Beach. Elements of the 116th Infantry and the 5th Ranger Battalion attempted to battle towards the Pointe, but the Germans kept them at bay. Relief for the Rangers would have to wait. Compounding the matter, late in the afternoon of June 7, "an unidentified Ranger officer from the 5th Battalion [incorrectly] reported to V Corps (G-2) that the Germans had retaken the Pointe." Fortunately, the 116th disregarded this erroneous information, but they still decided to wait until the morning of June 8 to push out from Grandcamp Les-Bains, a village near Omaha Beach, and link up with Rudder at the Pointe.

Not only were the Germans pressing on the Pointe's perimeter, the German's western flak guns were still active. Even the observation bunker at the tip of Pointe du Hoc remained in enemy hands. Rudder spent the day consolidating his position and attempting to remove these threats within his own perimeter.

The concrete observation post at the tip of the Pointe served as the eyes of Pointe du Hoc. From there, one could see most of the Cherbourg peninsula, and it also had a commanding view of Omaha Beach.

Rudder assigned Lieutenant Elmer Vermeer, a demolitions officer, with the task of eliminating the Germans still holding the observation bunker. "When the colonel asked me to blow the Pointe, I again called on my friend, Eberle, who had gone with me earlier on D-Day toward the machine gun nest. We found a twenty-pound sack of C-2 explosives and took about five other men from other companies who were at the command post with us to blow the Pointe. We stayed together and went from shell hole to shell hole until we came to the open ground. Then we moved as rapidly as possible and into position right behind the observation post. Eberle and I set the charge at the back door of the concrete bunker, and I hardly remember getting around the corner. We used a very short fuse, and I think the explosion probably lifted us right off the ground."

Not long after Vermeer and the men blew the doors off the bunker, eight Germans piled out shouting *"Kamerad!"* However, one of the Germans foolishly pointed a gun at Vermeer. Three or four rounds of rifle fire from the Rangers instantly cut him down.

The Germans' 37 mm flak gun, which continued to hit the Rangers, seemed to have an endless supply of ammunition. Big Stoop noticed Germans going in and out of a small hut located well behind their lines. He ascertained that the hut was an ammunition depot, and it was likely feeding the gun. Rudder once again tasked Vermeer and a crew of volunteers—including Petty, Sundby, and Fox Company Ranger Bill Anderson—with blowing something up—this time it was the ammunition depot.

Vermeer remembered: "We moved out very rapidly, and Lieutenant Wintz, who was holding the area that we went through, gave us a lot of fire cover so we could get to the ammo dump." One of the Dog Company men, Sigurd Sundby, who had been temporarily reassigned to Captain Masny and F Company and had volunteered to destroy the ammunition depot with Vermeer, gave him covering fire. "We gave cover fire for him, and then the Navy dropped some shells up along that area," Sundby remembers.

As they approached their target, the men could hear moaning. It came from George Schneller, who had a massive gaping wound on his back. Sundby thought to himself, *"There is no way this guy can be alive."* As the men attempted to pull his foot, Schneller suddenly sprung to his feet, astonishing everyone. For nearly two days, the Ranger had played dead while countless Germans passed him. The experience turned Schneller's chestnut-brown hair gray, but at least he was alive. Like Schneller, Sergeant Morris Webb, who had been bayoneted in the thigh near no man's land on D-Day, was also found by his Ranger comrades and brought back to the command post that night.

When the group of Rangers reached the ammo dump, which was really nothing more than a shed made of planks and tin, they all passed their Bangalore torpedoes to Anderson, who, as one Ranger recalled, was "even cockier than L-Rod Petty." He crawled towards the entrance and attempted to light the Bangalores' fuse.

According to Petty, "It seemed like it was taking an eternity to arm the torpedoes." Bullets filled the air around the men. Almost hysterical, Petty screamed down at Anderson, "Get the God damn things armed and let's get out of here. What the hell is the hold up?"

Anderson finished placing the charge and finally ignited the fuse.

German fire rained down on their position. Petty's adrenaline was pumping as he charged, once again firing from the hip. Anderson yelled, "Drop, L-Rod, drop! It's going to blow!"

Before Petty could react, Anderson tackled him to the ground.

BOOM! The ammo depot exploded. Steel, tin, wood and shells fell from the sky all around the men as they made their way back toward Ranger lines. The men returned to the command post and reported that the mission was accomplished.*

That afternoon, the Navy finally re-supplied Pointe du Hoc. Several LCAs brought in Ranger reinforcements, badly needed supplies, and ammunition. Vermeer remembers the first food that he had eaten in more than two days: "They also brought some bread, and Doc Block issued out jam sandwiches." The LCAs returned to the ships with German prisoners and many of the wounded Rangers.

As dawn crept across the Dog's defensive position near the coastal highway, Kerchner woke up to hear rustling in a nearby ditch. "I was scared. I figured it was the Germans digging us out. I was all set to try and defend myself when I realized they were Americans—two Americans from E Company that had been left behind.... So we weren't the only ones out there in this field. I think there were fifteen of us. These two men from E Company came in and joined us. They got in the hole with me."

---

*To this day, the surface of Pointe du Hoc contains several craters caused by explosions at various German ammo dumps that were located on the Pointe.

For the rest of the morning, the battleship *Texas* opened up its 14-inch guns on the field surrounding Dog Company. The ship's guns were targeting areas where the Germans assembled their men to launch a strike on Rudder's command post. Since there had been no word from Kerchner, Lomell, and their men, Rudder assumed that Dog Company had been entirely wiped out or captured. Huge shells from the *Texas* ripped open the fields around Dog Company. According to Kerchner, "a shell would land within fifty yards from where we were; it would dig a hole fifteen to twenty feet in diameter and four to five feet deep. You can imagine what a noise it made when it went off. And of course, you didn't know where the next one was going to land either. . . . I can say that I had a prayer book in my pocket. I'm a Roman Catholic. I did a tremendous amount of praying when I was in that ditch. I read that prayer book through from cover to cover, I suppose, half a dozen times, and I prayed very sincerely for protection. And actually, it's not apropos, since then I feel so guilty in all the things I asked for on D-Day and what I asked for the Lord to do for me, which was primarily to get me out of there alive. I've been so ashamed to ask for anything since then. I figure I used up all I had coming to me on D-Day."

CHAPTER 21

The Relief of Pointe du Hoc

After heavy shelling throughout the day and night of June 7, the big guns on the *Texas* eventually ceased firing. Miraculously, Dog Company managed to survive yet another night of deadly friendly fire and sustained enemy encroachment. On the morning of June 8, Kerchner and Lomell emerged from their foxholes where they had been holed up for the past two days. As Kerchner moved through the hedgerow, he asked, "Hey, is everybody alright?"

Twelve of his men were alive. Two men were wounded. Several men were dead, including Pat McCrone's best friend and fellow prankster, Larry Johnson. Still holding his M1, Johnson lay with his face pressed into the soft earth of his fighting hole. Devastated by his death, Staff Sergeant McCrone silently stood next to the fallen Ranger, reflecting on the many good times they had together at Camp Forrest. As he gazed down on Johnson lying motionless on the ground, something began to change inside of him.

Kerchner surveyed the devastation. The debris of intense battle surrounded their foxholes. Equipment and feces lay strewn about the hedgerow. Dog had not eaten for two days. To his surprise, Kerchner came upon Sergeant Mike Branley, who was hidden away in a hedgerow nearby, with his shoulder bandaged. Separated from the rest of Dog Company, Branley was so ecstatic to see the platoon leader that he "almost kissed Kerchner."

CLANK. CLANK. CLANK. CLANK. CLANK.

Suddenly, Lomell heard the sounds of steel tank treads crawling across the Norman coastal blacktop road that they had defended for two days. All of Dog Company, including Kuhn and Fate, who shared a foxhole, pointed their weapons toward the ominous oncoming sounds. Lomell thought the end was near: *"We're about to be overrun by the Germans!"*

The sound of clanking tank treads and marching boots drew closer to the men as they readied for battle. Joy replaced their fear when they realized that the tanks and men were American. Recalling the glorious moment, Kerchner said, "Right up behind the lead scouts was Colonel Canham, who was the commander of the 116th Infantry.... [He] came up this road with one hand bandaged up and had a weapon in the other hand.... We were so glad to see him. Colonel Canham was all soldier, and all he wanted to know was 'Where are the Germans?' All I wanted to know was 'Where are the Americans?'"

For two and a half days, Kerchner, Lomell, and what was left of Dog Company had tenaciously manned their roadblock, effectively cutting German communication and defending the road between Omaha Beach and Utah Beach.

The relief of Pointe du Hoc began in the early morning hours of June 8, when the five-inch guns of the USS *Ellison* opened up on German positions. D and E Company of the 5th Ranger Battalion took the high ground on the western side of the Norman village of Grandcamp. Meanwhile, the rest of Force C, men from the 116th Infantry, and tanks from A Company of the 743rd Tank Battalion moved down toward Pointe du Hoc.

Passing through Kerchner's position, the tanks approached Rudder's perimeter at about 11 A.M. The mines around Pointe du Hoc once again took their toll, destroying several tanks. Even worse, the tank crews were confused when they encountered the Rangers on the Pointe who were using confiscated German weapons. The tanks began firing on the Rangers next to Rudder's command post, tragically killing several.

Captain John Raaen*, CO of Headquarters' Company, 5th Ranger Battalion, and part of the relief force, remembers the desperate measures taken to halt the fratricide: "A lieutenant of the 2nd Rangers ran out of cover, jumped up on one of the tanks, beat on the turret until he got the attention of the crew, put a pistol to the head of the commander who opened the turret, and with that the attack of the 743rd stopped in its tracks."

In the chaos of friendly fire, the Rangers set off a recognition flare and even attempted to unfurl the American flag. As Lieutenant Vermeer recalls, "Again Colonel Rudder displayed his great courage and leadership as he helped the men in his command post hold up an American flag as high as they could, so the troops advancing would know that we were Americans and not Germans in the area. . . . I felt the pride of being a Ranger and of our accomplishments during the past few days."

At the same time, the *Texas* heard the tanks firing and radioed Rudder. "Are you being fired on?" Rudder replied, "Yes."

"Do you want me to fire on them?"

"No."

"Are you being hit by friendly fire?"

"Yes."

Suddenly, the firing ceased. "And then finally, later on the eighth, I went out of the aid station over the field. The firing had died down, and coming across towards us were the rest of the battalion," Frank South said of the wonderful moment. "Near the front of them, I recognized the tall figure and the peculiar loping gait of my closest friend, Bill ["Willy"] Clark, also a medic and also, at this time, not wearing a brassard but carrying an M1. It was a great sight, and relief. But then we started counting heads. Of the approximately two-hundred twenty-five men who had landed on the Pointe, there were fewer than ninety-five who could still bear arms."

*Raaen later rose to the rank of Major General.

CHAPTER 22

Survivors

CRACK!

Out of the corners of their eyes, the men caught the gleam of a captain's silver bars shimmering in the sunlight. As they turned to look in the direction of the gunshot, they saw a bloody bullet hole in the now-dead officer's head. Another soldier killed by a German sniper.

Dog had been on constant alert for snipers as they trudged into the tiny Norman town of Grandcamp-Les-Bains. On June 8 around four in the afternoon, what was left of D Company marched in a single column down the Isigny Road, which connected Omaha and Utah Beaches. Several mis-dropped paratroopers from the 101st and 82nd Airborne Divisions joined the haggard Rangers.

The carnage left by the sure-eyed German assassins surrounded them. Silent warriors, forever young, flanked the road. Years later, one Ranger re-lived that day with vivid memory: "The road is lined with dead American soldiers, mostly noncoms and officers. The snipers knew their targets.... A Jerry used the flash [of the captain's silver bars] as a target.... Most of all the dead in the town are shot in the head. Jerry is an accurate shot...We entered Grandcamp and are greeted in the streets lined with people.... It's hard to imagine snipers in this town, but due to constant halts and scattered shots, we know there are some up ahead."

Four hours earlier, the remnants of the 2nd Ranger F assembled near the Pointe. Companies A, B, C, and D moved ou One former Dog Company Ranger recalled, "I could not help but notice their thinned ranks from the wounded and dead lost."

At the bivouac area, battalion supply finally caught up with the men. Bedrolls, knapsacks, and other personal effects from the ships rejoined their owners. The supply chain from ship to shore was a long one. Many choice items from the packs "disappeared" into the hands of the other troops who transported the gear. Miraculously, Duke Slater's bedroll still contained a full bottle of Cutty Sark Scotch. Everyone assumed that Slater and all hands on the LCA 860 had been lost. The men reverently sorted these personal effects for shipment back to their families. They wanted to ensure that the last worldly items their comrades had touched would reach their loved ones. However, one artifact didn't make it. Gleefully, Bill Hoffman stowed Slater's bottle of Cutty Sark in his rucksack for safekeeping until the tenth, Jack Kuhn's birthday.

In the camp, the men had a chance to take a breather from the war and experience the bucolic Norman countryside. One Ranger recalled that he peeled away from the rest of his men. After climbing a stone wall, he reflected on the last several days of combat: "I sat in silence with deep thoughts. Then slowly I became aware of the soothing panoramic scene before me. A large green meadow sloped gently to meet a vast tidewater basin, and an incoming tide was surging rapidly to raise the water level almost to the tops of the saltwater reeds that bordered the shore. There was a village with assorted house colors enhanced by the later afternoon sun. It reminded me of the work of one of the famous French artists, but I did not know which. I became absorbed with what lay before me."

The short-lived respite ended in midafternoon on June 9. Dog resumed the march. Looking to their left and right after pulling into another Norman field to bivouac, the Rangers saw the debris and carnage of the recent invasion. The staccato sounds of battle filled the night air.

The next morning, Bill Hoffman broke the morning tension and anticipation of battle. He walked up to Jack Kuhn with a large smile, handed him the "liberated" bottle of Scotch whisky and said, "Happy birthday, Jack!"

Kuhn wasn't much of a drinker, but the acknowledgement of the birthday had a profound effect on him. He was alive. A survivor. Kuhn's expression radiated happiness. He decided to give the Scotch to the other men, who each took a swig and passed it around.

The next day, the Rangers continued their celebration of life by honoring the dead of both battalions. Father Lacy led the men in a prayer service.

Over the course of the next nine days, the 2nd and the 5th Ranger Battalions regrouped and were placed in close reserve. While the men waited for replacements, organization and training lapsed. In a rare break from the structured training regimen of the past, Rudder left the men largely on their own to do "whatever made them happy." During the downtime, the scars of battle remained fresh on their minds. Some shared their experiences with their brothers. For others, the experience throbbed like a raw nerve and, to soothe it, the men bottled the horrors of war deep inside, some for decades.

Predictably, boredom set in, and the men often found themselves itching for something to do. While in the camp area, Bill Petty and Herman Stein saw former D Company Ranger Sergeant William McHugh trying to start a dilapidated German motorcycle. Stein and Petty strolled over to lend a hand. As the two men approached the bike, a Frenchman approached the group at a hurried pace. The man kept holding up both hands and repeating, *"La Boche!"*— French slang for a German. Frantically waving his hands, he repeated himself and said what sounded like, *"Cinq! Cinq!"*—"five, five."

Petty and Stein thought the man meant "Five Germans!" The former Dog Company men shook their heads, which brought relief and laughter to the Frenchman. He said, *"Ami"* (friend), and he attempted to shake Stein's hand and kiss both cheeks.

Craving some action and wanting to kill the boredom, Petty said, "Well, what are we waiting for? Tell the frog to start hopping, and we'll hop with him."

Petty, Stein, McHugh, and a few other Rangers moved forward, expecting to encounter five Germans that they could take prisoner. Petty recalled the moment: "We set out with the buoyancy of the three musketeers on the way to an adventure."

The small group traveled about three quarters of a mile and stopped at the edge of a wide meadow. There they found a German bazooka with several projectiles around it. The farmer refused to go a step further. One of the men said, "Let's hit the woods and see what we run into."

L-Rod recalled the scene: "We entered the woods in a couple of minutes. About ten yards in we came upon a drainage ditch about fifteen-feet wide, four-feet deep. . . . As I bent my left leg and began to flex for springing power, I glanced down the left at the ditch, and what I saw startled me. It was packed with Germans leaning against the bank!"

Stunned, Petty landed flat on his belly and pulled the trigger back on his BAR. Not really aiming, but firing in the right direction and hoping to panic the Germans, he fired two bursts from the BAR.

The other Rangers opened up with their M1s. The maelstrom of lead wounded three Germans. Petty heard screams of terror as the Germans yelled *"Kamerad!"* Stein, Petty, and McHugh then moved forward to disarm the *"boches,"* who numbered far more than five. Two enemy officers and a dozen noncoms were armed only with Lugers. One of the Germans was badly wounded, "moaning and whimpering."

"Goddamn, what was a person who wept upon seeing kittens killed doing in this business?" Petty thought, *"I wished that I could help this young soldier, but I couldn't. I could only hope that he would survive the wounds that I had inflicted."* Just then, a sergeant who had accompanied the Rangers, chimed in, "I'm going to put this poor bastard out of his misery." The sergeant then stepped forward with one of the captured Luger pistols in his hand.

"Man, you can't do that. Doc Block is less than a mile away. Maybe he can—"

CRACK!

Before the words were out of Petty's mouth, a bullet entered the young man's head. He screamed and screeched.

In broken English, one of the German officers yelled, "You massn't [sic] shoot!"

The sergeant fired again—three more times—"until the soldier's screams ceased."

Petty reflected upon the scene: "I stood in stunned silence. It was a nightmare of horror in broad daylight. I had just watched and listened to [a killing] carried out on a human being within three feet of where I stood in disbelief. It wasn't much different than what I had watched inflicted on crippled horses as a boy... As a boy, I could weep. Here, I couldn't."

After the Ranger NCO killed the wounded soldier, the German officer was boiling over with rage, cursing and yelling, "Murderer!" The officer eventually calmed down, and the small group of Rangers then lined up the prisoners, about fifty-two in all. Petty then realized that the farmer had actually said "fifty-five," not "five." The prisoners didn't look like combat men to the Rangers. "They were part of a German regimental headquarters company and were trapped in the woods by the speed of the Allied advance." They hid for two days without food before making the decision to surrender. The Germans had sent the farmer to talk with the Rangers in an attempt to facilitate the end of the war for them.

Petty looked around and said, "Hell, Mac, I blame myself for this whole fuck-up."

"L-Rod, you can't blame yourself for the dead soldier," McHugh responded. "So you goofed in dealing with a frog. Tough shit, you're not God."

Petty responded, "I guess you're right, Mac, especially the part about me not being God, though I'm not sure he's doing so great a job himself if indeed he exists." Petty added, "Oh, hell, let's get up and get out of here. That dead young soldier is still lying in the ditch behind us, and I want to get him out of my mind."

When Petty, Stein, and McHugh returned to camp with the POWs, they found that replacements had arrived during their absence. To make up for the losses from Omaha Beach and Pointe du Hoc, new men started filtering in from England, where they had been held in reserve. As the fresh soldiers arrived, several Ranger officers, including Rudder, interviewed potential volunteers in nearby units since the allotted Rangers didn't come close to bringing the battalion up to full strength after all of its losses.

At first blush, Petty thought, *"These look like worthwhile men."* However, he soon noticed that one of the men was "only sixteen or seventeen." Some of the old-timers from Camp Forrest wondered if the greenhorns lacked training and if they could cut it in combat. It turned out some of the best men came from this group, Petty recalled.

Bill Petty remembers meandering around the encampment and shooting the breeze with his friends from the other company. "There was some concern from the early day originals in Camp Forrest on the possible lack of Ranger training on the new replacements. In my opinion, they overrated the combat value of such training. It was pretty much the same as the regular infantry, and not as tough as the paratroops. Actions during the invasion convinced me of that, though training was necessary. The key ingredients of good combat men were common sense and a good set of balls."

PFC Vince Hagg, one such replacement with boyish good looks, remembers a warm reception into the unit.* One of the other Rangers introduced Hagg to Jack Kuhn.

"Where you from?" Kuhn asked.

*Well into his eighties, Hagg is unusually young looking and appears to be in his late fifties.

"I'm from Tyrone, Pennsylvania," responded Hagg.

"Hell, I'm from Altoona!" exclaimed Kuhn.

Hagg felt an immediate, family-like bond with Kuhn and the rest of Dog. "They never looked down upon us. They welcomed us in, and we were one of them."

While they were in reserve, strafing and dive-bombing runs from several German planes hit the battalion. "We got an occasional bombing or strafing. I don't even think they were meant for us," recalled South.

Shortly after one of the German bombs exploded nearby, a bearded billy goat appeared over the top of the slit trench where South was holed up. "We all had cigarettes. Everyone smoked. During the strafing run, a homeless goat started snatching my cigarettes. It started eating them! I quickly lit a cigarette before he could get it, but he got it anyways! Maybe he liked Camels," laughed South.

On June 19, to the great surprise of everyone in the battalion, the ghosts of LCA 860 materialized in the flesh. Captain Morton McBride, Captain Duke Slater, and the nineteen other survivors from the doomed landing craft returned, bringing Dog Company nearly to full strength. In the makeshift reunion, the men traded stories of their survival at Pointe du Hoc, which contrasted with those of the "swimmers," who barely survived the cold waters of the channel. With his return, McBride replaced Kerchner as commander of Dog Company, while Slater became the battalion's operations officer.

On June 20, Dog Company and the rest of the battalion lined up in company parade formation. About a dozen men arranged themselves in front of the company. Their commanders had singled them out for awards. All too often, as a result of battlefield chaos, officers fail to complete the necessary paperwork, and many true heroes go unrecognized. But that wasn't the case on this occasion, when many heroes from D-Day received medals.

Lieutenant General Hodges approached First Sergeant Leonard Lomell, pinning the Distinguished Service Cross (DSC) on the breast of his field jacket. Rudder shook Lomell's hand and later said privately, "Len, this is your Medal of Honor."*

That day, Rudder also pinned the DSC on George Kerchner and Big Stoop Masny. Kuhn received the Silver Star. As in all wars, many men who deserved recognition were left out, including Bill Petty. Much later, Petty received a Silver Star for his heroism in the field of battle; however, most of his fellow Rangers felt his actions also merited the Medal of Honor.

After the awards ceremony, the 2nd Ranger Battalion remained in corps reserve, ready for special operations missions related to the Normandy breakout. Lieutenant Colonel Rudder consistently attempted to get his men unique, challenging missions suited for their training. Corps headquarters assigned the battalion to crack the German defenses in the Norman town of Cherbourg. However, the regular ground troops breeched the German lines before the Rangers got there, and headquarters scrubbed the mission.

Big Jim Rudder knew the limits of his men. During one of the long summer days, the battalion commander addressed Dog and the other companies. Standing in parade formation with the sounds of battle audible in the distance, his Rangers assembled near some hedgerows. Seeming to walk ten-feet tall, Rudder's calm presence and leadership resonated with the men who had carried out what many considered D-Day's toughest mission. "There is an end to your human endurance," he told them. "I will not send you on a suicide mission." Big Jim's pep talk was short and sweet. As Hagg recounted, "He was a gentleman. He gave you the facts. Before we came into Dog Company, he said, 'I hope you guys know what you're getting into.'"

*In 1942, the very first commander of 1st Ranger Battalion, William O. Darby, had issued the unwritten, inexplicable order that no matter how heroic the deed, no WWII Ranger would ever receive the Medal of Honor. Unfortunately, as a result, many courageous and outstanding actions that merited America's highest decoration went unrecognized.

The morning of June 25, a long column of trucks moved Dog Company and the rest of the battalion to Valognes. The battalion's mission was to serve as prisoner of war escort for First Army. The battalion's after-action report dryly noted the duty. "The mission was discharged in three phases: the picking up of the prisoners at the 4th and 79th Division cages in the city, processing through the enclosure, and the delivery to the First Army . . . located near Utah Beach. Working day and night from 25 June to 2 July, almost ten thousand prisoners were processed through this enclosure." George Kerchner reflected on his feelings toward the German prisoners, "When you're actually fighting, when you're shooting at them and they're shooting at you, every one of those men out there is your mortal enemy and you're just as anxious and trying just as hard to kill ever single one of them. When the fighting would die down, you would think about it, especially when you saw the German prisoners come through . . . you were bitter towards them."

From July 3 through August 7, Dog began an intense garrison and training period. For those few weeks, the men lived along the coast across from the German-occupied Guernsey Islands. The Germans would remain garrisoned on the islands in the channel throughout the entire war. Thousands of enemy troops waited for an invasion that never came. Likewise, Dog and the other companies in the battalion waited on the coast for an enemy raid from the Channel Islands that never materialized.

For six weeks after D-Day, the Germans seemed to have largely contained the Normandy beachhead. Losses for both German and Allied troops climbed as high as those during some months on the eastern front. However, the situation changed with General Bradley's breakout known as Operation Cobra, where the Allies ruptured a hole in the German lines.

Hitler responded to Cobra by launching Operation Lüttich, a counterattack at Avranches, located at the base of the Cotentin Peninsula in Normandy. In Lüttich, the Führer once again rolled the dice. The result was the near destruction of the German Army because he frivolously threw away his remaining armor reserve. American tactical fighter-bombers, which the Germans called *Jabos,* shot the tanks to pieces.

Command assigned Dog Company and the rest of the battalion to secure the right flank of the First Army near Mortain and to "repel any enemy attempts to withdraw... from the area." The ensuing German disaster at Mortain resulted in the collapse of their army at Normandy. After the German First Army counterattacked, American forces advanced towards Argentan, while British and Canadian forces advanced on Falaise. Hitler ordered his forces in Normandy to hold till the last man and the last round. However, the Allies cut off tens of thousands of German troops and forced their surrender. Enveloped by the Allied Forces, Germany effectively lost its Seventh Army in the Falaise Gap.

Bud Potratz vividly remembers the smell from the failed German breakout at the gap. "I will never forget the stench of death as we drove through," he recalled years later. "You get to certain places where there are certain types of odor and it brings it back quickly."

What was left of the German Army at Normandy retreated towards Paris. But Dog Company, subsumed in General Troy Middleton's VIII Corps, got ready for movement towards another large, resistant pocket of Germans entrenched in the heavily fortified coastal town of Brest.

CHAPTER 23

The Assault on Brest

Dog Company dismounted from the large olive green 6x6 trucks. The entire battalion had been driving along dusty Breton roads for hours. Most of the men had no idea where they were going or even what direction they were headed. With their new replacements in place, Dog was back up to strength. The old-timers from Camp Forrest started to sing a ditty they had learned back in England.

It was a hot August day in France. As the company pushed farther down the bucolic farm roads, the sun beat down on their backs. Captain McBride made an astute observation: further back from the front, there were more downed telephone wires and electric wires, some lying in ditches or across the road. As McBride explained, "When there's no wire at all, you know you're ahead of your own troops and probably in Jerry territory!"

Most of the men looked around and noticed the wires were gone. Peering across the hedgerow, about a football field away, Dog Company suddenly saw a five-man German patrol. "Hold your fire!" barked McBride.

As the patrol moved closer, paralleling the Rangers, the Americans got the order and opened fire, cutting three down immediately. The company's primary mission was to secure the village of Loc Maria Plouzané. Rather than pursue the wounded Germans, they pushed forward with their objective. "As Dog Company approached, French civilians ran out into the street and greeted them with flowers, glasses of wine, and kind words."

Ruggiero remembers that the French women mixed with both the German soldiers and American soldiers scattered throughout the area with equal gusto. "They were all friendly. They were mingling [among] us. They were bumming cigarettes and candy bars," recalled Ruggiero.

However, on at least one occasion, the timing of the visits from their new French girlfriends seemed suspicious. Several of the women came down to chat with the Rangers, and one was even giving haircuts. "She was a big hippo, very heavyset. She had black hair that was cut like a bowl around her head," remembered Ruggiero, laughing.

As the afternoon wore on, the women suddenly announced, "We have to leave."

"They left, and it was maybe an hour after, all at once, the shells started to come in." The Rangers realized, to their horror, that their new French "friends" had tipped off the Germans to their location.

The capture of the hamlet Loc Maria Plouzané was but one of many forgotten skirmishes in the Allied operation to take control of the channel ports. Dog Company formed part of a vanguard of over eighty thousand troops in VIII Corps, which headed into the Breton Peninsula to capture its largest ports, most importantly the port city of Brest. After the successful Allied breakout in Operation Cobra and the German collapse at Falaise, the Germans were in full retreat into Paris and northern France. Interestingly, the unexpected speed of the German collapse had strained the Allied supply chain. Initially, they brought supplies in on artificial harbors known as "mulberries." But a storm destroyed one of the mulberries at the Normandy beachhead, creating an acute shortage of everything—beans, bandages, bullets, and gasoline. The Allies always intended the mulberries to be a temporary solution before they could capture many of France's great ports along the English Channel—Brest, Saint Nazaire, Cherbourg, and Le Havre. However, Hitler knew the importance of the channel ports to the Allied supply efforts and ordered the German garrisons within them to fight to the last man. Before the Norman port at Cherbourg capitulated, German forces blew up and sabotaged the port's facilities.

Having anticipated an Allied attack for several years, German construction crews fortified the French coastal port towns with bunkers, encasements, and heavy guns. One of the most formidable fortresses along the Atlantic wall was Brest. Fifty thousand German troops ringed the antitank positions, machine gun nests, and bunkers around the city. Those troops included two German infantry divisions, currently unassigned U-boat crews, Russians pressed into service with the German army, and at its core, the vaunted 2nd Fallshirmjäger Division.

General Hermann-Bernhard Ramcke commanded the German forces. The highly decorated officer was one of only twenty-seven people in the German military ever to receive the prestigious Knight's Cross of the Iron Cross with Swords, Oak Leaves, and Diamonds. Ramcke also held the rare distinction of having served in all three branches of the German military. In Operation Merkur, the airborne attack on Crete, he personally led a Fallschirmjäger (paratroop) regiment. Ramcke fought in North Africa and later served in some of the more hard-fought battles in Italy and along the Russian front.

The Allies didn't want the daring and resourceful Ramcke hitting their vulnerable supply lines from behind. As General Omar Bradley noted, "I went ahead with the costly siege of Brest with Eisenhower's approval, not because we wanted the port, but because Ramcke left us no other solution."

The 2nd and 5th Ranger Battalions became part of VIII Corps, which was dedicated to neutralizing Ramcke and taking fortress Brest. It was a formidable task considering that the Germans were dug in and waiting, and the Allies did not have the three-to-one advantage an assault force typically needs to remove an entrenched enemy.

Protecting the port facility of Brest, the Germans had arrayed several powerful guns, including the Lochrist Battery with four 280 mm

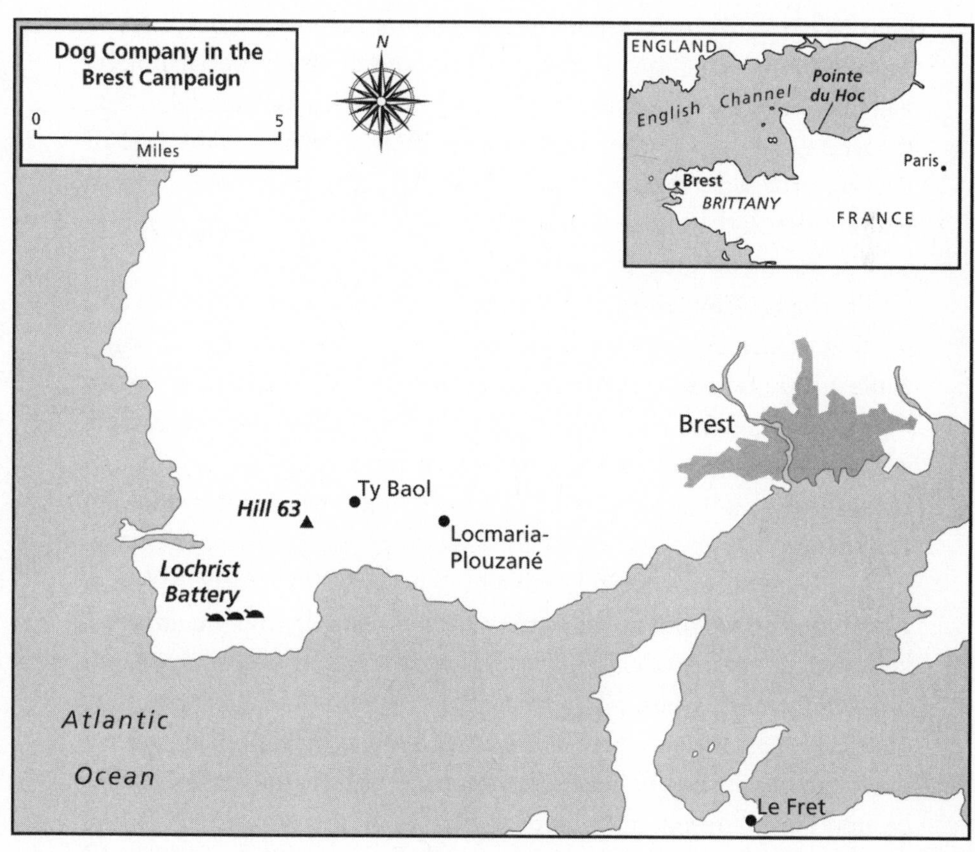
Dog Company in the Brest Campaign
0
5
Miles
N
ENGLAND
English Channel
Pointe du Hoc
Paris
Brest
BRITTANY
FRANCE
Brest
Ty Baol
Hill 63
Locmaria-Plouzané
Lochrist Battery
Atlantic Ocean
Le Fret

Krupp guns, each with a bore measuring eleven inches in diameter. Before moving the guns to Brest, the Reich originally placed the artillery on one of the Friesian islands off the northern German coast. The Germans dubbed the guns the "Graf Spee Battery" because they matched the size of the guns on the infamous German cruiser, or "pocket battleship," with the same name. In fact, the Germans originally built the guns for the *Braunschweig* class of warships. In addition, the magazines bore the semblance of a battleship buried under tons of Breton earth. Like their mission at Pointe du Hoc, taking out the guns became the 2nd Ranger Battalion's primary objective. And reminiscent of Pointe du Hoc, it was nearly mission impossible.

The battery formed the main strong point of Germany's western portion of the Brest defenses. Located in the wilds of Le Conquet peninsula, known to the French as *Le Finistère* (the end of the earth), the rugged terrain served as home for a handful of isolated inhabitants with a culture all their own. The French farmers in the area largely spoke Breton, an ancient Celtic dialect passed down from generation to generation.

The Graf Spee Battery resembled the Hollywood-imagined *Guns of Navarone,* but looking at the battery from a distance, you would never know it. The command post of the battery appeared to be a large mound of pastureland in a farmer's field, with a portion of the superstructure, draped in camouflage nets, poking from the top of the hill. Massively thick, the reinforced-concrete structure contained several stories underground. The command center, or fort as it was known, included telemetry and range-finding equipment, crew quarters, underground magazines, and even a hospital. Flanking the fort were six fortified pillboxes and one large gun emplacement fitted with antiaircraft guns to ward off any pesky low-flying Allied fighter-bombers. A long, underground tunnel connected the fort to several of its outlying bunkers.

Located 700 yards from the command center, the Spee's four 280 mm guns fired 626-pound shells that sounded like freight trains when traveling to their targets. A mushroom-like dome of earth covered one of the gun casements, making it difficult to identify from the air and nearly impervious to aerial and shore bombardment. Circular concrete casements, similar to those at Pointe du Hoc, concealed the other batteries. The Germans had turned the entire complex into a deathtrap, ringing it with barbed wire, minefields, and machine gun pillbox nests with interlocking fields of fire. The Rangers would have to enter this kill zone to neutralize the guns.

The fort's guns initially worked as the Germans intended, keeping Allied warships, even the venerable old lady HMS *Warspite,* at bay. A veteran of the World War I battle of Jutland, the *Warspite* shelled the fort but turned tail and steamed away after huge geysers of water from near misses formed around the warship and shrapnel hit the superstructure. Against land-based targets, three of the large battery's guns could rotate 360 degrees and fire shells capable of vaporizing an entire Breton hedgerow filled with dug-in Rangers.

The defense of the Graf Spee fell on the shoulders of recently promoted, forty-one-year-old Colonel Martin Fürst. Over one thousand German troops who manned the battery and the supporting defensive positions reported to Fürst. The German commander received his commission during the days of hyperinflation in the Weimar Republic. Ironically, the officer had ties to America; Fürst's brother immigrated to America, becoming a citizen and a successful businessman. Despite his family ties in the States, Fürst prepared to hold his ground and execute his duty as a German officer.

The Allied attack on Brest and its guns began on August 25, 1944, without fanfare because the liberation of Paris occurred on the same day, eclipsing news of the battle. For the assault, the battalion broke into several smaller task forces. Dog Company formed part of Task Force Slater, named for The Duke, who commanded the group. The motley crew included D, E, and F Companies, along with one platoon and five scout cars of the 86th Cavalry Recon Squadron, seven light tanks, and French resistance fighters from the FFI (French Forces of the Interior). Since the third week of August 1944, Dog Company had been riding on the backs of tanks, screening the 29th Division's right flank and probing German positions in the Le Conquet peninsula located on the western side of Brest.

For many of the replacement Rangers, the attack marked their first taste of combat. In his diary entry for August 25, 1944, Second Lieutenant George Kerchner noted, "1st Platoon surprised [a] large Jerry patrol at dawn and drove them off of Hill 95. This was the first time under fire for more than sixty percent of my platoon, and they behaved exceptionally well."

The wild and rugged terrain of the Le Finistère made an ideal hiding place for the FFI. To support the resistance, the OSS had dropped several Jedburgh Teams into the area. With expertise in demolitions, the Jeds, forerunners to U.S. special operations troops, organized and trained insurgents to ambush and harass the Germans. A typical team's composition was tri-national: a Frenchman, an Englishman, and an American.

One such three-man team, code-named Horace, worked with the 2nd Ranger Battalion. Major John W. Summers led the team. Earlier, Summers had engineered the daring escape of more than two hundred Russian prisoners of war who had been pressed into service for the Wehrmacht. Those Russians now fought for the OSS and FFI. The Jedburgh Teams' knowledge of the terrain and the additional manpower helped augment Task Force Slater.

In order to accomplish their mission, the battalion would have to secure the right flank of the 29th Division, cut the German lines of communication to Brest, and most importantly, neutralize the guns. To get to the guns, the Rangers would have to break through about three miles of fortifications that arced out from the battery. A key piece in the defenses was the tiny Breton town of Ty Baol and its nearby Hill 63, which loomed over a crucial road junction several miles north of the Lochrist Battery. It formed an important part of the supply lines back to Brest.

Vince Hagg remembers the day that word filtered down that Dog Company would attack Brest. In a forgotten farmer's field that served as Dog's bivouac the night before, Jack Kuhn and Len Lomell approached the rest of the company.

"Boy," they said, "do we have a job." Kuhn and Lomell were always among the first to pick up on rumors.

"We're going to come in behind Brest," they announced, excited. Hagg recalled, "They loved action almost like we were going on a Sunday picnic! They were looking for action. Colonel Rudder was the same way."

Probing the German defenses involved numerous small skirmishes over the course of a week. On August 27, Kerchner wrote, "While awaiting orders, Jerry patrol tried to get into our lines. Drove them off, killing or capturing seven out of eight.... 1st platoon took on the mission of securing Hill 63 and clearing road up to Hill 63. Looked like [a] suicide job, but it was cancelled.... While setting up lines, Jerry patrol walked into ambush with undetermined number of casualties. Area was heavily shelled and mortared all night, inflicting several casualties."

Bill Hoffman recalls that one attempt to avoid the shelling resulted in a bizarre run-in with the Germans. "We were starting to get shelled. I jumped into this house. I ran down into the cellar. I looked down there and there was about four or five Germans who were sitting around on barrels." Huddled around a candle, the men were sharing a large can of sardines. Their rifles lay stacked in a nearby corner.

As Hoffman came tearing down the stairs to get away from the mortar fire, the Germans looked up at him, wondering what he would do.

"What the hell?" exclaimed the sergeant, taking in the scene.

One of the largest men in the room looked up at him and asked for a cigarette: *"Haben Sie eine Zigarette?"*

Hoffman looked at him blankly. *"Zigarette?"* the German repeated. He looked down at the can of sardines and, smiling, offered some of it to the Ranger.

The Ranger reached into his cartridge belt and took out one of the five packs of cigarettes he was carrying.

"Danke! Danke!" the enemy soldier thanked him.

And that was that. "I just turned around and went back up the stairs and got with the rest of the guys," Hoffman recalled.

On August 28, the men spent the night in tents. Kerchner noted that it was their "first time under canvas for four days. Men were very much on edge, and rest did a lot of good."

Task Force Slater set off for Hill 63 on the morning of August 29. However, by the afternoon, massive storm clouds and blue lightning obscured the strong rays of the Breton sun. Even worse, blinding rain pelted the company, halting their advance. To avoid the deluge, the tanks and the men pulled off the road into a nearby field flanked by hedgerows. Yet there was no escaping the freezing rain, which chilled the men to the bone. With Hill 63 still looming ahead, the force dug in for a miserable night in water-filled foxholes.

CHAPTER 24

Hill 63

On the morning of August 30, the task force resumed its trek toward Hill 63. Bogged down in a morass of thick, brown mud, the tanks carrying Dog Company could progress no further. Led by Captain McBride, Dog advanced on Ty Baol without the armor. After slogging through the muck, Dog rounded a bend in the road and spotted Germans laying mines and barbed wire. A large farmhouse sat next to the road, guarding the entrance to the village, which was about a quarter of a mile away.

"Before we knew it, we thought we saw a German forward group, five or six them, trying to sneak in where we were," remembered Ruggiero. "One of the other guys spotted them. We chased them out of there all right. They jumped over the fence. I think I hit one of them in the butt, right in the ass."

Not too long after, Ruggiero made another memorable shot. As the platoon was working its way toward the farmyard, McBride pointed towards a haystack and whispered, "Hey! Take a look at that!"

"What is it?" asked Ruggiero, who didn't see anything there.

The sandy-haired Scotch-Irishman handed over his binoculars, and Ruggiero could just make out a German soldier crouched behind the pile of hay.

"You want me to take a crack at it?" asked Ruggiero.

Knowing Ruggiero had the iron sights of his M1 zeroed in, McBride told the expert marksman to take the 300-yard shot. With no better way to brace his weapon, Ruggiero balanced his rifle on McBride's shoulder. Without a telescopic sight, he could only make out a faint blur where the soldier stood.

CRACK!

The shot rang out, and the soldier disappeared from sight.

"Jesus! He's gone!" exclaimed McBride.

"Did I hit him?"

"We're going to find out." With McBride and Ruggiero on point, the platoon headed towards the farm.

Spotting Dog Company, the Germans made a beeline for the barn. No sooner had the Germans dashed to the building than an enormous amount of automatic fire erupted from the structure. In order to get as close to the barn as possible, the Rangers crouched down and "duck walked" up to a stone wall that flanked the building. Not seeing them, an SS trooper behind the wall made a break for it, trying to join his fellow soldiers. "He didn't make it," remembered Ruggiero. "McBride and I both nailed him. My bullet hit where his belt buckle was, and he was moaning and groaning. McBride went in and finished him off."

With the Germans holed up in the barn and the Rangers crouched down outside, a Mexican standoff of sorts ensued. To break the stalemate, McBride called in Dominic Sparaco, who carried one of the platoon's M1's fitted to fire rifle grenades. "The barn door was left open in the middle. In other words, they weren't closed tight," explained Ruggiero. McBride turned to Sparaco, "Hey, do you think you could put it through there, get those krauts out of there?"

Sparaco launched the grenade right through the opening, but it didn't go off. "The Germans didn't know that," grinned Ruggiero as he explained what happened next. "They came scurrying out. There was one behind a hayloft. They had about four or five storm troopers in there. They put up a fight, but we got them all."

After clearing the town of a few snipers, Dog Company approached a crossroads on the gentle slope of Hill 63. A few hundred

Leonard "Bud" Lomell, legendary first sergeant and later lieutenant and platoon leader in Dog Company. The "mainspring" of Dog Company, Lomell rendered inoperable five of the guns atop Pointe Du Hoc. Historian Stephen Ambrose would later claim that after General Eisenhower, Lomell was the most important individual of D-Day because his actions saved countless lives. *Photo courtesy of Tom Ruggiero.*

Captain Harold "The Duke" Slater, Dog Company commander. Known for his winning spirit, fearless bravado, dashing good looks, and his uncanny resemblance to the actor Lee Marvin, Slater helped mold Dog Company into one of the finest Ranger companies in history. *Photo courtesy of Tom Ruggiero.*

On the left is Captain Morton McBride, Dog Company executive officer and later its commanding officer, known for his keen mind, and acerbic wit. On the right is Sergeant Antonio Tom Ruggiero, "Ruggie." Prior to the war, Ruggiero was a professional tap dancer under the stage name, "Tommy Knight." Known for burning up the dance floor to entertain his fellow Rangers, Ruggie was also known for his deadeye as one of Dog's snipers. *Photo courtesy of Tom Ruggiero.*

First Sergeant Jack Kuhn (right), standing next to an M8 Greyhound armored car, and Tom Ruggiero (left). Kuhn had a great sense of humor and often did stand-up comedy to help relieve the tension of battle. He assisted best friend Lomell in taking out the big guns of Pointe du Hoc. *Photo courtesy of Tom Ruggiero.*

With back turned, Captain Morton McBride (left), Duke Slater (center), and a smiling Tom Ruggiero (right). *Photo courtesy of Tom Ruggiero.*

Herman Stein and his best friend L-Rod Petty. The Ranger buddy system and brutal combat forged friendships that continue to this day. *Photo courtesy of Deborah Stein-Caldwell.*

D-Day Rangers from Dog Company, taken shortly after the Battle of the Bulge: (Left to right, starting with top row) Morris Webb, unidentified, Jack Kuhn, George Schneller, William Kruz, unidentified, John Riley, Captain Mort McBride, (front row) unidentified, Melvin Sweany, Tom Ruggiero, Joe Devoli, Sigurd Sundby, Gordon Lunning, (above Lunning) Edwin Secor. *Photo courtesy of Tom Ruggiero.*

Vince Hagg, who joined Dog Company shortly after Pointe Du Hoc in June 1944 and fought with the unit through the rest of the war. *Photo courtesy of Vince Hagg.*

Bill Hoffman, one of the original members of Dog Company from its earliest days. He fought in Dog's major campaigns and later retired from the U.S. Army as a master sergeant. *Photo courtesy of Bill Hoffman.*

The legendary leader of the 2nd Ranger Battalion, Lieutenant Colonel James Rudder. The photo was taken on Pointe Du Hoc. The discoloring in his uniform is due to a near miss from an Allied naval shell which contained Explosive D or Dunnite, a yellow powder that was pressed into the shell. The friendly fire wounded Rudder and killed the man standing next to him. *Photo courtesy of National Archives.*

Rangers training at Camp Forrest, Tennessee. They are crossing a rope bridge with a controlled explosion detonating nearby to simulate combat. *Photo courtesy of National Archives.*

Full-scale dress rehearsal of the Rangers' amphibious assault which included live fire from Allied ships. *Photo courtesy of George Kerchner.*

Dog Company training on cliffs in England in preparation for their D-Day mission. The Rangers perilously scaled 100- to 300-foot cliffs without the protection of safety harnesses nearly every day for six months before their assault on Pointe Du Hoc. *Photo courtesy of Tom Ruggiero.*

Training photo of Rangers scaling steep cliffs during a larger training exercise prior to D-Day. *Photo courtesy of George Kerchner.*

Members of the 2nd Ranger Battalion marching to their embarkation area in Weymouth, England, where they boarded ships for the invasion of France. *Photo courtesy of National Archives.*

An American bomber over Utah Beach. The Rangers' objective at Pointe Du Hoc was one of the most heavily shelled and bombed targets on D-Day in a futile attempt to neutralize the Pointe's six heavy guns that could hit the invasion beaches or Allied ships. Hundreds of tons of ordnance turned the top of Pointe Du Hoc into a cratered moonscape, but failed to destroy the guns, which were later taken out by the Rangers. *Photo courtesy of National Archives.*

The approximately 90-foot cliffs of Pointe Du Hoc. Dog Company had to scale the cliffs in a frontal assault under murderous German MG-42 machine gun and grenade fire. *Photo courtesy of National Archives.*

The Germans booby-trapped the cliffs of Pointe Du Hoc with "roller mines" (IEDs). They suspended this French shell on the side of the cliff. *Photo courtesy of National Archives.*

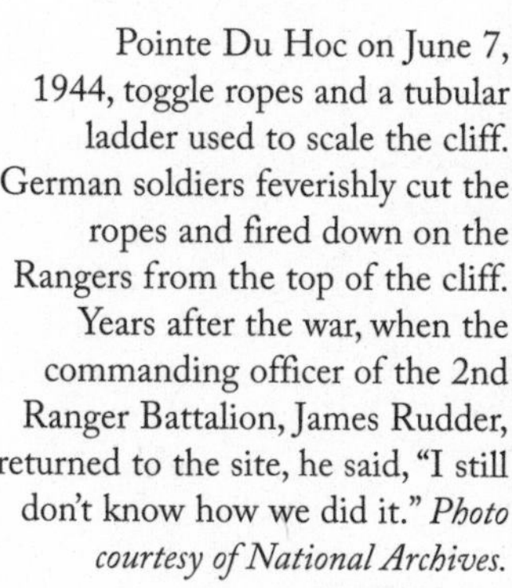

Pointe Du Hoc on June 7, 1944, toggle ropes and a tubular ladder used to scale the cliff. German soldiers feverishly cut the ropes and fired down on the Rangers from the top of the cliff. Years after the war, when the commanding officer of the 2nd Ranger Battalion, James Rudder, returned to the site, he said, "I still don't know how we did it." *Photo courtesy of National Archives.*

One of the six guns at Pointe du Hoc. The guns posed a significant danger to the Allied invasion, and knocking them out became a top priority. Hundreds of tons of bombs and naval shells failed to destroy the guns; however, two men from Dog Company disabled five of the guns. *Photo courtesy of Paul Woodadge.*

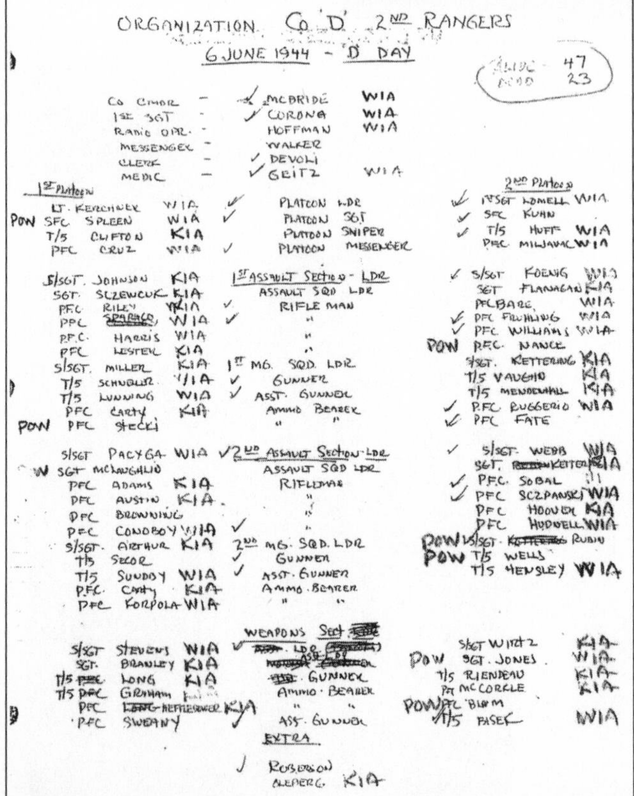

ORGANIZATION CO 'D' 2ND RANGERS
6 JUNE 1944 – 'D' DAY

ALIVE – 47
DEAD 23

CO CMDR – ✓ MCBRIDE WIA
1ST SGT – ✓ CORONA WIA
RADIO OPR. – HOFFMAN WIA
MESSENGER – WALKER
CLERK – ✓ DEVOLI
MEDIC – ✓ GEITZ WIA

1ST PLATOON
LT. KERCHNER WIA ✓ PLATOON LDR
POW SFC SPLEEN WIA ✓ PLATOON SGT
T/5 CLIFTON KIA PLATOON SNIPER
PFC CRUZ WIA ✓ PLATOON MESSENGER

S/SGT. JOHNSON KIA 1ST ASSAULT SECTION – LDR
SGT. SLZEWCUK KIA ASSAULT SQD LDR
PFC RILEY WIA ✓ RIFLE MAN
PFC SPARACO WIA ✓ "
PFC HARRIS WIA "
PFC LESTER KIA "
S/SGT. MILLER KIA 1ST MG. SQD. LDR.
T/5 SCHNULLR WIA ✓ GUNNER
T/5 LUNNING WIA ✓ ASST. GUNNER
PFC CARTY KIA AMMO BEARER
POW PFC STECKI " "

S/SGT PACYGA WIA ✓ 2ND ASSAULT SECTION LDR
POW SGT MCLAUGHLIN ASSAULT SQD LDR
PFC ADAMS KIA RIFLEMAN
PFC AUSTIN KIA "
PFC BROWNING "
PFC CONOBOY WIA ✓ "
S/SGT. ARTHUR KIA 2ND MG. SQD. LDR
T/5 SECOR ✓ GUNNER
T/5 SUNDBY WIA ✓ ASST. GUNNER
PFC CARTY KIA AMMO. BEARER
PFC KORPOLA WIA " "

WEAPONS SECT.
S/SGT STEVENS WIA ✓ LDR.
SGT. BRANLEY KIA ASST. LDR
T/5 LONG KIA GUNNER
T/5 GRAHAM AMMO. BEARER
PFC HEFFLEBOWER KIA " "
PFC SWEANY ✓ ASST. GUNNER

EXTRA
✓ ROBERSON
CLERK KIA

2ND PLATOON
✓ 1ST SGT LOMELL WIA
✓ SFC KUHN
✓ T/5 HUFF WIA
PFC MILJAVAC WIA

✓ S/SGT KOENIG WIA
SGT FLANAGAN KIA
PFC BARE WIA
✓ PFC FRUHLING WIA
✓ PFC WILLIAMS WIA
POW PFC NANCE
S/SGT. KETTERING KIA
T/5 VAUGHN KIA
T/5 MENDENHALL KIA
✓ PFC RUGGERIO WIA
✓ PFC FATE

✓ S/SGT. WEBB WIA
SGT. KETTERING KIA
✓ PFC. SOBAL "
✓ PFC SCZPANSKI WIA
PFC HOOVER KIA
PFC HUDNELL WIA
POW S/SGT. RUBIN
POW T/5 WELLS
T/5 HENSLEY WIA

S/SGT WINTZ KIA
POW SGT. JONES WIA
T/5 RIENDEAU KIA
PFC MC CORKLE KIA
POW PFC BLUM
T/5 PASEK WIA

Hand written notes given to the Author by Len Lomell, detailing the extensive losses Dog Company sustained on D-Day. Nearly every man in the company was killed, wounded, or taken prisoner as a result of the intense fighting on Pointe du Hoc. *Courtesy of Len Lomell.*

Rangers from the 2nd Ranger Battalion. Note the helmet with the distinctive insignia with a diamond containing the number two. The men are in a massive crater caused by aerial bombardment or the 14-inch guns of the USS *Texas*. The Rangers are manning a 30-calibar machine gun while fending off one of the numerous German counterattacks on their position. *Photo courtesy of National Archives.*

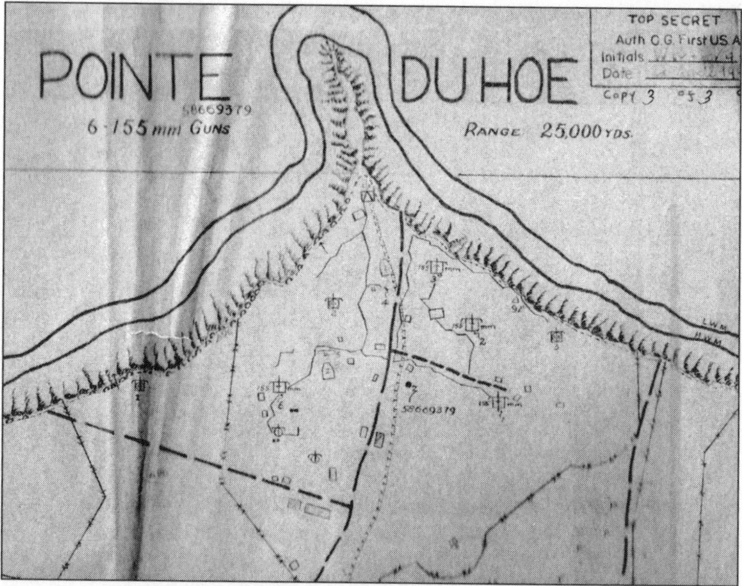

An original map detailing the fortress-like defenses and minefields atop the Pointe. To reach the guns located about a mile from the cliffs, Dog Company had to fight through closely knit machine gun nests and 37mm anti-aircraft guns, while avoiding dense minefields. *Map courtesy of National Archives.*

Rudder's command post, which the Rangers set up in a flak bunker on the eastern side of Pointe Du Hoc. An American flag lies draped over the side to prevent friendly fire from roving Allied fighter-bombers. *Photo courtesy of National Archives.*

A small boat ferrying needed supplies to Pointe Du Hoc. The photo was taken at low tide, showing the massive shell holes created by the Allied bombardment. Several members of Dog Company fell to the bottom of the huge underwater craters as they exited their landing craft on the morning of D-Day, while Germans fire rained down on them from above. *Photo courtesy of National Archives.*

Close-up of men near Rudder's command post on top of Pointe Du Hoc. The Ranger drinking from the canteen is communications officer Lieutenant James "Ike" Eikner. The bandaged officer in the right corner is British Commando Lieutenant Colonel Thomas Trevor, who helped train the Rangers. *Photo courtesy of National Archives.*

The Ranger without a helmet with the Thompson submachine gun on the far left is Staff Sergeant Jack Kuhn. The large Ranger standing next to the soldier with Red Cross medical armband is Captain Otto "Big Stoop" Masny. *Photo courtesy of National Archives.*

The Coast Guard rescuing survivors of a small vessel which capsized off Normandy. A similar fate befell LCA 860; the landing craft capsized on its way to Pointe Du Hoc, drowning several men on board, while nearly a third of Dog Company struggled to stay afloat and battled hypothermia in the cold waters. *Photo courtesy of National Archives.*

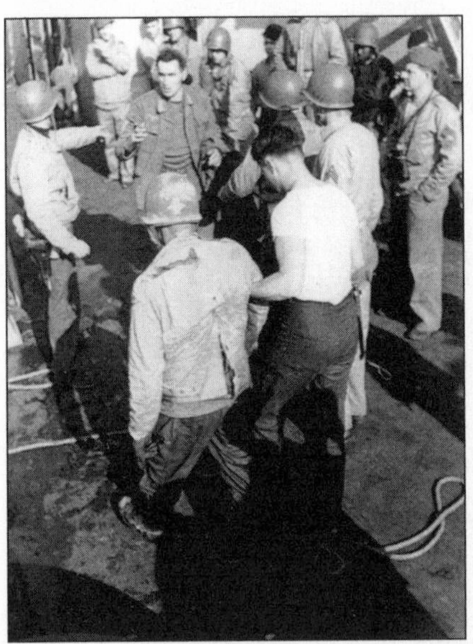

The mighty 14-inch guns of the USS *Texas* provided crucial shore bombardment, defending the Rangers, and the battleship also provided hospital and medical services to wounded Rangers, including the survivors of LCA 860, and several German prisoners of war captured at Pointe du Hoc. (Two pictures.) *Photo courtesy of National Archives.*

What turned out to be Dog Company's toughest objective, Hill 400. At approximately 7:28 a.m. on December 7, 1944, Dog and Fox Companies of the 2nd Ranger Battalion launched one of the few bayonet charges of World War II. After charging across a 100-yard open field into the teeth of MG-42 machine guns and artillery, the Rangers stormed up the 400-meter hill where they withstood a two-day, all-out assault by German units, including elite troops. The author snapped the photo at dawn after spending the night on the hill during one of his battlefield tours. He attempts to visit all the places about which he writes, to walk the battlefields and trace the steps of the participants. *Author photo.*

A large troop shelter located atop Hill 400. The shelter became the focal point of German counterattacks intended to reclaim the hill from the Rangers. It provided some refuge from the thousands of rounds of German artillery fire that poured down upon the hill once the Rangers seized it from their enemies. *Author photo.*

A German soldier captured near Hill 400 during the brutal fighting in the Hürtgen Forest, one of the longest and bloodiest battles the U.S. Army would ever fight. A G.I. is questioning him. *Photo courtesy of National Archives.*

A heavily armed, battle-hardened grenadier of the *Waffen SS*. While pushing into Germany, Dog Company often fought the SS. The German soldier in the center of the photo draped with bandoliers of machine gun ammunition is holding the dreaded MG-42, which had a rate of fire that approached 1,500 rounds per minute. The Rangers faced the murderous "bone saw" throughout the war. *Photo courtesy of National Archives.*

Members of the 2nd Ranger Battalion prepare for a mission inside Germany. *Photo courtesy of National Archives.*

A patrol of the 2nd Ranger Battalion inside Germany. *Photo courtesy of National Archives.*

Former Dog Company member Herman Stein after scaling the cliffs of Pointe Du Hoc in his youthful sixties, shortly before President Reagan's famous speech commending the "Boys of Pointe Du Hoc." *Photo courtesy of Deborah Stein-Caldwell.*

Herman Stein, always a Ranger, 2010. *Photo courtesy of Deborah Stein-Caldwell.*

yards from the road junction, the gentle slope turned into a steep cliff. Surprisingly, there were few Germans defending the hill, and the Rangers summarily seized it and hunkered down. In his diary, Kerchner wrote, "[We] settled down to what promised to be long stay on Hill 63."

The next day, the Rangers attacked a nearby German position in what would be platoon leader George Kerchner's last action. As he and his men assaulted a machine gun nest near the hill, an MG-42 opened up, and a single bullet dug deeply into his shoulder, ripping it apart. As a medic carried him off the field, Kerchner thought the wound might be critical enough to send him home. Indeed, Kerchner was right. "It was the last time we ever saw him," recalled Ruggerio.

Hill 63 proved crucial for both the Germans and the Rangers. For an entire week, Dog Company tenaciously clung to the hill as the Germans launched countless counterattacks and relentlessly pelted the Rangers and their French allies with artillery. The most deadly came from the Lochrist Battery. The 88 mm artillery could easily reach Hill 63, but the 626-pound shells delivered by the big guns from the battery proved even more deadly. "My God, the damage those shells could do! I've seen whole hedgerows disappear before my eyes," recalled Hagg. "Of course, the 88s were boom, boom, boom, but the shells on the Graf Spee were not as fast, but they were way bigger. You could actually see the shell as it was coming at you."

The gun battery was not the only danger the Rangers encountered on the Hill. Throughout the week, the Rangers also sustained self-propelled artillery, sniper, and mortar fire. One day, Ruggiero and his friend Joe Flanagan were lying behind a hedgerow discussing an incident that had occurred earlier in the week when someone yelled, "Ruggie, get over this hedgerow and bring that [SCR-]536 radio."

At only five-foot-three, Ruggiero looked up at the much taller, prickly hedgerow and said, "How the hell am I going to get over that?"

"Come on Rugg, I'll put you over it," offered Flanagan. "Keep your feet together, and when I count to three, straighten them out."

Ruggiero later recalled, "He gave me a hell of a shove. I just caught the hedgerow, the top of it, and got one leg over, and that mortar came right in. It sailed right by me, only inches from my body. It cut Flanagan right in half. I got a couple splinters in me. I was so concerned about him. Oh, Jesus, what a mess."

Ruggiero radioed for help, and Lomell soon arrived in a Jeep bearing a Red Cross flag. "Are you alright, Rugg?" asked Lomell.

"I don't know. I got some splinters in my ass, but it's no big deal," he answered.

Amazingly, Flanagan was still alive. With his glasses covered in blood, Flanagan started yelling, "Clean my glasses, I can't see anything. I can't see, I can't see! Clean my glasses!"

"My God, we knew he wasn't going to survive," explained Ruggiero. "We got him on the Jeep as best we could, what was left of him. We covered him up, and Lomell drove him to the field hospital. He was dead before he got there. It was completely horrible to see a guy get hit like that. You ask yourself, *Why him and not me?*"

In the place where Flanagan had been lying, Ruggiero found a German Iron Cross that Flanagan had held onto as a souvenir. When the war was over, Ruggiero looked up Flanagan's family. Although it took him decades to track him down, Ruggiero eventually delivered that Iron Cross to Joe Flanagan's brother.

Unfortunately, many other Rangers would face similarly horrific fates during the week Dog Company spent on Hill 63. On September 3, direct firing from the 88s and 280 mm shells from the Lochrist killed and wounded twenty-one Rangers. Perhaps the worst day of shelling came on September 5. That night, a shell the size of Ruggiero buried a squad of men alive. Using their helmets as entrenching tools, the other men of Dog Company dug out their brothers, who were traumatized from the shock of nearly dying. The severe enemy shelling forced the FFI to retreat.

On several occasions, the Americans captured or killed German soldiers. A two-man patrol led by Sergeant Ed Secor snared over a hundred Germans. The quiet, mild-mannered Ranger teamed up with the animated Staff Sergeant Joe Stevens. Stevens, called "Steve" by the men, usually kept a cigar clamped tightly between his teeth. He was steady and cool under fire, but if you "fucked up, he would hammer you," said Hagg.

Hagg recalled an incident involving Stevens when Hagg and his mortar man Jake Jakubiak took a prisoner. "At the far end of the hedgerow, you could see this white flag appear. A German came out, surrendered, coming across the field, you know. He got maybe thirty or thirty-five yards from me and Jakubiak. Getting German pistols at that time was the big thing. I think Jakubiak may have seen a pistol on the German." Jakubiak jumped up to approach the German. A bullet, probably from a sniper, instantly struck him dead. Hagg later reflected, "It was the first friend that I had seen killed."

Staff Sergeant Joe Stevens witnessed the incident. He grabbed Hagg by the shoulder. "Hagg, don't worry about Jake anymore," he said with his unlit cigar clenched in his teeth. "Jake is dead. He doesn't have to worry about the war. He doesn't have to worry about the hard times. Just forget about it."

But Hagg couldn't forget. "I was only nineteen years old. It's one of the most vivid things I can remember."

On September 6, all companies opened fire on the German positions in front of Hill 63. A haunting scene served as the backdrop for the attack, the memory of which is seared into the minds of many men who were there. Lightning arced across the sky, but "you couldn't tell if the lightning bolts were shells or lightning bolts." As the men climbed the slope, "one shell came in pretty close. We all hit the ground. It was raining like hell. One of the guys got hit. It was Dominic Sparaco, who fired the rifle grenade [through the barn door]."

When the thunderstorm finally stopped, it was pitch black. The Rangers advanced over a thousand yards with McBride, Ruggiero, and Cruz in the lead. "Finally, we got into the German positions. The Germans had moved back, to the back of the hill," remembered Ruggiero. However, the rest of the Ranger platoon had fallen far behind.

McBride looked at Ruggiero and said, "Tell the platoon leaders to come up here. You and Bill Cruz go back and don't come back unless you bring the company with you."

"That was scary because you didn't know where the Germans were hiding," recalled Ruggiero. Cruz and Ruggiero split up after first settling on a whistle they could use to signal to each other. Creeping through the eerie buildings, Ruggiero eventually heard some talking.

Ruggiero whistled to signal Cruz. To his surprise, Cruz's whistle came back from about fifteen feet away. "Stop whistling and come on over here," said Ruggie.

In the darkness, Ruggiero, McBride, and the other members of Dog reformed and continued their advance towards the guns.

CHAPTER 25

The Fabulous Four

Sprawling hundreds of yards in front of the battery stood several well-placed signs reading *Achtung: Minen!* (Attention: Mines!) Hundreds of anti-personnel and tank mines guarded the entrance to the guns of the Lochrist Battery. Navigating that death trap required balls of steel: one step—one inch—in the wrong direction would blow off a body part, or if you were lucky, kill instantly.

"I believe I see a passage through that minefield." Ranger Lieutenant Bob Edlin from A Company looked carefully at the minefield, and told his Rangers, "Maybe we can work our way up to that pillbox."

Known for his audacity and daring, the twenty-something Texan decided that, rather than risking his entire platoon, he would take three of his best men—Sergeants William J. Courtney, William Dreher, and Warren D. "Halftrack" Burmaster. Collectively, these men became known as the "Fabulous Four," achieving legendary status within the battalion.

Jumping off at 8:30 A.M. on September 6 with "instructions to move as rapidly as possible to permit the enemy no time in which to organize his defenses," the 2nd Battalion had moved in the direction of the Lochrist Battery. Able, Baker, and Charlie Companies made the main thrust of the attack. Fittingly, although all the Rangers approached the fort, only one small group would force the surrender.

Like at Pointe du Hoc, a band of individual Rangers acting on their own initiative changed the course of the entire battle.

Just before the small, daring team began their trek through the minefield, Edlin ordered a mortar to drop smoke on the field. With their hearts racing, the Fabulous Four dashed across the field through the cloudy, gray haze of smoke and fire laid by the artillery. As Edlin instructed, the men carefully concentrated on the well-worn foot path that unfolded in front of them, which was used by French civilians to deliver goods to the fort. Pushing their backs against the pillbox, they moved towards the door. "We could hear them talking and laughing inside," recalled Edlin.

In a swift, fluid motion, the strong, wiry Texan kicked the door open. Courtney barked in perfect German, *"Hände hoch!"* (Hands up!)

Stunned, the paratroopers threw their hands up. None of the twenty went for their machine guns and assault rifles stacked in the corners of the pillbox.

Edlin shot Courtney a quick glance, "Talk to somebody. See who's in charge here."

Before Courtney could get the words out, Edlin's German counterpart, a twenty-something lieutenant came forward. "Sir, I speak fluent English. I went to college in America."

Surprised at the Germans' behavior, Edlin chimed in, "You guys seem like you're glad this thing's over with."

"We're glad it's over with," replied the same German. "We've been bombarded with artillery, and the bombers, then here, and the fighter planes, and now we're going to be overrun. It's a shame we're going to lose a lot of men. Of course, you're going to lose a lot of men too."

The Fabulous Four had captured one of the outlying pillboxes that formed part of the larger fortifications guarding the battery. Audaciously, Edlin pressed the German officer. "Will you lead us to the fort commander?"

The English-speaking German responded with a sharp, *"Ja."*

Rather than risk all of his men to the hazards of war, Edlin decided to go only with Courtney acting as his translator. "It was a tremendous risk, and I didn't see any point in risking anyone other than myself. But I needed an interpreter in case they were lying to me."

Edlin told Burmaster, "Get on the radio and contact Colonel Rudder to lift all artillery fire and planes, all fire on the fort."

Burmaster spoke firmly into the microphone on his SCR-536 radio and repeated Edlin's command. The message stunned Len Lomell, the battalion sergeant major, when he heard it come in. No one could believe that the lieutenant and his men had survived the deadly minefield and infiltrated the Germans' fortress. He recalled Lieutenant Arman from F Company saying incredulously to Rudder, "The fool lieutenant of yours is up there already!"

The "fool lieutenant" was audaciously pressing his luck. Edlin, Courtney, and the German lieutenant were making their way through yet another minefield to reach the main fort entrance. As they walked, Edlin casually spoke to the German officer about college in the United States, his tommy gun slung on his soldier to avoid the appearance that he was taking the German prisoner.

The men entered a long, concrete tunnel and approached a pair of massive metal doors, which opened electrically. Through the doors, they first entered a cavernous underground hospital, equipped with state-of-the-art medical equipment. Nurses and doctors and wounded soldiers filled the ward. Courtney commanded, *"Hände hoch!"* Hands went up.

Immediately, chaos broke out. "They were yelling at us, and they sounded the alarm. Courtney hollered something at them in German. This lieutenant started talking, and they quieted down. Courtney was interpreting to me, and he was telling them that we were going to talk to the commandant and possibly end the situation."

Shaped somewhat like a buried skyscraper, the fort included a number of elevators for reaching its deep underground levels. The trio approached one such elevator and found several men guarding the door. The American-educated German lieutenant ordered them to lower their weapons.

He then led the Rangers to Colonel Martin Fürst's office. Their German guide was about to knock on the door when Edlin barked, "Don't knock! Don't touch the door! Just step back!"

Edlin turned the knob, and he and Courtney bolted through the door. Seated behind a large mahogany desk, Martin Fürst looked up as the Rangers crossed the room. Edlin yelled *"Hände hoch!"* as he shoved his tommy gun at Fürst. Shocked and stunned, the alarmed colonel stammered several words in German asking what was going on.

Fürst calmed down quickly, though, and Edlin thought, *"This is one of the coolest characters I've ever seen."* The colonel got up, walked over to a table, poured a drink, and asked in German, "What do you want?"

Courtney attempted to stammer something in German, and the colonel condescendingly said, "You don't need your interpreter, lieutenant, I speak excellent English."

Edlin responded, "Fine. Why don't you just surrender the whole fort and all your prisoners and get this whole thing over with." Edlin added that he had taken the pillbox and wanted to discuss surrendering the fort, which would avoid a lot of casualties.

Fürst demurred.

Edlin then tried to convince Fürst of the futility of the situation. "You're completely surrounded. There's Rangers all around you. And the Air Force is going to bomb you." While part of this strategic situation was true, Edlin really had no idea. He tried to drive home the bluff powerfully so that Fürst could save face.

Fürst looked at Edlin and said, "I'm not going to surrender." The colonel picked up the telephone near his desk, asked a question in German, and hung up. Within a matter of seconds, the black phone buzzed. Fürst picked up the receiver. Edlin's stomach tightened and his heart raced. The colonel looked up at Edlin. "Ah!" he said.

On the call, he had determined that there were only four Americans in the fort. "Well, there are only four of you, so you're my prisoners."

Outnumbered by eight hundred Germans, Edlin continued the unbelievably audacious bluff with a poker face—one that would fool the most cunning riverboat gambler. "The thing that happened, I have no explanation for it whatsoever." It was then that, out of his ass, Edlin pulled one of the gutsiest stunts of the war. The odds were eight hundred to four, but at that moment in time, he knew he was all in. "I had a tommy gun and a pistol on my hip and a knife on my boot. And I reached over and grabbed a hand grenade from Courtney and I pulled the pin on it. And I stuck it between his legs."

Edlin looked directly into Fürst's eyes. "You either surrender right now, or I'm going to release the pin, and you'll be a dead man!"

Fürst played his last card. "You know, if a grenade goes off, you die with me."

Edlin was prepared to die. He responded, "Yeah, but it'll be worth it. I'm gonna count to three and on three, I'm gonna release the grenade."

Fürst caved in by the count of two. "All right, all right, I'll surrender," he stammered.

Edlin told the colonel to get on the PA system and order the entire fort to surrender.*

With a tommy gun to his head and a live grenade near his crotch, Fürst got on the microphone that linked to the fort's PA system. He ordered the garrison to surrender, hand over their arms, and take no hostile action against the Americans. Through Burmaster, Edlin contacted Rudder, who facilitated the surrender of the Lochrist Battery. The entire 2nd Ranger Battalion assembled outside the fort. The

*When Edlin was seventy-seven years old—an older, wiser man—he reflected upon that moment. "I know what I would do now. I would put the pin back in the grenade and surrender to him. But at that time—I don't know, nobody knows. No one will ever know. I think now over a cold beer that in my braver moments I would have released that pin. But I don't know if I would have or not. I very likely would have barricaded the office and killed him and hoped that he would die without a sound."

Germans hoisted several white flags around the area and in the defensive positions of the fort. Dog Company and the other companies within the battalion stood at attention as the Germans began surrendering their weapons. "Initially, I thought only several hundred Germans would surrender. In all, eight hundred and thirteen Germans began stacking their arms."

Fürst and his fellow German officers exchanged salutes with Rudder and surrendered the fort at 1:30 P.M. on September 9, 1944. Notably, Fürst's surrender of the Lochrist Battery effectively eliminated a crucial redoubt in the western portion of Germany's Brest defenses. For his actions, his superiors recommended Edlin for the Medal of Honor.*

Mopping-up operations continued for the next two weeks. The Rangers cleared the Breton town of Le Fret, which contained a German "hospital plant" that held Allied prisoners of war. In accordance with the Geneva Convention and to avoid fratricide, the Allies employed highly restrictive rules of engagement, which prohibited the firing of artillery nearby. Despite these restrictions, the soldiers cleared the area largely without incident. They captured forty German soldiers and rescued four hundred Allied POWs.

In the third week of September, Dog Company and the battalion assembled to prepare for a mission that would involve a seaborne assault on the last remaining German strongpoint on the peninsula. But similar to the events at Cherbourg, Allied ground forces overran the defenses, making the seaborne attack plans moot.

On September 18, the German garrison in Brest surrendered. The long and bloody campaign in Brest ended with a final act of defiance. In the surrender ceremony, German General Hermann-Bernhard Ramcke smartly approached newly promoted American Brigadier

*Thanks to the dogged persistence of Rudder, who recommended Edlin for the Medal of Honor, the ballsy Texan eventually received the DSC.

General Charles Canham. On D-Day, Canham commanded the 116th Infantry Regiment but now served as assistant commander of the 8th Division. Months earlier, with the 116th, Canham relieved Dog Company on the coastal road near Pointe du Hoc. Swagger stick in hand and wearing full dress uniform, Ramcke approached Canham with a cocksure attitude. "Let me see your credentials," Ramcke demanded with disdain.

General Canham locked his steely gaze with Ramcke and pointed at his men. "These are my credentials."

CHAPTER 26

Interlude

Pat McCrone looked through the cracks in the walls of the rotting, old boxcar that had seen service in World War I. Time, like the endless French countryside, passed by in a blur. McCrone thought back to the days he had spent with his best friend Johnson, everything from training at Camp Forrest to his final days at the Pointe. He reflected on the carnage he had seen for the past several months. Killing became easy; so did vengeance.

Shortly after the fall of Brest, Dog Company crammed into French boxcars known as "forty-and-eights," named for their ability to carry forty men or eight horses. The uncomfortable journey spanned four days. Dog Company traveled 430 miles without incident to a train yard in the small Belgian town of Foy.

After de-training in Belgium on October 4, command assigned the battalion the mission of acting as a mobile counterattack force to the Ninth Army. Specifically, their role was to neutralize a German airborne attack.

Dog Company then went into an enhanced training schedule where, as in Brest, they received reinforcements. On October 6, they held a battalion review. Rudder pinned gold lieutenants' bars on Leonard G. Lomell, and the sergeant major* made history as the first

*After D-Day, Lomell was promoted from first sergeant to sergeant major of the 2nd Ranger Battalion.

enlisted Ranger of the 2nd Battalion to receive a battlefield commission. "It was a proud moment," recalled Lomell sixty-five years later. Lieutenant Lomell became a platoon leader for Dog Company's 1st Platoon.

On October 9, the battalion formed an honor guard for the commanding general of the Ninth Army. "These sixty men, selected for uniformity of height and proficiency in the manual of arms, were to act as an escort of honor."

The men then trucked to Arlon, Belgium, where they were billeted near King Leopold's hunting preserves. A seemingly magical place, the forest was a maze of tall interlocking fir trees with a dark carpet of green moss covering its floor. The mythical setting seemed a million miles removed from the horrors of war. Doctor Block couldn't resist the temptation to organize a hunting party.

On October 12, Lieutenant Colonel Charles Taylor and Master Sergeant Forrest Pogue rounded up Dog Company and other members of the battalion and interviewed them in a nearby farmer's field for the War Department Historical Section. Taylor and Pogue later became legends in the historiography of the war. Taylor sat down with men like Lomell, Kuhn, Cruz, Slater, and Edlin and captured their stories while they were still fresh and vividly burning in the mind's eye of each soldier. Using crude maps, the historians cross-examined the Rangers, verifying their stories and reconstructing the Battles of Pointe du Hoc and Omaha Beach in the green field at Arlon. When Taylor departed a few days later, he remarked that "he had come with the idea of writing a chapter on the battalion in his account of the D-Day action, but was leaving with the material for a book!" While the story was fertile ground for a movie, an official book on the subject wouldn't go to press for several years.

The men returned to the humdrum tasks of garrison duty. McBride and the other company commanders departed for a tour of the Siegfried Line to "see firsthand the job they would have to do."

During the respite, Rudder cleaned the dead wood out of the battalion, "transferring a number of undesirable men to other units in the

Ninth Army." Even during this interlude, the battalion remained at a high level of readiness, serving as part of a counterattack force. "Two companies were held on constant alert while the remainder of the battalion [continued training]."

On November 2, command ordered the 2nd Ranger Battalion, including Dog Company, to move north to the Hürtgen Forest, which would culminate in what many would consider their longest day.

CHAPTER 27

A Factory of Death

As the sun went down, white flakes of snow pelted the faces of Dog Company as they trudged through ankle-deep mud. Twisted hulks of trees flanked the fire trail cut into the forest. Rotting remains of the front half of a horse sprawled across the trail. One of the tragedies of war are the innocent animals caught in the crosshairs of battle. Helmets, equipment, and the debris of a lost battle littered their path. As Dog marched through the mud and snow, a boot caught Morris Webb's eye. He kicked it aside, and a dead man's bone fell out of the worn leather and rested in the muck.

The macabre scene continued as the men spotted a burned-out Jeep—a lone sentinel guarding one of the forest's many destroyed churches. Hit head-on by an 88 mm round, its lifeless driver seemed to welcome Dog Company into one of the tiny hamlets that were scattered inside Germany's dense Hürtgen Forest. The charred corpse sat in the rusted vehicle with its blackened hands affixed to the steering wheel. Only the dead soldier's torso and skull remained intact. He dutifully wore his M1 helmet, which had been scorched to a charcoal-indigo color by the shell that had engulfed him in flames. The odd grin on his unrecognizable face exposed shiny ivory teeth that gleamed in the sun's fading rays that filtered through the diffused clouds of the gray November sky. Dog Company fixated on the driver;

the spectral figure eerily pointed the way to the remains of an old building which would become their new command post.

A mile or so from the Jeep, nearly a battalion of doomed Americans and their burned out trucks, tanks, and even an intact aid station hauntingly remained frozen in time, stuck there behind German lines on the gorge-like Kall River trail. A violent German counterattack had sealed their fate.

Like moles, the Rangers clambered into the cellar of the nearby structure after nearly stumbling over a headless German soldier still wearing his boots and tattered field-grey uniform. A starving black cat had crawled inside the body and poked its face out where the soldier's head should be. "Get out of there, you son of a bitch!" A Ranger kicked the cat away from the corpse.

Several days earlier, the Rangers had moved to Germany's Hürtgen Forest. They were attached to V Corps and nominally under the control of the 28th Division. Dog Company was about to engage in one of the U.S. Army's most protracted battles fought on German ground during World War II, and one of the longest single battles in the Army's history. A flawed strategy would also make the battle in the Hürtgen one of the most deadly of World War II. The number of men killed and wounded—a staggering 40,000—approached America's losses for the entire Vietnam War. Worse, it was largely a battle that didn't need to be fought. As legendary Major General James Gavin, whose 82nd Airborne Division fought in the forest, noted, "For us, the Hürtgen was one of the most costly, most unproductive, and most ill-advised battles our army has ever fought." The Allies could have bypassed the forest. Instead, they rushed headlong into a German meat grinder.

The Hürtgen Forest covered a rectangular area: each side roughly twenty miles long, with the city of Düren in the corner to the northwest and Roetgen to the southwest. In the southeast corner were several hydroelectric dams on the Roer River, which snakes through the dense forest. The area includes more than fifty square miles of lush hills and deep ravines with very few roads and many fortified positions. Gigantic conifer trees blocked the sunlight from reaching the thick, green, mossy floor.

Rain and fog, dense trees, deep ravines, and the ever-present shelling transformed the Hürtgen into a dark green hell. Ernest Hemingway described it as "Passchendaele with tree bursts," referring to the World War I battlefield where heavy artillery turned the field into a charnel house littered with the bodies of hundreds of thousands of butchered men on both sides. The forest's trees magnified the killing power of the German artillery. The combatants deliberately detonated shells across the forest's canopy, causing a deadly rain of shrapnel and razor-sharp conifer splinters that sliced through flesh and bone.

Throughout the forest, the Wehrmacht had carefully constructed a factory of death. Pillboxes, bunkers, and barbed wire blocked passage through much of the forest. Across the vast forest floor, the Germans had also strewn hundreds of thousands of mines intended to kill and maim American soldiers. Almost every position within the forest was preregistered by German artillery. Several towns within the forest were located on key terrain, and many guarded approaches to large river dams. These dams were crucial to the outcome of the battle. As long as the Germans controlled the dams, they controlled the Roer. By opening the dams' floodgates, they could flood large swaths of land in the Hürtgen, making it impassable. Only after months of needlessly sustaining enormous casualties did the Allied high command finally recognize the strategic importance of the dams. But by that time, it was too late for the tens of thousands of American soldiers who died in the battle.

High ground located in the forest also overlooked one of Germany's best-kept secrets of World War II: within the nearby Ardennes Forest, Hitler had established covert assembly areas for troops that were to carry out the powerful counteroffensive Hitler was preparing. For months, Hitler had amassed tens of thousands of men, tanks, and artillery in the nearby Ardennes forest. He was planning an operation on the Western front, designed to change the tide of the war. If Allied forces penetrated Hürtgen's high ground, they would lift the veil of secrecy surrounding Hitler's operation. Unbeknownst to the Americans, the Germans were therefore prepared to defend this territory at all costs.

The key towns within the forest were Hürtgen, Germeter, Vossenack, and Schmidt, all of which sat on important positions overlooking the river and its dams, some near the Bulge assembly areas. Schmidt was adjoined by a high ridgeline, which linked it to the town of Bergstein, the location of Hill 400, one of the area's highest hills. The top of Hill 400 provided a crucial vantage point of strategic importance. The Germans called the hill Burgberg or "Castle Hill" since it purportedly contained the ruins of a medieval fortification.

Since September 1944, the Allies had been battling in this death trap. The Hürtgen's narrow roads and trails made it almost impossible to maneuver tanks and neutralized the Allies' dominance in firepower. With their blinders finally off, the Army recognized the importance of controlling the dams. Into this dark and bloody killing field would march the men of Dog Company.

Trained as an offensive strike force, the Rangers prepared for a mission to clear and hold key terrain near Schmidt after the armor units had taken it. "The mission assigned on November 4 was to reinforce the CCA (Combat Command A of the 5th Armored Division) in a three-day attack which was to pass through the ruptured west wall at Lammersdorf and, sweeping in an arc to the south, assault an enemy-held portion of the Siegfried line from the rear. Intelligence showed that more than 100 fortifications were located in the area.... The plan of the attack hinged on the 28th Division's ability to take and hold Schmidt, an important enemy road center."

The 2nd Ranger Battalion formed into three teams for the operation. Dog and Charlie Company took an inner track "of the sweep and were to hole up for the first day." The overall plan "was to then swing south and west in a semicircular drive, with the Rangers mopping up

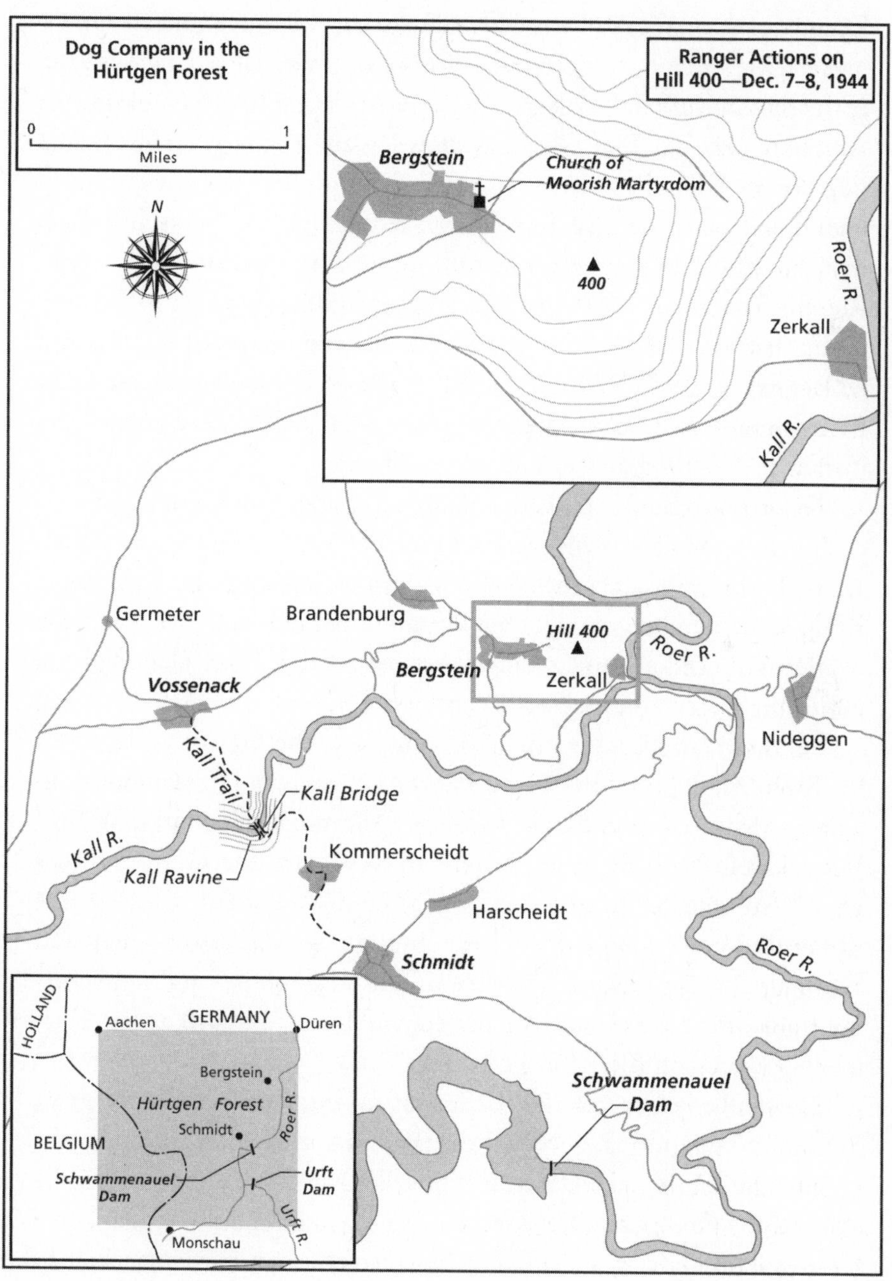

Dog Company in the Hürtgen Forest
0
1
Miles
N
Ranger Actions on Hill 400—Dec. 7–8, 1944
Bergstein
Church of Moorish Martyrdom
400
Roer R.
Zerkall
Kall R.
Germeter
Brandenburg
Hill 400
Bergstein
Zerkall
Roer R.
Vossenack
Nideggen
Kall Trail
Kall Bridge
Kall R.
Kall Ravine
Kommerscheidt
Harscheidt
Schmidt
Roer R.
Schwammenauel Dam
HOLLAND
Aachen
GERMANY
Düren
Bergstein
Hürtgen Forest
Roer R.
Schmidt
BELGIUM
Schwammenauel Dam
Urft Dam
Urft R.
Monschau

all resistance bypassed by the two armored infantry spearheads. Flamethrowers were to be used freely during the operation."

Yet Dog's role in the proposed plan never materialized, because the 28th Division suffered a staggering defeat at Schmidt. On November 1, All Souls' Day, the 28th Division, known as the Pennsylvania Keystone Division or "Bloody Bucket," attacked Schmidt and the crucial ridgelines dominating the area. In what was named the "All Souls' Day Battle," the 28th fatefully descended into the misty, wet, and dark forest. Rounds from hundreds of machine guns and pillboxes tore into the men as they battled their way past the abandoned and destroyed vehicles and tanks from the 9th Division's failed attack on Schmidt in September. Muddy roads and trails, as well as hundreds of shell-craters, greeted the men as they battled dug-in German positions.

The Bloody Bucket's 112th Infantry Regiment took the lead in securing the crucial towns of Kommerscheidt and Schmidt, which guarded the approach to key Roer dams. Crossing the Kall River Bridge, the men had to negotiate several minefields and face hundreds of prepared bunkers and redoubts—most hidden from plain sight—until the decimated unit finally captured Schimdt.

Because of Schmidt's crucial importance, the Germans deployed the 89th Infantry and the 116th Panzer Division, or "Greyhounds," in an impressive counterattack. In one of the most devastating World War II defeats dealt to an American regiment, the German units forced America's 28th Division out of Schmidt and cut it into pieces as the division attempted a retreat through the Kall river valley and across the bridge towards Vossenack. The steep gorges and icy, winding trails of the Kall made the perfect site for an ambush as the Germans pounced on the Pennsylvanians.

The unlikely hero of the battle was a German doctor. In a great display of humanity, regimental doctor Captain Günter Stüttgen negotiated an unofficial truce near the Kall River Bridge that mercifully allowed the Americans and Germans to evacuate their wounded, preserving thousands of lives. The German medics, in particular, helped save many American lives.

On November 8, the U.S. military stopped fighting. At night, the 300 remaining troops of the 112th Infantry Regiment withdrew after losing 1,900 soldiers. The total losses of the 28th Infantry Division amounted to more than 6,000 men out of approximately 25,000. Sharing the same fate of the 9th Infantry Division earlier, the 28th Infantry Division was mauled in the forest.

In the midst of this defeat, the Rangers went on a grueling, five-mile forced march during the second week of November. They slogged through the snow and mud to the town of Vossenack, where they relieved the remnants of the 28th Division. Following headquarters' decision to scrub the Rangers' mission, due to the 28th Division's failure to capture Schmidt, the Rangers became a quick reaction force. They were placed on two-hour alert as a "counterattack force in the Vossenack area," and in the event of a German breakthrough, the Rangers would go in to plug the breach in the American lines. Now in the front lines of the Hürtgen, Dog Company and the entire 2nd Ranger Battalion were under constant attack from artillery, mortars, and aggressive German patrols.

Dog Company occupied nearby foxholes and the basements of several old buildings. They created a perimeter defense with tripwires, barbed wire, and flares. Each side probed the other; frequent German infiltration patrols hit the Ranger perimeter, sometimes tripping the flares—as did wayward animals. When a flare went off, "it could have been a cow or a German patrol. We had to go out and reset it again," explained Bill Hoffman.

Portions of the Hürtgen Forest, initially a deeply lush and forbidding place of soaring conifers, had become what Hoffman called "the land of six-foot trees," because "tree bursts and artillery just chopped up everything."

★ ★ ★

WHOOSH!

The shell came sailing through the night air, exploding near the Dog's command post. The German 88 mm guns and self-propelled artillery, which frequently bombarded the positions, had pre-registered the coordinates of the buildings that Dog Company occupied. As shrapnel tore through one Ranger's helmet in several places, Webb and Hoffman sprung into action to save their wounded comrade.

The two men drove through the winding trails of the Hürtgen in a Jeep with the injured man. Hoffman remembered, "We laid the guy across the windshield of the Jeep, which was folded down. He was in a litter. Morris held onto him, and I drove." The men made the hellish ride in the dark with artillery bursting on both sides of them. They passed through a T-junction, which the men referred to as "Purple Heart Corner" because the Germans had preregistered the crossroad and frequently shelled it. Hoffman and Webb successfully ran the gauntlet at Purple Heart Corner, but the heroic journey would be in vain. The men delivered the wounded Ranger to Doc Block's aid station, but he died of his wounds shortly afterwards.

In another act of heroism, Ruggiero attempted to rescue a Ranger who had been wounded near the perimeter. Running back to a Ranger-occupied house, he yelled into the basement, "Tell that medic to get his ass up here, right now!"

The new medic came up carrying his bag and wearing a helmet painted with red crosses. "One of the guys got hit up there, right up by the hill up there," Ruggiero told the greenhorn. "You run the same way I run. Stay right on my fanny. Run as fast as you can."

As the two men took off, the shelling resumed. "They could see us," Ruggiero recounted. "Shells landed nearby, but we finally got up to the guy. The heel of his foot was almost blown off. We moved him into a ditch, just so we could get out of their sight. I didn't bank on it, but I thought that the red cross on the helmet might stop the German shelling, but it didn't."

"Let's bring him into that house over there," the medic said, pointing at the house where 1st Platoon was.

"No, no. Lomell's in that house," said Ruggiero. "We run into there, the Germans will know that there's guys in there. You stay here, do what you can for him. I'm going to make a run for it [to find transportation]."

The nimble dancer started to run as the shells fell around him. Popping up near the door to one of the other houses, McBride waved him in. Ruggiero recalled, "I hit one hole after another. I dove into them to avoid the shells. It was pretty hot. You couldn't see every hole. I ran down one, popped up, and went into another." When he finally neared McBride, Ruggiero made a dive for the commander and knocked him right down the steps.

Dusting himself off, McBride got up and said, "God damn you, Rugg, what the hell are you doing? I don't know whether to give you a kick in the ass or put you in for a medal." McBride then brought out a Jeep that they used to rescue the fallen Ranger and the medic.

As the artillery took its toll on Dog, German wonder weapons, subsonic V-1s, eerily buzzed through the air overhead. The V-1 attack was concentrated on Liege and Antwerp, miles away. Mist and fog enshrouded the forest as exploding shells from German artillery blasted the trees—or what was left of them—producing deadly tree bursts. The constant bombardment resulted in cases of shellshock. After being hit, one Ranger didn't know his name and couldn't speak or recognize anyone. He lapsed into a chronic vegetative state and was sent back to the rear.

The brutal and cruel conditions acted as a catalyst, as the men's hatred against the Germans grew and intensified like a volcano about to erupt. Vengeance seized the hearts and souls of the men. The abysmal living conditions didn't help matters. Mud, snow, and dampness from living in the foxholes and moving around in the morass resulted in frozen feet or trench foot for many of the Rangers. Hoffman explained: "We lived a dog's life. The holes weren't real deep, but they were enough to lay down in. You couldn't really sit up in it. We'd lie in the inside in blankets. We found a couple of old German canteens, which we filled with gasoline. We put a wick in it. It was a really smoky light, and it only provided a little bit of light. You couldn't wait to put the thing out it was so smelly. It was a little bit of comfort as opposed to being in the dark. The logs provided some overhead cover. They were shelling the area. Trees were coming down."

Life in the buildings wasn't much better than conditions in the foxholes. "The living conditions were terrible," Ruggiero confirmed. "Most of the houses were blown up and hit pretty hard. There was no place to go when you had to go to the bathroom." To remedy this, the previous unit that had occupied the house set up a large bathtub in the living room as a makeshift toilet. Most of the newly arrived Rangers also made use of the tub. "I wouldn't do it. No sir," Ruggie vowed. "I noticed there was a big hole in the roof where a shell had come through. Another one comes through, I don't want to be squatting over [the tub]."

Instead, the sergeant held onto his K-Ration boxes and used those as a toilet. "In that particular place, I got kidded an awful lot about it." But one night, he really needed to go. "I was looking for a place to go. I wasn't going to fool around with that big tub that was chock full. Every now and then the Germans would fire that damn 88. Those shells would come in pretty close. I had to go pretty bad, so I found a nice soft spot by the door of this particular building. I said to myself, *If I can't hold it anymore, I'm just going to have to stick my fanny out of the door.* I went out and did my duty." When he came back in, the sergeant advised his men to do the same if they needed to go to the bathroom, but none of them did.

The next morning Duke Slater came walking in and asked, "Hey, which one of you guys took a shit by the door?"

The men all looked at Ruggiero, who admitted, "Yeah, I thought it was the safest spot."

Slater shot back, "Yeah, it was safe all right, go on out there and take a look."

Ruggiero hadn't noticed at the time, but then remembered the headless German body lying buried underneath the snow.

Slater said, "Jesus Christ, Rugg, I know you like to shoot the Germans, but don't shit on them."

On the night of November 18, command alerted the Ranger battalion for the potential relief of the 28th Division's 109th Infantry. At the same time, Fox Company received a direct hit on their command post but, miraculously, took no casualties. The men of the 109th weren't so lucky.

WHAM! WHAM! WHAM!

As they passed through the Ranger lines, 120 mm German mortar fire fell on the close column of outgoing 28th Infantry Division troops. Doctor Block and the others in the medical section, including Frank South, rushed to their aid. The Rangers brought in nineteen Americans from the 28th. Nine soldiers had been killed on the road, including a full-bird colonel. Morris Webb recalled Doctor Block's attempts to rescue the wounded men. In the pitch-black darkness, the doctor began feeling around their bodies. Then he "pulled up a handful of teeth and brains." The normally stoic Block lost his composure and vomited on the muddy road.

By November 21, orders came for 2nd Ranger Battalion's Able and Baker companies to link up with the 12th Infantry Regiment. Since November 17, the 12th Infantry Regiment had been part of Operation Queen. The advance was very slow and bloody, as German antitank guns gored the unit. The Rangers remained in a counterattack position for possible deployment to exploit a breakthrough created by the 28th. In addition, the Keystone Division directed the Rangers to send a patrol to "determine the exact location of the right flank of [the 12th Infantry Regiment's] 121st Infantry Battalion."

Captain Sid Salomon's B Company moved out late at night to probe an area of the forest that was still thickly wooded in an attempt to find the battalion's right flank held by K Company of the 121st Infantry Battalion. According to Salomon, it was so dark "you had to put your hand on the shoulder of the man in front of you. If you put your hand in front of your face, you couldn't see it. The forest was so dark in general that even in the daytime you had a hard time seeing."

The Rangers first linked up with a scout, a sergeant who was given the task of leading them to K Company. "He was supposed to guide us in. He wouldn't get out of the dugout. My first sergeant, Ed Andrusz, told him to get out, and when he didn't, he just yanked the sergeant by the collar and gave him a bash to the jaw." The sergeant still refused to move.

B Company then moved in the direction they thought was the location of K Company. But the men walked straight into a dense minefield near Germeter. Every step became a matter of life and death. Mines went off one after another. Screams of wounded Rangers pierced the air. Several men lost their legs, and another man was killed. In the midst of the chaos, Salomon ordered the company to halt, dig in, and pull out their trench knives to gently probe the positions around them for the deadly mines. As B Company held their position in the minefield, the men "received intense mortar and artillery fire." One direct hit on a foxhole used as the company's command post added to the twelve casualties during the period, "[including] one [that] was fatal." The company also repulsed an enemy patrol attempting to "turn their right flank."

At sunrise, the men made their move. "When dawn came, we pretty much looked to find out where we were. We grabbed a couple of [Germans and took them prisoners] as they made their way through the minefield. They were scared to death." As Salomon recalled, "I was pretty rough with them because I was absolutely livid that so many of my men had been hit." The captain had taken German in high school and barked an order in German at one of the prisoners: "Start calling names. Call Fritz, Johann, and everyone else. Start calling the names of your comrades," he commanded in an attempt to lure the other Germans from their hiding places.

Thankfully, A Company and portions of D Company helped rescue Salomon's trapped and wounded men. During the relief of B Company's position, a heavy firefight ensued between the combined forces of A and D Companies and the Germans. "For almost forty-five minutes, B Company was trapped under a three-way crossfire, but fortunately, no casualties were incurred during this action. [However,] intense enemy artillery caused seven more casualties this day; the company was now down to less than fifty percent and many of the top NCOs were hit."

When the firefight was over, medic Bill Geitz, who punched Lomell on D-Day, helped evacuate the casualties. As Geitz was moving to tend to a wounded Ranger, he stepped on a mine, which blew off his leg. Ruggiero recalled the heroic efforts to bring out Geitz and several of the other wounded Rangers. "With men laying on their stomachs, Dog Company formed a human chain where we reached out in front of the other guy and probed the area with our knives to make sure we didn't step on any more mines."

Down to half strength, Salomon's B Company retrograded back to the battalion perimeter near Vossenack. Salomon bore witness to the intense brotherhood within the battalion. "The other men had heard what we were undergoing up there, and we didn't have to dig a foxhole. The foxholes had already been dug [for us] by the battalion." Salomon's men returned to Vossenack right around Thanksgiving Day. "When we got back, we all got a good night's sleep that night. The mess sergeant had saved a hot turkey dinner for us. We didn't eat anything while we were up there, so we all ate ravenously. Wouldn't you know it, we all had the GIs [the runs]."

On November 26, the battalion received orders from the 8th Division: "Reconnoiter areas taken yesterday, Hürtgen and Kleinhau, with view of occupying said areas. Make recommendations as to whether movement into the area should be made by day or by night." With Operation Queen in full swing, V Corps had pierced the heavily defended German lines. At great cost, they occupied the villages of Hürtgen and Kleinhau and looked to continue on to Schmidt. The butcher's bill for the attack was enormous—the Germans mauled the 8th Division "Golden Arrows" just as it had done to the 9th and 28th Divisions. In a maddening on again, off again situation, the Rangers had received orders to act, only to be told to stand down. From the 445th

Antiaircraft Battalion, twenty "deuce-and-a-half" trucks were attached to the 2nd Ranger Battalion as troop transports in preparation for a counterattack mission.

When the reconnoiter orders came in, Rudder tapped Bob Edlin to scout Schmidt. The hero of Lochrist and the rest of the Fabulous Four ditched their noise-making steel helmets and stealthily entered the forest armed with tommy guns and trench knifes. The men slipped through Kommerscheidt and into the outskirts of Schmidt without seeing even one German. At the edge of the town, the Ranger from Texas had a premonition to enter the town alone.

"Hold here," Edlin told the other members of the Fabulous Four.

He slipped into the village of Schmidt alone, tommy gun in hand, hugging the buildings for cover as he probed deeper into the crucial German city, which had earlier been the focus of two massive battles. "I was sneaking around buildings. Absolutely nothing. There should have been some self-propelled weapons in sight, some activity somewhere.... It smelled like a trap."

Edlin rejoined Courtney, Dreher, and Burmaster. "I've had enough," he explained. "Let's get back to the battalion as quick as we can." Edlin reported back to Rudder his suspicions about the seemingly empty town; Rudder relayed the information up the chain of command and continued to hold his position.

On December 5, Captain McBride and the other company commanders submitted names of the men recommended for rotation back to the United States, giving some hope for relief. Unbeknownst to the men, they were on the eve of another of their greatest battles. To the men's dismay, Colonel Rudder received orders to report to First Army headquarters. Rumors ran rampant as to why the "old man received his summons" and was leaving his beloved Rangers.

CHAPTER 28

Moving Out

"Rack it up! Get ready in twelve minutes!"

Feverishly, the men of Dog Company crammed their personal items into duffel bags and prepared for battle. They broke open crates and grabbed ammo bandoliers and fresh supply of Mk 2 olive drab pineapple grenades.

Dog Company got ready quickly and then waited. Several of the seasoned noncoms who had brought them this far disappeared into the company command post. There they received an urgent message from the commanding officer of the 28th Infantry Regiment: "Battalion alerted for movement to Bergstein." The 2nd Ranger Battalion's executive officer and Rudder's replacement, Major George Williams, expanded on the new orders: "The battalion is to move to Bergstein with the mission of securing the town and taking the hill to the east. Companies A, B, and C will go into defensive positions in Bergstein. Companies D, E, and F will take and hold Hill 400."

Lieutenant Len Lomell recalled, "They had a special mission for us." After meeting to plan details, noncoms and officers from Dog Company emerged from the command post and ordered the battalion to "Mount up!"

Dog Company's 1st Platoon climbed onto the olive-drab trucks of the 445th. The platoon was a shell of its former self. As rifleman Bud Potratz explained, "We had gotten a new sergeant named

Mike Sharik—a staff sergeant. He was initially a sergeant in the 2nd Platoon, but we had so few men that we had a lot of replacements. . . . Our platoon leader [George Kerchner] was severely wounded in Brest. Then we received Len Lomell who took over our platoon. . . . Ed Secor [was] our BAR man, and his assistant [was] Johnny Goreman."

It was a moonless night—perfect for hiding the movement of troops. But just as the men started to entruck, one of the mobile field kitchens burst into flames. The men worked furiously to douse the bright blaze, looking over their shoulders for the German artillery that they were sure would be landing any second. Luckily, the fire hadn't caught any enemy eyes, and German guns didn't respond.

At 11:30 P.M., the truck engines of the 445th roared to life. Stretching back over a quarter of a mile, a score of trucks carrying Dog Company and the rest of the battalion drove through the darkness. Lomell recalled, "We rode through the forest in darkness, lights out." The trucks carefully maneuvered through the winding roads of the Hürtgen Forest.

The men of the 2nd Ranger Battalion rode for nearly two hours through the inky blackness of the forest. The trip was relatively uneventful until the lead truck became mired in the mud of a shell hole. Quickly, the Rangers clambered out of their deuce-and-a-halfs and attempted to push the truck out of the mud. Within moments, German antitank fire lit up the area, forcing the Rangers to abandon the lead vehicle. The rest of the convoy moved around it.

The cavalcade eventually reached the small German hamlet of Kleinhau. Leaving the relative comfort of the trucks, the men faced a grueling march through a sloppy, wet mess. Mud covered their boots up to their ankles. Sleet and rain pelted their faces.

Describing the march, Potratz said, "We had our packs on. We had a blanket bedroll over the tops of our packs and ammunition belts and grenades, bandoliers, [and] a rifle. And we all had overcoats on. When these things got wet, the wool overcoats became like a ton of bricks on your shoulders. We just trudged through that darkness."

Bill Hoffman recalled, "If you didn't see the guy in front of you, you didn't know where you were going. If you dropped your rifle, you would never find it again because of the mud. It was deep mud."

Suddenly, German artillery shells streaked through their position, lighting up the dark night sky. Someone hissed, "Spread out! Keep it spread out!" The men staggered about five yards apart—if they bunched up, a well-placed shell could take out several Rangers at once.

For many of the Rangers, one moment stood out on the long, dreary march toward Bergstein. As they left camp, a lone figure stood in the middle of the road and shook the hands of the men of the battalion as they passed.

"Good luck," Rudder told each of them, also giving advice here and there.

"Good luck," they replied.

As one of his last actions as their commanding officer, Colonel Rudder offered each Ranger words of encouragement. Even as he was leaving, Big Jim made time for the individual needs of his men. When Harry Fate passed, Rudder said, "Harry, I understand you are up for a furlough?"

"Well, I'm not sure I'm going take it," Fate dithered.

"You are going to take it. I will make sure of that," Rudder insisted,*

Universally, the men of the 2nd Battalion hated to see Rudder leave, but he had immediate orders to report to the First Army Headquarters. As they later learned, he would take command of the 109th Infantry Regiment, which was in desperate need of new leadership.

In the previous five weeks, Rudder's new regiment had sustained 6,184 casualties fighting the Germans in the Hürtgen, racking up one of the highest casualty rates suffered by an American regiment in the entire war.

*True to his word, Rudder ensured that Fate left Dog Company on the furlough. The colonel's intervention may have saved Fate's life.

The distance between Kleinhau and Bergstein is only about a mile as the crow flies, but it seemed much farther to the Rangers, who traveled the route at a snail's pace. They stopped and started frequently in order to avoid becoming an easy target for the German artillery.

When the gleam of a German flare outlined the charred silhouettes of several burned-out buildings, they came to a dead stop for five minutes.

The glowing embers, crimson and menacing, from one burning house were etched in Bud Potratz's memory. "I will never forget the burning buildings there, and curtains were blowing through what was left of the window frames," said Potratz. "It cast an eerie feeling. It was a haunting feeling. Very haunting. When we started to make the trudge to Bergstein, we saw hulks of destroyed American tanks. That was very disheartening. So was the sight of the GIs whose bodies were blackened and charred in the tanks."

Being near tanks, even destroyed ones, meant danger. According to Bill Hoffman: "The first tank, I almost bumped into it. The Jeeps up there were burned out. There was something ominous and weird about seeing the blackened hulks of the tanks. If you are anywhere near a tank, you are going to draw artillery fire."

"You don't get immune to it," Hoffman added. "For me, the worst was the smell, the smell of blood. That is a God-awful smell. One guy, two guys, and then you see a whole bunch. It's not normal to see dead people. I remember seeing the body of a young guy, [a] German soldier."

★ ★ ★

The Rangers were on their way to reinforce Combat Command R (CCR) of the 5th Armored Division, which was barely hanging onto its foothold in the German town of Bergstein in the face of fanatic German counterattacks.

CCR, originally a regiment-sized unit, had been reduced to the equivalent of a reinforced company after fighting through a gauntlet of German villages on the way to Bergstein. CCR's capture of Kleinhau and the nearby village of Hürtgen marked the beginning of the end for one of the bloodiest battles in American history. Four American divisions and a host of attached units fought to seize the corridor of villages from Hürtgen to Bergstein running along a plateau that extended to the Roer River crossing. Bergstein and the high ground behind the town were crucial to the battle: "Possession of the two villages spelled control of a sizable segment of the only good road network between the Hürtgen Forest and the Roer [River] and . . . the Brandenberg-Bergstein ridge, the most commanding terrain in the vicinity. Capture of the ridge would enable the V Corps to gain the Roer [River] . . . and at last provide the long-sought secure right flank for the main drive of the VII Corps [into Germany]. The Brandenberg-Bergstein ridge also was important to any drive that subsequently might be aimed at the Roer River dams."

The butcher's bill for clearing Kleinhau and the nearby town of Hürtgen would end up costing approximately 1,247 American dead and wounded.

CHAPTER 29

Bergstein

Two days earlier, December 4, 1944, Combat Command Reserve's attack on Bergstein

Task Force Hamberg, an element of a Combat Command Reserve unit (CCR), advanced up the road from Kleinhau to their objective—Bergstein. The officers dispatched a twelve-man patrol to locate barbed wire entanglements and mines and to determine the size of the German force in the town. Hugging the ditches to avoid the German mines and booby traps, the patrol crawled through the darkness until it reached the edge of Bergstein.

After mapping the location of the German observation posts and positions, the patrol returned to report and then waited for the jump-off time for the first attack.

Soon after, the attack on Bergstein began. GIs from several companies rode on the backs of M4 Sherman tanks moving toward the town.

The Germans were waiting. From their observation positions on top of Castle Hill, they fired a massive artillery barrage, forcing the American soldiers to dismount. The Germans had also positioned several 75 mm antitank guns in the town. A direct hit from one of those guns destroyed the task force's lead tank.

"The companies plowed into Bergstein, firing with every gun they had, then veered to the left edge of town. The two platoon sergeants of the leading C Company platoons were killed in the attack and their platoons were disorganized."

The fighting devolved into house-to-house and hand-to-hand combat. A German officer rose from his foxhole near one gun and "raised his gun to fire on the advancing infantrymen. Private First Class Lester Aurand shot him squarely in the forehead before he could aim his gun." The GIs captured one antitank gun with a round still in its breach.

★ ★ ★

The German defense of Bergstein fell on the shoulders of the 2nd Battalion, Grenadier Regiment 980, which was led by a remarkably able officer, Captain Adolf Thomae.* Commanding from a reinforced-concrete Westwall bunker about one hundred yards north of Hill 400, Thomae attempted to defend the town from the Allied onslaught and later organized the German counterattacks following the loss of the hill. He would receive the Knight's Cross, one of Germany's highest military decorations, for the defense of the town.

Bergstein and the high ground behind it, Hill 400, or Castle Hill, were crucially important to the Germans. The American attack on Bergstein fell less than two weeks before the Germans were scheduled to launch Operation *Wacht am Rhein*, their major winter offensive in the Ardennes. As they continued to battle in the Hürtgen, the American army was completely unaware of Hitler's imminent counteroffensive.

On a clear day, an observer on Hill 400 could see six or seven miles into the German rear areas, all the way to Düren, Germany, and other nearby towns, where a huge German force was secretly massing. American capture of Hill 400 could possibly expose the northern portion of the *Wacht Am Rhein* buildup to American eyes and spoil Hitler's strategic surprise. If the Americans could reach and cross the Roer River, which was just beyond Bergstein and Hill 400, they could "jeopardize the execution of the Ardennes offensive."

With the American penetration so close to the staging area for their upcoming offensive, the Germans immediately began a counterattack to take back Bergstein.

---

*Brilliant and charismatic, Thomae later earned a doctorate and became a prominent German industrialist.

CHAPTER 30

Counterattack

Close-in fighting raged in Bergstein. As one exhausted, German NCO described: "Tank against tank, hand-to-hand combat, tanks burning… [One of my men] shot a Sherman with a Panzerfaust (antitank weapon), but the warhead fell off in midair, rendering it useless. [During the attack he] was immediately killed by the tank. Loud noise of duels between men armed with Panzerfausts and tanks… Burning and exploding tanks, men falling everywhere. My people shot up [another] Sherman, which started to burn. One of the crew members staggered out and stumbled to the side of the burning tank. I screamed, 'Don't shoot, he's defenseless!' Then I ordered someone to bring him to safety before the tank exploded. They brought him to me and he appeared unwounded, although he was blinded."

Directing Germany's counterattack at the strategic level was one of her greatest field marshals and the Reich's best defensive tactician, Field Marshal Walter Model. Known for recovering from desperate situations, Model could turn the tide of war.

To recapture Bergstein, Field Marshal Model released his only available reserve, the 272nd Volksgrenadier Division.* Volks-

---

*People often confuse the Volksgrenadier Divisions (VGDs) with the *Volkssturm*, which were the German home guard and militia consisting of young boys and grenadier divisions, including the 272nd, carried the latest German small arms, in particular the MP-44, the forerunner to the Soviet AK-47. In single-shot mode, the MP-44 had an effective range of 400 meters, but more significantly, when on full auto, the weapon was deadly. With its thirty-round magazine, the MP-44 provided firepower far surpassing the bolt-action Mauser 98K, the rifle carried by most German soldiers.

Volksgrenadiers received a strong dose of Nazi propaganda that their leaders hoped would inspire courage, initiative, and leadership in battle: "A brave heart is the prerequisite for troop leadership. One must bring this talent with him. It cannot be given to him through training or professional development. . . . The Führer wants soldiers who distinguish themselves by their courage, their willingness to assume responsibility, and whose worthiness as leaders has been tested and further developed [in combat]."

At this time the Volksgrenadiers were highly motivated—the recent Allied advance had crossed onto German soil, so the men of the 272nd were fighting to protect their homeland. In preparation for Hitler's counteroffensive in the Ardennes, the 272nd created special assault companies within each regiment. As described by a pamphlet, which included instructions for the unit's combat leaders, "Assault companies are to be set up, armed, and trained under the command of the best-suited leaders. They are to be reinforced by the addition of mine clearing, tank destruction, and flamethrower teams, as well as by the addition of artillery forward observers. . . . Their mission is to overcome, take out, or cut off the enemy's forward outpost line and individual strong points."

---

old men. In contrast, the German military leadership conceived the VGDs as a new elite corps of troops that would be equipped with some of the finest weapons in the German arsenal. In reality, their "elite" status never materialized. They were often staffed by former personnel from *Luftwaffe* and *Kriegsmarine* units, as well as some experienced NCOs from German army units.

★ ★ ★

At precisely 6:34 A.M. on December 6, a massive German artillery bombardment rained down on Bergstein. A few minutes later, the Germans' only armored reserve in the area spearheaded a counterattack with orders to retake the town at all costs. Ten tank destroyers—four StuG IIIs and six Jagdpanzers—rolled around the serpentine road at the bottom of Hill 400 and linked up with 520 men from Germany's 1st Battalion of Grenadier Regiment 980. With the self-propelled guns in the woods near the hill, the Germans would have to cross an open field to make their way toward a church and into the heart of Bergstein.

The men of CCR who were manning positions in Bergstein waited for the Volksgrenadiers to come within twenty-five yards before they opened up with everything they had. The battle became a slaughter as .30- and .50-caliber machine gun bullets cut down the grenadiers. Nevertheless, the German armor pressed on and penetrated the village. The fighting in Bergstein resembled the battle for Stalingrad as German infantry and tanks counterattacked in the blackened rubble. The fighting raged house to house as American tanks found themselves hunted by Panzerfaust-wielding German infantry. Despite taking heavy losses, the Volksgrenadiers recaptured portions of the eastern and southern sections of the hamlet.

The Germans counterattacked the Allied-held town repeatedly. Tank destroyers took on tanks at point-blank range, just fifty to seventy-five yards apart. Most of the American M-4 Sherman tanks were armed with low-velocity 75 mm main guns, whose shells bounced off the sloped armor of the German tank destroyers. As one American soldier vividly remembered, "My eye could see the shells hit the German tanks and glance off into the air. My heart sank."

CCR was barely holding on to its foothold in Bergstein. Company A alone lost twelve of its seventeen tanks. All the armored infantry companies had been reduced to platoon strength. Only one each of the unit's twelve M-10 and M-36 tank destroyers were still serviceable. Exhausted, CCR appeared to be on the brink of annihilation.

In desperation, CCR called on the walking wounded in the aid station. Unarmed and feeble, the men scrounged for weapons from their dead comrades. Their efforts were largely ineffective; many were too weak even to hold a rifle.

"Virtually all the men in the CCR were in a state of shock," wrote one eyewitness from CCR. "Their nerves were shot; their physical energy had long since disappeared. They crouched dazedly in their foxholes and basements, loading their guns and waiting for the Germans to come back. They could never hold another counterattack like the last one. There simply were not enough men left." Another survivor recalled, "Had daylight arrived fifteen minutes later, they would never have been able to hold Bergstein."

The German assault force, however, had suffered grievously as well. By 12:40 P.M., the German commander, Captain Rhein, who started out with 520 men, could only muster 150. In addition, the Allies had destroyed seven of the priceless German tank destroyers—what was left of the German assault force was forced to move back toward Hill 400.

With CCR barely able to hold its own, the only unit available to take the rest of Bergstein and Hill 400 was the 2nd Ranger Battalion. Under V Corps' control and attached to the 8th Division, its commanding officer, Major General William G. Weaver petitioned Lieutenant General Leonard Gerow's V Corps to release the Rangers from corps reserve.

CHAPTER 31

The Church

One of the CCR officers described the arrival of the Rangers: "We sat down for the counterattack, which we expected would come in the [next] morning. We had a faint promise from [V] Corps of the Second Rangers, but we weren't too hopeful. About midnight, a guy came down the road, and two others—each one five yards behind the other. They were three Ranger lieutenants. They asked for enemy positions and the road to take. They said they were ready to go. We talked the situation over with the officers. They stepped out and said, 'Let's go, men.' We heard the tommy guns click, and without saying a word, the Rangers moved out. Our morale went up in a hurry."

The CCR had defended Bergstein valiantly, but they were a spent force by the time the Rangers arrived. The Combat Command had suffered many casualties and was greatly reduced in strength.

In the early morning hours of December 7, Dog Company and most of the 2nd Ranger Battalion started filtering into the cellars of Bergstein. With just a small part of the town under American control, the Allied position resembled a very thin stiletto that had pierced the German lines. Only the road back toward Brandenburg was available for withdrawal. German troops surrounded the U.S. troops on three flanks.

Accompanied by F Company's "Big Stoop," Lomell attempted to find Duke Slater, who had set up Ranger headquarters in one of the cellars. After wading through several flooded basements, Lomell and

Masny eventually located Slater. From his watery command center, The Duke ordered a reconnaissance patrol to determine the best way to attack the hill. "I was given that patrol," Lomell explained. "As the patrol leader, I was to take five men with me. F Company was also to choose five men. It was led by a young lieutenant, McClure was his name. This was about 3:00 in the morning of December 7. We were to go reconnoiter Hill 400 and its environs—the approach to it, and everything—and bring back that information to the staff officers at battalion headquarters who were in a cellar nearby. My duty was to take my patrol and reconnoiter the right side of Hill 400. Visualize it cut in half—F Company on the left and us on the right."

Lomell's five-man patrol took off down the street. Crouching low and hugging the buildings to avoid detection, they moved into German-occupied Bergstein. Passing a partially burned building, Lomell turned around and noticed that one of his men's flashlights had started shining in the hip pocket of his combat jacket. Sternly, Lomell whispered, "Mack, for God's sake, put out that light."

Quickly, the man doused the light, but within fifteen seconds, three mortar rounds landed where the light—and the patrol—had just been. The men scurried down the street towards the edge of town, near a stone Catholic church dedicated to the men who had died in the Crusades: the Church of Moorish Martyrdom.

As the small group approached the church, they ran into what they thought was an American outpost. Lomell asked the GI manning the position if there were any Germans between him and the church. The GI responded that he didn't think so and that he didn't think any Germans were left in the town. The group then proceeded to the church where they were greeted cryptically by a low voice saying, "Halt."

Sensing that the speaker was probably German, Lomell chose to ignore the command. The patrol made their way down toward a sunken road in front of Hill 400. Named by the Allies for its elevation of 400 meters, Hill 400 loomed in front of them like an "upside down ice cream cone." Hill 400 was the crucial promontory in the Brandenberg-Bergstein ridge, the "most commanding terrain in the vicinity."

Lomell recalled, "When we got there, the two patrols, we decided to do it a little bit differently. In each group, we decided to leave three down below, which would total six to patrol the base of the hill to determine where the German machine guns were positioned or any other positions. We were to do this and not be caught or be heard, not be seen. It was supposed to be very quiet. We moved very silently and didn't breach security at all. I took a couple men and went up the right side and McClure took a couple men up the other side. We went up towards the top of the hill, at least as far as you could get without getting caught. After we reconnoitered, we decided to make our way back to the base of the hill." The ten-man group from F and D Companies then made its way back to Slater's command post and reported its findings.

Based on the Corps' and Lomell's reconnaissance reports, Slater decided that the best way to attack would be to approach the hill in a frontal assault, since it "offered the best chance of success," rather than hit it from the sides, which had been heavily mined. Like Pointe du Hoc, it was to be a frontal assault—another potential suicide mission.

According to the plan of attack, Easy Company would jump off at 5:40 A.M. to clear out the rest of Bergstein. Fox Company and Dog Company would move up to the sunken road. At 7:30 A.M., Fox and Dog would cross the hundred-yard field to assault Hill 400.

As Easy Company pushed through the town early in the morning, they "surprised a number of the enemy at breakfast in a Bergstein home. One grenade burst sufficed in the taking of thirteen prisoners." While Easy Company secured Bergstein, the men of Dog Company, sheltering in the town's cellars, prepared for battle. Bill Hoffman recalls descending into a cellar. "It was like a swimming pool with a house on top of it. It had eighteen inches of water in it with a concrete floor. The water was up over the top of my Corcoran jump boots. I will never forget how dark it was in there."

While stuck in the watery cellar, Hoffman experienced an inconvenient need to defecate. "*Where am I going to go? I don't have any toilet paper.* So I got my pants down, and I just squatted down and let her go. I think I got it on my legs, I don't know. I used my handkerchief—threw that away."

Sitting near Hoffman, Bud Potratz perched on a pile of coal. "We took off our packs and our overcoats and we cleaned our weapons and got ready." Potratz could smell the heavy odor of cigarette smoke. He had recently received a carton of cigarettes from his aunt for Christmas and had distributed them to his squad. As the men were smoking and cleaning their weapons, Potratz's squad leader turned to him and said, "We're going to attack something called 'Sugarloaf Hill' [Hill 400]."

Sergeant Hank Zyrkowski or "Zeke," a replacement who joined Dog Company's mortar platoon near Brest, also sat nearby. He later reflected, "The basement was flooded with water from the rain and snow. The homes were hit and they were opened right down to the basement. We got down there and I just tried to stay dry, but my boots and legs were in water."

As Potratz looked down at his watch, he noticed the hand approaching 7:30 A.M. Sharik then shouted, "Let's go!"

Vince Hagg later described the scene: "When the guy opened the door on top of the stairs, it seemed the Germans knew we were coming. Flares all over the place. The artillery came in like hell. I started down the street. A shell came in. Kenny Harsch was hit. The lieutenant behind me was hit. Captain McBride shouted: 'Hagg, take care of Harsch.'"

The men of Dog Company clambered up the stairs of the cellars. "The minute that we came out of the buildings, it was daylight," Ruggiero remembered.

In his mind's eye, Ruggiero can still see the picture of the first platoons heading for the hill in his mind. *"My God, I don't think anybody is going to get through this as far as the church,"* he thought. "Guys were getting hit. Guys were crawling, holding their leg in their arm. That's when McBride said, 'Are you ready, Ruggie?'

"I'm about as ready as I'm gonna be."

Potratz passed Captain McBride, who pointed at Hill 400 in the distance and said, "There it is."

As Dog Company hit the streets, German shells and mortar rounds rained down upon them. Potratz recalled that "it was coming down from all sides because Bergstein was like a finger" poking into the German lines.

Fox Company's Herm Stein recalled crouching in a street next to a burned-out house, "Captain Slater was dashing up and down the column with words of encouragement. . . . He outwardly had more dash and abandon than Rudder, but not the caring and concern and that know-how of the right decision."

WHAM!

A shell landed in a squad of Dog Company men, striking Bill Hoffman, Lieutenant Lawrence Schelper, and Kenny Harsch.

Hagg saw Schelper lying on the ground. "I asked him if he was hurt or anything. He couldn't hear. He was lying there in a position where he was shaking." Also stunned by the shelling, Bill Hoffman blacked out. With the help of several of his foxhole buddies, Hagg got Schelper, Harsch, and Hoffman into the house. Harsch had sustained a massive wound on his face, gouging out his eye. Inside the house, they ran into Zeke Zyrkowski.

Harsch turned to Hagg, "Vince, I think I lost an eye."

Hagg played down the wound, saying "You'll be OK," but knowing full well that the injury would end the promising baseball career Harsch had begun before the war.

Shell-shocked, Hoffman wouldn't wake up until two days later. "I remember somebody saying sleep was the answer. I spent two days sleeping in our rear area [at Hill 400], remembering nothing." He returned to Dog about a week later.*

*Sixty-seven years later, in April 2012, Tennessee Governor, Lamar Alexander, presented Hoffman's long overdo Purple Heart. In Lamar's speech he reminded the audience Hoffman refused the medal during the war: "This year, the Army has awarded Bill a Purple Heart. But not for the first time. During World War II, the Army tried. But Bill, in an Army ward surrounded by soldiers that had lost arms or legs in the fighting, believed that his wounds didn't measure up and said, "I don't think so." The governor fittingly closed his speech in Hoffman's words, "They say, 'Ranger friendships are forever.' It's true."

"The Germans were using white phosphorous in their shells," remembered Zyrkowski. "It burned right through one man's overcoat, but it didn't penetrate to his skin." To avoid the fire, Zeke and his companions quickly dodged into another house.

"Holy crap! That was close!"

D Company continued moving toward the jump-off point near the base of the hill. They saw several German soldiers with their hands behind their heads, surrendering as they ran toward the rear.

The Rangers passed by the Church of Moorish Martyrdom. As Morris Webb turned to his left, he noticed three dead Germans sprawled across the stones steps leading into the church courtyard. The men passed under a Gothic archway and looked up, noticing that the church's steeple resembled a witch's hat. They made their way toward their next objective, a sunken road near the foot of Hill 400.

Dog moved through the cemetery adjacent to the church as German artillery fell on them. Potratz noted the constant need to keep running: "We lost a lot of men in the cemetery from German mortars. I remember the tombstones were knocked over; some of the graves themselves were ripped open. We just kept moving. It was touch and go all the way. . . . I could see our aid man . . . coming up. . . . He was patching these guys up. We just kept moving."

D Company started to line up on the right side of the road, while F Company took the left. Within a few minutes, the companies were in place. Looking ahead, they could see an open field. Potratz recalled, "The terrain was about 75–100 yards of open field. There were two buildings over there that were pretty much gutted from shellfire." Despite the heavy mortar fire raining down on the field, Dog could see their objective—Hill 400.

CHAPTER 32

The Charge

Nervously, Sigurd Sundby studied the woods at the far side of the open field and mentally marked the German machine gun positions waiting for them. The Ranger next to him, John Conaboy, soberly noted, "Just like *All's Quiet on the Western Front*."

The sunken road where they crouched provided an embankment about three feet high that stretched about two hundred yards in front of Hill 400. The road provided some protection from small arms fire, but the Rangers were exposed on their flanks and to the rear.

At this point, the assault companies had dwindled to fewer than 120 men. In front of them loomed their objective: the rocky, scarred summit of Hill 400. German machine gun nests and bunkers dotted its slopes. Although pockmarked by artillery shell holes, it remained largely covered in pine trees.

To get there, the men would have to cross about one hundred yards over an open, frozen field laced with mines. It offered no protection from German machine gun fire, mortar shells or artillery rounds. Lomell described it as "a level table-top field that was filled with snow and ice."

Suddenly, a German soldier at the edge of the woods near the hill jumped up, fired a flare into the air, and made a mad dash toward a German pillbox. Most of the Rangers took pot shots at the German but missed. As the Rangers readied their positions, Morris

Webb remembered being told, "Keep firing as you walk and don't stop walking no matter what happens. If they pin you down in the field, you're done for. Keep moving and keep firing. And watch out for the mines."

As the Rangers waited behind the earthen wall, German mortar shells began falling behind them. The barrage of death was creeping closer and closer. According to L-Rod Petty, "The first mortar burst exploded about seventy-five or one hundred yards behind us and seemed to be coming from our left front. While [the Germans were] establishing their range and lateral adjustments, the bursts began to creep nearer. You could feel the tension building up in the lines in the voices grumbling about why we didn't charge. Of course, we could not because almost simultaneous with the German artillery fire, our own artillery commenced to shell the hill. I think every man on the line was convinced that mortars would reach us before our artillery lifted."

Caught in an area less than two hundred yards between the two opposing barrages, tension was building up to the exploding point. As the two walls of heavy artillery closed in on the men, the Rangers listened incredulously as a newly minted F Company officer barked to Sergeant Petty, "Send out a scout!"

Herm Stein no doubt echoed the thoughts of many of the men as he muttered, *"Why? Are they nuts—sending a scout into the face of obvious fire?"*

Petty snapped back, "Fuck you, no way!" The officer yelled the order several times and received the same response. He then barked to Sergeant McHugh, "Send out the scout!" McHugh barked, "Fuck you!"

The men of Fox Company knew it was suicide.

The officer then turned and yelled the same order to Private First Class Gerald Bourchard and screamed, "That is an order!"

McHugh and Petty both yelled, "Don't go!"

Bourchard obeyed the order. He stood up and started walking across the open field. In stunned silence, the men of Fox watched the sickening scene unfold. After taking no more than four steps, Bourchard collapsed, taking a rifle shot to the belly. "This was the fuse that ignited the explosion of the Ranger charge."

Fox Company commander Big Stoop yelled, "Fix bayonets!"

But the men would not wait. Two minutes before the official jump-off time, F Company's McHugh waved his tommy gun over his head, and screamed, "Let's go get the bastards!"

On the Dog Company side, Captain McBride shouted, "Go!"

With their M1s, the Rangers fired a tremendous volley into the German positions to keep the enemies' heads down as they charged across the field.

"WA-WOO-WOOHOO, WA-WOO WOOHOO!"

Screaming something similar to the "Rebel yell," Dog and Fox Companies charged into a hail of bullets and mortars.

In Petty's opinion, had the Rangers waited until the prescribed time, the encroaching German mortars would have killed many of the men along the sunken road before they jumped off for the attack. Petty believed that the German machine guns "would have mowed us down" as the Rangers hit the wide-open field. "It's doubtful that any or very few would have reached the woods," concluded Petty.

"We were supposed to move at 7:30," Petty related, "but we felt that if we didn't make the move beforehand, we'd get slaughtered by the German mortars. We stood up just like in a movie. It was like seeing a wave in the football field. It started with F Company and moved across into D Company. We went over the field as one."

Private Bud Potratz admitted his mouth turned "dry as cotton" as he charged across the field, firing his weapon at the German lines, and yelling "Heigh ho, Silver!" at the top of his lungs. Shooting from the hip, the Rangers rushed headlong through the same icy, snow-dusted killing field that Captain Rhein's company had fatefully attempted to cross only one day earlier, leading to their slaughter in their failed attempt to recapture all of Bergstein. Most of the Rangers' thoughts were simple: *"How do I get across this field and onto the hill in the woods?"*

BOOM! BOOM! BOOM!

Artillery shells were landing all over the field, wounding and maiming Rangers—though many of them kept up the charge. It was all or nothing. German machine guns opened up from a nearby bunker and other positions. Halfway across the icy expanse, the Ranger charge grew staggered because some men ran faster than others. According to Petty, "it became a disarrayed assault with no one in command. It would have been impossible to do so."

Potratz recalled a few men who froze and did not join the rest of the company on the charge. "I hate to say this, but [some of the men] never got up. I never knew what happened to those guys but they didn't make the charge."

But all the others, Lomell remembered, "were running as fast as we could and running at the base of the hill. The Germans called in mortar and artillery fire. They started a crawling fire effect behind us. It made us move faster. It followed us right up the hill."

At the sight of more than one hundred crazed, screaming Rangers tearing across the field, charging at them with their cold, steel bayonets pointed and guns blazing, many of the Germans began to surrender.

One German soldier who had been firing on the Rangers stood up and shouted, *"Kamerad!"*

Festering with rage, one of the Rangers snarled back, "You son of a bitch!"

As Stein recalled the tragic incident, "I got about halfway across the field. A German was coming with his hands on his head to the right of me." The German was being waved back to the American lines "until he met up with one of our men who was cussing him out and hollering at him. The German promptly got on his knees, pleading for his life. But this Ranger, with a wild gleam in his eyes, shot him through the head."

According to Webb, "[he] shot him even though he had his hands up. I don't agree with that kind of stuff, but when you are being shot at you have all that tension, I guess you want revenge. I don't agree with it. I saw that a couple of times, but it's a sad sight to see. It shouldn't be."

As the Rangers continued to charge, more Germans abandoned their pillboxes and machine gun positions and ran for their lives up the hill. "I guess if you see one-hundred twenty men acting like a bunch of Indians coming at you, you think *'These guys are nuts.'* We were yelling like crazy, the 'Rebel yell.'"

Petty reflected on the moment, "With bayonets shining, hip firing, and yelling a battle cry that probably goes back into the eons of time, we charged into the jaws of death. I know that I will never see a more brave and glorious sight. It was for me indeed a moment of being proud to be a Ranger."

To Ruggiero, "It was something straight out of Hollywood. Someone yelled, 'Fix bayonets,' and we screamed and took off. The Germans didn't know how many men we had. At that time, we were shorthanded. To take that hill with Fox Company and Dog Company was quite a feat. It was less than 120 men, for Christ's sake.... I didn't see any sun at all, there was so damn much smoke."

"As we moved out," Ruggerio continued, "we were taking sniper fire from a nearby building window. The round hit right near McBride's foot. They were sniping at us. Mack would hear it every time the bullet would hit in front of us. He shouted, 'That son of a bitch is up in a window to the right.' I almost emptied an entire clip of my carbine into the window. At that instant, an artillery shell hit the window. Something big hit it, and it just blew up."

McBride and Ruggiero then moved to a small mound of earth on the edge of the open field. "The first hummock was about seventy-five yards maybe from the back end of the church," Ruggie related. "All I know is that when we got out of the church, right after the tail end of 1st Platoon, [Dog] was making their way across the field at the foot of the hill. We went through the churchyard and there was this big, high hummock-like thing. Myself, McBride, and Joe Stevens, who was the mortar sergeant, we were up against this hummock. We were watching the guys go across. Every now and then a shell would come in right in back of us."

Even worse, explained Ruggie, "the Germans started using that six-barrel thing. A Nebelwerfer, a rocket launcher. We could tell that's what it was. One dropped between Mack and Joe Stevens and me, just in back of us. That's when I got blown over that hummock."

After the blast, Ruggiero wasn't able to move. "McBride threw me over his shoulder. He had to run back to the church with me over his shoulders. That's when I threw up all over him." As McBride was carrying Ruggiero across the field, McBride was shot in the buttocks.

Fortunately, the Rangers did not fall victim to the same carnage that had befallen the Volksgrenadiers on December 6. Smoke from the artillery barrage partially obscured the Germans' field of vision. In the murky haze, the scores of screaming, bayonet-wielding Rangers swiftly rushing toward the 980th caught them by surprise.

As World War I had proven, a bayonet is usually no match for a machine gun. However, the timing and circumstances of this charge—the heavy smoke, the premature charge, and the narrow gap between the two artillery barrages—miraculously created a window of opportunity that would allow the Rangers and their bayonets to overcome the Volksgrenadiers' entrenched machine gun positions.

Only as the men of Dog and Fox closed the final ten yards of the field did the Volksgrenadiers begin to fire their weapons.

By that time, it would be too late.

CHAPTER 33

Hill 400

The Rangers hit the stunned men of Captain Thomae's 2nd Battalion like a tsunami. Cresting and breaking the German defensive positions, the Americans struck with bayonets and rifle fire. In the official history, a single sentence deftly summed up the scene: "It was one wave of shooting, screaming Rangers."

"As we entered the forts at the foot of the hill," said Petty, "the force of the charge carried us into our own shelling. It was still in full barrage. We temporarily escaped the enemy, but were being slaughtered by our own friends." When they realized what was happening, some of the men bridled in confusion.

"We ran into our own artillery and experienced casualties," Petty continued. Three Fox Company Rangers were dead, and many more were seriously wounded. The dead and wounded were piling up in Dog Company as well. "The situation was in turmoil. There were people trying to help the wounded. Others were hesitant to move forward."

Several burned-out buildings lay in the path of D Company's assault near the base of Hill 400. "I was so damn scared," Potratz admitted. "I just moved forward, firing from the hip. I was trying to figure out where these guys were dug in. They had machine gun nests set up just south of these buildings. How we never got hit, God only knows."

Sundby also charged toward the buildings. "Everyone was screaming and yelling. Jerries came out of the house [and surrendered]. I believe there were about twelve or thirteen of them."

Potratz related, "Then I saw [Private] Mack Durrer . . . from the first section, throw a white phosphorus grenade into the second story of one of the buildings that the Germans were firing from. I don't know if Mack got hit or what happened to him, but he never made it up the hill. Then Al Komits, who was a BAR man from the first section, was hit and killed. And around the side of the building—he scared the living daylights out of me—came a guy by the name of Carr. He was our bazooka man. He was screaming 'I'm hit!' I grabbed him by his cartridge belt, and said, 'Stay down.'"

Conaboy turned to Sundby and said, "I'll beat you to the top of the hill." With that, Sundby, Conaboy, Lomell, Sharik, Potratz, and others charged up the Dog Company side of Hill 400. In the confusion and heat of the assault, unit cohesion fell away. Platoons and companies intermixed as the men pressed on up the slope.

Adrenaline and training overrode the Rangers' fear. Fighting hand-to-hand, the men of Dog and Fox pushed forward in small groups. "Each man was on his own," explained Petty. "The twelve or fifteen men who had carried the company since we landed at D-Day [carried the assault]."

On the Dog Company side of the hill, Lomell was moving as fast as his legs could carry him. As he charged, one thought kept running through his mind: *"Get to the top of the hill as fast as I can and run the Germans off."*

Fighting their way toward the crest, the men moved through an obstacle course of steel rain, downed trees, and Germans. The artillery took its toll. Axis and Allied shrapnel shredded the evergreen canopy of Hill 400, knocking down pine trees and turning the green hill bald. The artillery tree bursts sent down deadly, dagger-like wooden splinters.

Sliding, falling, and shooting as they climbed, the Rangers overran the Germans positions. "I was using my rifle as a staff because the hill was so steep," remembered Potratz. Looking over his shoulder, he saw several men. Up front, Lomell, Sharik, Potratz, and most of their fellow Ranger officers led Dog's charge. "Ranger officers are up front. They don't lead from behind, they lead the charges," affirmed Lomell.

Lomell and Sharik were among the first men atop the hill. Petty, Anderson, and Big Stoop soon joined them.

The top of Hill 400 offered a commanding view of the Hürtgen Forest. A large observation bunker sat on the crest of the hill. Built in the early years of the war as part of the "West Wall," the reinforced concrete bunker protected German artillery observers. From this commanding position, Germans had been able to see several miles on either side of the hill and call in artillery fire on Bergstein or the other nearby German hamlets.

Passing in and out of artillery barrages, Sergeant Petty, Private First Class Anderson, Captain Masny, and several men from F Company reached the bunker first and "went for it." When they received no fire from the bunker, they entered the German strongpoint.

Petty and Bill Anderson* ran into an eight-foot hallway and encountered another large steel door leading into the heart of the bunker. Affixed to the door was a small metal slot "like a mail flap." Petty opened it and jammed his BAR into the slot. Pulling the trigger, he emptied the entire magazine while Anderson lobbed two grenades through the aperture.

Anticipating the blast from the grenades, L-Rod tried to yank his BAR back through the hole, but the front sight of his BAR was hung up on the flap. He left it hanging in the door. As the two men scrambled down the hallway and out of the bunker, an artillery shell burst within ten feet of them. The blast from the shell blew Anderson into Petty's arms. "As I clutched him to hold him up with my hands across

*Bill Anderson's twin brother Jack also served in F Company. A clone of Petty, Anderson was one of the "bravest men of the battalion" and frequently challenged his superiors, one of whom busted him in rank.

his chest, the force of the blood from his heart... blew my hand about a foot away. He never knew what hit him, and I let him down."

Stunned by the loss of Anderson and dazed by the explosion of the shell, a shaken Petty stepped aside as Captain Masny and other F Company men moved into the bunker. With his "big foot against that pillbox door, [Masny] broke it down, and pitched in a pineapple grenade."

Several surviving Germans shouted: *"Kamerad! Kamerad!"* The Rangers accepted their surrender.

According to Potratz, Masny then pointed to him, Lomell, and Sharik and barked, "Go over the forward slope and set up a line of fire."

Mike Sharik and Bud Potratz slid down the eastern side of Hill 400 toward the Roer "on their butts." As they careened down the hill, Potratz lost their shovel, which had been anchored to the back of his cartridge belt. "I saw the shovel slide down the hill rapidly. I had no time to retrieve it since our eyes were glued to the terrain looking for Jerries. Upon hitting the base of the hill, we could see the river in the distance. On the other side of river there was another hill where the Jerries had dug in some artillery. We knew the Jerries were looking down our throats."

Potratz noted, "We set up a line of fire, and it was quiet then. Sharik and I were lying on our tummies, because we couldn't dig in."

With Rangers swarming on top of Hill 400 and the observation bunker out of German hands, Thomae, who had been ordered to hold the hill at all costs, took desperate measures. He picked up a field phone from his forward command post in West Wall Bunker 320a, about one hundred yards north of Hill 400, and called in the artillery, practically on top of his own men.

The Germans, using artillery one Ranger described as "belt-fed, like a machine gun," rained fire down on the hill. "The entire hill shook" under the awesome weight of German ordnance falling on 400, killing Rangers and Germans alike.

Four shells hit the side of the bunker where Petty and Big Stoop stood, "knocking us helter-skelter. Amazingly, neither of us was hit."

However, the deadly shrapnel seriously wounded several other Rangers, tearing into flesh and bone. One man snapped and went "hysterical." Petty sharply slapped him across the face in an effort to bring him back to his senses. It didn't work, so the staff sergeant moved the agitated man into the newly captured observation bunker.

The Germans moved several tank destroyers into position to fire upon the Rangers. Armed with the potent 75 mm main gun, the Germans placed direct fire on the Americans.

At 8:30 A.M., Masny reported the top of Hill 400 secure. However, while the Rangers held the crest of Hill 400, hundreds of Thomae's men were hanging onto a protected ravine near the wooded, eastern side of the hill. The Volksgrenadiers also stubbornly clung to portions of the reverse slopes on the northern and southern sides of the hill.

Hidden in the very midst of the enemy, Sharik, Potratz, and Lomell, along with two men from F Company, lay face down, sprawled on the frozen ground. Digging in on the icy slope was nearly impossible because of shale and tree roots.

Suddenly, a shell landed in front of the men and felled a large tree, fortuitously providing some badly needed cover from the incoming shells. "The tree saved our lives," recalled Potratz. Chain-smoking Lucky Strikes, the men nervously hoped the next shell wouldn't hit them.

After a slight lull, shells began to bombard the hill from three sides without warning, and throughout the ensuing carnage, the Rangers "could hear our comrades trying to dig in above. There were screams of dying men, and the voices of the wounded tore our hearts."

Within a quarter of an hour, the barrage lifted, and an eerie silence took hold on the hill. Dense, acrid smoke burned the men's eyes and nostrils.

"I'm going up to the top to see who's left, and I will get some help," said Lomell. Still chain-smoking, Potratz and Sharik huddled together for another hour and waited for word from Lomell.

German infantry doctrine called for an immediate counterattack after an enemy captured a position. The Rangers knew it was only a matter of *when*, not *if*, the Germans were coming. Taking a drag from his Lucky, Potratz turned to Sharik and said: "When the Jerries counterattack, we would be in better position to fight if we were on higher ground."

Sharik nodded and told the Fox Company men to move toward the left side of the hill where he thought Fox had deployed. On their way to the crest, Potratz and Sharik passed a portion of the hill with a steep drop-off of exposed rock. The two men pushed to the southeastern portion of the hill. Climbing the rocks, they found the mangled bodies of PFC Frank Lewis, Staff Sergeant Michael Branley, and PFC Jack Trout. A single shell had taken out all three men, whose remains could be identified only by their dog tags.

Close by, Potratz spotted the lifeless body of Pat McCrone. "He was on his knees, and his helmet was blown off. He had a shovel in his hands. And his brain was exposed." In death he was reunited with his lost buddy, Larry Johnson.

Surveying the haunting, still scene, Potratz wondered, *"Are we the only survivors?"*

As they pushed farther up the hill, Potratz and Sharik finally came upon other surviving Rangers: Lester Arthur, Dick Martin, and Pop Adams. Arthur, wounded on Hill 63, had come back just days before the attack. Desperately tending to Sergeant Leroy "Pop" Adams, the oldest Ranger in Dog Company, Arthur pressed a bandage down on his carotid artery, which was bleeding profusely. Potratz jammed a morphine syrette in Pop's leg to numb the pain and tried to console him as he died.

As they neared the top of the right side of the hill, Potratz and Sharik joined Lomell, who was now in charge of what was left of Dog. The Germans had captured Captain Masny while he was going for reinforcements. And Captain McBride had been wounded.

Later, Lomell would describe how the barrage had whittled down the men of Dog Company: "We got to the top and took charge of everything on the right side of the hill. One platoon lost its officer, and the company commander got wounded. My own platoon sergeant got wounded, but he got back up after he was treated. I was acting company commander since I was the most senior officer on the hill at the time."

On the F Company side of the hill, the barrage also took its bloody toll, with wounded Rangers screaming for help:

"L-Rod!"

"L-Rod!"

"L-Rod!"

"I spent the next thirty to fifty minutes getting wounded people disentangled from downed trees and into the bunker. Screams for L-Rod never seemed to stop," Petty recalled.

Petty and the other ambulatory Rangers carried the wounded, including Bill Anderson's twin brother Jack, into the safety of the reinforced concrete walls of the bunker. The shrapnel from the shelling cut deeply into Jack's limp body; Petty knew the remaining twin was dying. After he set Anderson's broken body down inside the pillbox, the Ranger died. "I had the dubious distinction of having held both brothers while they were in the process of dying within an hour's time."

Despite the severe losses, Lieutenant Len Lomell, Staff Sergeant Joe Stevens, and their runner, Private First Class Sam O'Neal, told the men of Dog to dig in. The Germans were on three sides of Hill 400.

Sergeant Ed Secor and Private First Class Ellis Lawson established themselves in a commanding position underneath a large overhanging rock. Staff Sergeant Morris Webb dug a foxhole nearby. They and the last remaining men of Dog Company scanned the front of their positions and waited for the Germans to come.

CHAPTER 34

Their "Longest Day"

The bitter stench of cordite permeated the air. Broken tree limbs, dust, and rock littered the scalded surface of the hill. The haunting moans of the wounded echoed across Castle Hill's crest on December 7, 1944. Dog and Fox companies readied their weapons and hacked away at the frozen rocky hill, waiting for the German counterattack, which they knew would be swift and brutal. As the Rangers chopped at the gnarly, thick tree roots embedded in the icy, unyielding ground, they scraped their hands raw trying to dig their foxholes just a few inches deeper in preparation for the inevitable German onslaught.

Cautiously lifting his head above his foxhole, Bud Potratz scanned the trees at the base of the hill, his heart pounding in anticipation of the battle.

Someone yelled, "Here come the krauts!"

At approximately 9:30 A.M., scores of Thomae's grenadiers, augmented by several companies of the elite German paratroopers, charged from the southeast portion of the hill. The Germans had sent elements of a Fallschirmjäger battalion to the north of Bergstein into the maelstrom on Hill 400. The Fallschirmjägers had long been a nemesis of America's elite units, including the 82nd and 101st Airborne Divisions on D-Day and later, during Operation Market Garden.

The Germans swarmed the hill like a colony of ants, attacking in small six- to ten-man groups. The German assault glanced off Fox, which was arrayed in a semicircle, and stormed toward the bunker where the wounded were holed up. The woods on the F Company side of the hill screened the German assault. "In some instances, the attack was discovered just as the enemy was about to the rush the last few hundred yards to the bunker," remembered Lomell.

With the Germans on top of them, the men of Dog chucked grenades and squeezed back on the triggers of their Garands, BARs, and tommy guns, using everything they had to repel the oncoming field-grey tide.

"There were a lot of gray uniforms coming up, with that distinctive German helmet," said one Ranger.

The focal point of the attack was Lawson and Secor's foxhole. Protected by the massive boulder that overhung their position, the two Rangers fired hundreds of rounds into the Germans. Suddenly, Secor's weapon took a hit from a German round.

CRACK!

Secor cast his "smashed and useless" BAR aside. The usually mild-mannered sergeant charged out of the fighting hole and ran to recover weapons from several dead German soldiers lying nearby. After grabbing two German MP-40 machine pistols,* Secor madly charged into the oncoming Germans. "With a captured machine pistol under each arm, he stood up to turn twin streams of demoralizing fire upon the close-in enemy."

Morris Webb, who was dug in near Secor's foxhole, also noted Secor's selfless heroism: "He stood up with both machine pistols under his arms and let the lead fly. It takes a lot of courage to stand up and shoot like he did. He then put both machine guns down when he was out of ammo and picked up his pistol and started to shoot at the

*It's possible that the weapons were MP-44 assault rifles because the unit was heavily equipped with that weapon; however, the after-action report states that they were machine pistols.

Germans. This time when they attacked Secor, it was company-sized. They were attacking all the way around the hill. I credit Secor in repelling that attack."

In fact, the official Ranger after-action report concisely summed up this extraordinary act of bravery. "[Secor] turned the tide of the battle."

Lomell reflected on the first attack. "They came right at Dog Company. There were paratroopers on foot that tried to drive us off the hill with bayonets and other combat arms such as machine guns and whatever else they could carry. We were surrounded at times. We were outnumbered tremendously."*

The defense of Hill 400 rested on the stalwart shoulders of the few remaining men of Dog and Fox Companies. Lieutenant Lomell moved over to the F Company side of the hill to ensure the two companies' lines were tied together.

As Lomell passed Sergeant Herman Stein, Stein asked, "Jesus, where are the guys from D Company?"

Lomell replied, "Well, they're right down the hill there." Lomell lifted his arm and his hand, which was bloodied from a shrapnel wound. One of Lomell's fingers was dangling from a tendon, "half dropping off," as he pointed to the D Company section of the hill.

Lomell directed Stein and his two foxhole buddies to move closer to Dog Company. Stein, Moss, and a stray Dog Company Ranger made their way down the hill. But in the smoke and twisted remains of trees, they became disoriented, and discovered that they actually moved away from Dog Company and toward a gorge near the Roer River. Oddly, as he tried to get his bearings, Stein spied a Mercedes sedan filled with laughing German officers across the river.

---

*Lomell recalls, "I took my survivors and went back to Hill 400 in 1989. We met a class from the German Military Academy. We went over their book together. They were awfully nice guys. Their book said that they were outnumbered by us Rangers. [Even decades later,] they did not know that there were so little of us on the hill that survived."

Suddenly, the Rangers also spied a German patrol emerging from the gorge and starting to cross a nearby trail. "Along comes a German patrol, and they were paratroopers. We could tell by the camouflaged ponchos they had on. The German patrol was about a dozen men. They looked pretty sharp, and they were well spread out," remembered Stein. He turned to Moss and the other Ranger. "Should we take them on? Shit, should we bother?" Stein continued, "Jesus, we ain't got no support at all. Hell, no."

Sensing that they would be overwhelmed by the paratroopers, Stein let the patrol pass. Time seemed to tick by slowly. Nothing happened for more than half an hour. Stein then told the other men, "We better get our asses back up the hill."

As the men moved towards the summit, Germans manning a self-propelled gun spotted them and opened fire. Moving in and out of cover, the Americans made their way back up toward the observation bunker on the crest of the hill and dug in.

Herm Stein's best friend, L-Rod Petty, was conducting reconnaissance toward the base of the hill. Along with Whitney Barowski, he observed that the Germans were preparing to attack again, organizing their men into five- or six-man squads. The two men quickly returned up the hill and pulled all of the able-bodied Rangers out of the observation bunker. Even the wounded, anyone who could still fire a rifle, came out of the post to fight off the attack. Petty and another Ranger, Lieutenant Thomas Rowland, were the last two men out of the pillbox.

According to the after-action report, "enemy forces advanced so close that it was necessary to shoot one's way out of the bunker."

Scrambling out of the pillbox, Rowland immediately charged into the midst of the German attack. "The Germans were either prone or kneeling," Petty remarked, "but all of the Rangers were either standing or moving to meet them. I began trying to get people down, but to no avail. All of their combat training had gone to hell in the excitement."

In his headlong charge, Rowland took several German bullets in the chest.

A brief lull in the fighting allowed Barowski to bring Rowland to safety. With Rowland bleeding profusely from the chest, Barowski carried the fallen Ranger on his back up the hill toward the command bunker. L-Rod carried another wounded Ranger, Garness Colden. Fearing he would not survive D-Day, Colden confided in Petty on the eve of the invasion. Now, tragically, Colden was bleeding to death in Petty's arms and would later succumb to his wounds in the pillbox.

As he trudged up the slope, a rifle shot jerked Rowland's head back, instantly killing him. "They're firing from the trees!" Barowski screamed.

Petty then looked up at the few trees that remained standing. The Germans weren't firing from the trees, but from a higher location on the hill. "Reading it as a flanking movement to get above us, a brand new kid named Shannon had moved across to cut them off. I was running at full speed with Shannon only a couple of steps behind. We came upon a German only twenty feet away in a prone position and a rifle aimed dead center on me. I saw him too late. I fired, but a second too late. He must have flinched because the bullet passed through my right shoulder and into Shannon's chest," recalled Petty.

Petty then emptied his BAR into the German. With a gaping bullet hole in his shoulder, he attempted to lift the weapon and reload it. Seriously wounded, Petty and Shannon then retreated toward the bunker, where they encountered Herman Stein. In a state of shock and losing a lot of blood, Petty snapped, "Who's gonna take my BAR? Who's gonna take my BAR?" Most of the sergeants in Dog and Fox carried BARs because "the BAR, to us, was the best gun you could get."

Stein replied, "I'll take the BAR," but thought to himself, *"What am I going to do with two BARs?"*

Stein got Petty and Shannon into the pillbox and jammed a morphine syrette into each of them.

As the Germans continued to attack the hill, back in Bergstein's church, Lieutenant Howard K. Kettlehut, a 56th Armored Field Artillery forward observer assigned to Duke Slater and the Rangers, unleashed a deadly ring of artillery fire around the hill. Taking his life in his own hands, Kettlehut remained in the church's bell tower while the church miraculously withstood "eighty-two direct hits" from German artillery. Using his field glasses, Kettlehut coordinated with the men on the hill, carefully plotting targets, as he called in American artillery fire practically on top of the Rangers. His exacting skill in placing fire was noted after the battle: "[Kettlehut] performed superior service in placing the fire where it was wanted. At times, due to nearness of the enemy approach, the troops called for fire almost on their positions."

With both German and Allied artillery raining down on the hill, Dog Company soldier Sheldon Bare never knew which side hit him. Bare had recently rejoined the unit after recovering from a wound suffered on D-Day. "I was never a smoker, but I always had chewing tobacco in my mouth. I had some in my mouth when the artillery hit me. I thought my foxhole buddy hit me in the back of the head. I thought he gave me a crack for something I had said. It happened so quickly." Bare spat out the chewing tobacco as he tried to regain his senses.

His foxhole buddy, Sigurd Sundby, said, "Come on, Bare, it's just a concussion. You're OK, it's just a concussion."

Bare felt the back of his neck and revealed his bloody hand to Sundby. "Does this look like a concussion?" he asked.

"Jesus, you're going to the aid station."

Sundby recalls Lomell giving the men orders to dig in deeper and telling Sundby to go take care of Bare. "I can still see Len walking on the top of that hill, his blood coming from his hand and carrying his tommy gun. A leader like that we would do anything for."

Sundby took Bare to the troop shelter, where he received a shot of morphine before his evacuation. Razor-sharp shrapnel had torn into Bare's neck, barely missing his spine. The metal shards remained in his neck for years after the war before they were finally removed at a VA (Veterans Affairs) hospital.

Meanwhile, with the few Rangers he had left, Lomell worked strategically to defend the hill. He explained, "We had outposts so that we would know where the attack was coming from. And I'd get the guys on the hill to charge towards that point so that we could meet the German counterattack. All other positions were vacated or abandoned; we didn't have enough men to cover everything."

With so many radios damaged from shrapnel hits, the men had to devise other means of communicating when outposts came under attack. "One guy would see a counterattack forming and break away from his post and say there were one-hundred and fifty of them coming, and we would get ready for them," Lomell remembered. "We were always helping each other. We would use hand signals, whistle, or slip down away from the position. Believe me, if we had to stop breathing, we would have stopped breathing to prevent being caught or heard."

D and F Companies were expected to hold the hill for about twenty-four hours, but miraculously held it for almost forty hours, thanks to their mobile defensive tactics. "The outposts would hold them off as long as they could until we arrived. The Germans didn't understand how they were getting such a large response, when in fact we were just shifting forces around to meet each counterattack. This is why they thought we actually outnumbered them. If the Germans had known that we only had fifteen or twenty men from each company, forty men in total, they would have rolled right over us from every angle."

Having been promised prized Iron Crosses and leave from their command if they could re-capture Hill 400, the Germans relentlessly probed the defenses on the hill. "These were pretty smart troops. They were paratroopers that were trying to take us by surprise," explained Lomell.

Observing the battle from the steeple of the Church of Moorish Martyrdom, Duke Slater knew his men badly needed support. Not an armchair officer, the Ranger commander with the "looks and demeanor of Lee Marvin" confidently strode up the hill to visit his men. Slater's presence bolstered the Rangers' sagging morale as he surveyed the hill and gazed upon the Roer. After climbing down the hill and returning to the church at 12:42 P.M., Slater reported, "Only seventeen men of Company F and fifteen men of Company D were still in fighting condition."

A second attack came from the northeast, east, and southeast. A rainstorm of German artillery preceded the assault. The artillery was so violent the entire hill seemed to lurch again.

"The artillery fell like rain," Lomell attested. "Have you ever been out in a torrential rainstorm? All right, picture yourself on a hill. Now picture yourself trying to hide from those raindrops. You can't dig in. You might try to hide on one side of a stump of a fallen tree. But instead of rain, it's falling shrapnel. Deadly shrapnel rain. But the shells, mortar shells or 88s, when they hit the tops of those trees they send down a shower of shrapnel and wooden splinters. You just have to hope and pray they don't get you."*

Once again, a wave of German paratroopers and Volksgrenadiers ascended the hill and closed upon the men of Dog and Fox. "A large enemy [self-propelled gun] was parked on the east side of a building in the near distance. We could see the burst of fire as the tank zeroed in on our position. We felt helpless," recalled Potratz.

---

*Addressing the author, Lomell expanded on the point: "Pat, no one ever seems to get this right: we were continually under barrages that rained tons, and I mean *tons* of shrapnel. It was an enormous amount of artillery that came down on us. No one knew there were tens of thousands of Germans that were hidden there ready and waiting for the Ardennes to launch the Battle of the Bulge. And that was just a few miles up the road from us. No one in Army intelligence or in the Hürtgen Forest knew that there were tens of thousands of Germans massing for the Battle of the Bulge. There were thousands of tanks and battalions of artillery prearranged for the Battle of the Bulge. In just three days before we made this assault, five thousand men from the 5th Armored Division and 8th Division tried to take Hill 400, and they failed—just the day before we launched our attack. You should have seen the mess there. There were burned-out tanks, burned-out trucks—heavy stuff that was burned out. They don't talk about the Hürtgen Forest. Why? Because there were a lot of mistakes that were made. There were tens of thousands of casualties, including a hell of a death list. The reason that I am saying this is because no one seemed to know where all this artillery came from. And then half of us are gonna get all busted up. And then the Battle of the Bulge breaks out."

At 4:06 P.M., Len Lomell sent the following message: "Counterattacks on hill all afternoon; very heavy artillery; only twenty-five able-bodied men left; help needed badly; we are surrounded."

In the din of battle, Lomell heard the screams of men crying out to their mothers. "They were dying.... And this went on for hours," related Lomell, still deeply affected by the tragic scene fifty-five years later.

There was no way to get the wounded off the hill in daylight. Frustrated, the former first sergeant did his best to rally the men, despite their desperate situation. "Don't worry, things are going to get better. We're gonna hold," Lomell told his men. "Listen, we are doing the best that we can. As soon as we get more medical supplies, Kinmuth, the medic, is going to come around and take care of you. All I can say, guys, is that we are doing the best that we can."

After enduring several more hours of hearing the cries of his men, the lieutenant reached an emotional breaking point. Only seventeen Rangers were left in Dog Company and a handful in Fox Company. Lomell gathered those who could still stand to attend what amounted to a council of war and posed a hypothetical question. "We have been fighting together for six months, and we have always known the Germans to give first aid to wounded Americans," Lomell began. "What if we draw down, let the Germans have their God damn hill back, because there are more of them? They have the muscle and the vehicles to take the wounded off the hill very quickly and get them back to their hospitals and so forth."

Lomell's Rangers wouldn't hear of it. "Nah, Nah, Len! Nah!"

Lomell retorted, "You want to walk around, check these guys like I've been doing?"

But the Rangers stood firm, "No, no. Don't give an inch." Lomell stopped arguing. He nodded his head, "OK."

Decades later, he recalled how badly the situation had affected him. "And that hurt. Maybe emotionally that was the lowest point that I have ever been in combat. I was so helpless, and they were so helpless. All we could do was hold the ground on the goddamn hill.

No matter how many tons of goddamn shrapnel were dumped on us."

At 4:52 P.M., Lomell sent a final, urgent call for help to Duke Slater. Not having a reserve platoon, Slater cobbled together a platoon from E Company, which stretched his defenses in Bergstein to the breaking point.

But sending in these Rangers to fortify their brothers on the hill broke the German counterattack. According to the after-action report, "the attacking enemy force withdrew in the face of these onrushing reinforcements." At 5:35 P.M., Lomell was able to report, "Everything is quiet on the hill." But the lull was only temporary.

The Germans still occupied portions of the reverse slope of the hill, as Sergeant Bud Potratz and his foxhole buddy, Private First Class James Brown, could attest. "Brown got straight up and stretched in the darkness. I pulled on his leg to get him down. Just plain stupid! Within seconds, a potato masher grenade bounced off the top of our foxhole, and the impact was in the front of the hole. We were lucky."

The Germans continued to probe the hill, sending out small reconnaissance patrols to test the Ranger defenses. Initially, the German high command was skeptical that Burgberg had fallen. Accordingly, they dispatched a scouting party consisting of several officers. The officers climbed the hill and confirmed that the crest was in Allied hands.

CHAPTER 35

Nightfall

The moans of the dying filled the air as the dark gray rays of dusk clawed across the scarred face of Hill 400. Sleet and icy rain pelted the men, turning their holes into miserable, mud-filled, soupy messes. As night descended on the hill, the Germans regularly tested the Ranger defenses. At this point, Fox Company was down to six men; Dog Company had just over a dozen. Many of the severely wounded were barely clinging to life after lying exposed to shrapnel for hours. Only the lucky ones had made it inside the troop shelter of the bunker. German snipers, artillery, and the direct fire from self-propelled guns made the evacuation of the wounded impossible in broad daylight. Knowing that time was running out for the dying men of Dog and Fox, Slater and Lomell organized a rescue mission for the wounded.

When darkness fell, Rangers in Bergstein formed into teams of litter bearers and ascended the hill to evacuate the casualties. The bulk of the evacuation efforts fell on the men in the 1st and 2nd Platoons of Charlie Company, who had spent the earlier part of the day manning a roadblock midway between the church and the base of the hill. Men from Dog's mortar section, including Zeke Zyrkowski, joined the rescue party climbing the hill.

Out of breath from the steep climb, Zyrkowski and Dog's other mortar men, who had been stationed near the church, reached the crest of the hill unscathed. Walking toward the bunker, Zeke turned to his right and gazed at fallen Rangers McCrone, Lewis, and Branley. "There were several bodies in the hole, crimson blood all over them."

The smell of blood and sweat permeated the bunker's gray, dank, reinforced-concrete walls. Inside, Zeke found Lomell with a deep wound on his upper thigh and his shrapnel-mangled hand.

Lomell and Petty, who was suffering from sharp and piercing pain from the gunshot wound to his shoulder, both needed evacuation. Petty nudged the medic, who administered another shot of morphine. "After the injection, I was high as a kite and feeling no pain," Petty later recalled. Despite their severe wounds, both men did what they could to encourage the other Rangers.

Typical of Ranger leadership, Lomell and Petty managed to supervise the evacuation, despite their severe wounds. This was a perilous exercise, considering that the Germans remained ready to pounce, lying only several dozen yards or so on the reverse slopes of the hill. The stretcher bearers set out in groups of one or two pairs, each accompanied by an armed, able-bodied Ranger. Several men made round trips from the top of the bunker down to the church.

Zyrkowski placed the seriously wounded Frederick Dix in a litter. With Dix in the stretcher, Zeke and another Ranger named Bill descended 400. "Trees were knocked down and we had to scramble over them. The hill was very steep. Bill was in front of me and I was in the back and Dix was in the litter."

Suddenly, Bill's hand slipped. Dix tumbled out of the litter and rolled down the hill. In the fall, Dix's helmet fell off. Writhing in pain, Dix blurted out:

"Fuck! You mother fuckers! Give me my fucking helmet back. Give me my fucking helmet." Knowing the outburst would alert the enemy to their position, Zeke and Bill tried to calm the wounded Ranger down. Then they gently lifted Dix back on the litter and continued down the hill.

A few mortar rounds fell near them as they approached the frozen field they had charged with bayonets earlier that day. "We started to run. There was an opening at the bottom on the way to the church." In full stride, and halfway across the field, Bill asked, "Can we stop?"

Exasperated, Zeke retorted, "Run, you son of a bitch, run!"

Eventually, the men made it into the church where the seriously wounded Dix received medical treatment, which helped him survive the war. Not all of the men evacuating the wounded made it to the relative safety of the church. German officers sent to reconnoiter the hill captured two litter bearers.

By 9:40 P.M., all Ranger casualties were off the hill and grouped behind the stout, stone walls of the church, which acted as a triage station for the wounded.

When the litter bearers carrying Petty arrived at the church, German shells were falling in the streets. The Rangers carried him carefully down the stairs of the church's cellar. "After descending the stairs to the basement," Petty explained, "the first thing I saw when I went in was the first sergeant sitting against the wall smoking. I don't know why it infuriated me so much, for the entire company had known he was yellow since D-Day, but I went nuts and began kicking the hell out of him. By the time they got me under control, I had the satisfaction of giving several other officers my opinions of them. I can assure you it was not complimentary. I would personally take my three days [at Pointe du Hoc] as an annual holiday compared to my one day on the hill. The trauma to me was deep and lasting. The battle will always be yesterday. Sound bitter? You bet your ass—unforgiving, after forty-three years."

Later that evening, a three-man, heavy machine gun crew from the Army's 8th Infantry Division approached Dog Company's part of the hill. Heedless of the extreme danger surrounding them, the men were complaining loudly about their plight. Concerned that their griping could expose their position to the Germans, Potratz hissed, sotto voce, "Pipe down and be careful where you're walking. There are three dead Rangers next to us." The machine gunners became "stone quiet" and moved thirty yards to the right of Potratz's position where they began to dig in.

CHAPTER 36

December 8

As the first rays of the sun crept over the hill, the heaviest concentration of artillery fire of the entire battle fell on Bergstein and Hill 400. "At dawn, all hell broke loose! The Jerries hit us with everything they had: artillery, mortars, and tank fire. I had never experienced such a long and hard barrage that they laid down on us that morning of the eighth," Potratz reflected.

"The artillery fire was so heavy that it seemed to have a 'drumming' sound," the Ranger after-action report noted direly. The barrage that fell on the hill was "of such a density that one explosion would cover the sound of the next approaching shell." Shells hit the splintered and broken remains of the trees on the hill, creating the all-too-familiar deadly tree bursts on the Rangers' positions.

Sharik yelled out, "I'm hit in the leg!" He hollered again, "I'm hit in the leg!"

Brown, in the foxhole next to Potratz, screamed and held up his hand. His thumb had been sheared off—only a bloody stump remained. The two wounded men stumbled toward the bunker.

Under his heavy clothes and overcoat, Potratz felt a sickening burning on his upper hip. Despite the wound he remained in his hole, wondering, *"I know I'm hit, but to what extent?"*

Suddenly the shelling stopped. Potratz tried to inspect his leg but had trouble maneuvering in his foxhole and couldn't remove his heavy clothes. Fortunately, a medic arrived. He began cutting off Potratz's uniform, revealing mangled, bloody flesh from the shrapnel wound. He dumped powdery sulfa on Potratz's hip, stuffed a white gauze bandage into it, and "disappeared." He had many more casualties to tend.

Potratz braced himself in his foxhole and reflected on the lack of men holding the hill. "The guys in the machine squad were all killed. That left only Secor, Lawson, Martin, Arthur, Robertson, myself, and two guys that came up the hill on our side the very late afternoon of the seventh. Eight men on our side. There was a big gap now on our right. We had no idea the number of men left on the morning of the eighth in F Company."

The German counterattack started in earnest. The elite Fallschirmjäger once again joined Captain Thomae's Volksgrenadiers. Potratz recalls how paratroopers attacked his position. "We just kept firing at the black helmets, and I thought I'd burnt out my M1." After the counterattack, Dog reported "only ten men left."

Shaking and almost exhausted from the first attack, Potratz gulped water from his canteen, took an inventory, and readied his weapons for the next attack. Noticing he was low on ammunition, he and the other men of Dog Company quickly crawled out of their foxholes and stripped the weapons and ammunition off their dead comrades and any dead Germans close by.

On both sides of the crest of the hill, the men had arranged their foxholes in a rough semicircle. Like groundhogs, men burrowed in their individual holes to weather the deadly storms of shrapnel and tides of Germans. The front of Herman Stein's foxhole resembled a dealer's table at a militaria show. Arrayed before him were two BARs, an M1, a Colt .45, and half a dozen pineapple grenades.

All too soon, the Germans again assaulted D Company's position. From their superb position under the large boulder, Secor and Lawson once again contributed decisively to repulsing the German attack, even taking a prisoner.

A forward observer from the 8th Division arrived to provide crucial support. The observer "came to our position and laid in artillery support from the tanks to our south."

The Germans were right on top of the Rangers' foxholes. In desperation, the forward observer called American artillery directly on the Rangers' location. "Once that observer called artillery in on our own positions, they got slaughtered—the Germans were just slaughtered. Germans were in the open and did not have cover." The observer then directed a barrage at the self-propelled gun that had been firing on Potratz's foxhole since the previous day. "I'm sure he got the tank, because we never had any more problems from it later. Then we had the Air Force with a P-47 dive-bombing the enemy on the north side of hill near the F Company sector. God, what an uplifting sight that was," Potratz declared. Thomae's determined grenadiers and the paratroopers hit the Rangers again at dusk. "Another German attack started right at sundown," said Stein. "As soon as they stopped with their artillery, I looked out of my foxhole, and there were a couple of guys [Germans] not far in front of me, maybe fifty feet walking up the hill. They didn't know I was there. They looked like they were kidding with one another. Naturally, they didn't kid any longer once I got them with the BAR . . . One of my men, who we called the 'Mad Russian,' got wounded, and we had to get him back into the pillbox. But he stayed with us all night."

Captain Slater and Major Williams both pleaded with headquarters for reinforcements. The mission—take Hill 400 *and* be relieved in twenty-four hours—was being stretched well beyond the breaking point. In desperation, from his basement command post in a burned-out building, Williams sent Lieutenant Frank Kennard to broach the issue of reinforcement personally with headquarters.

"When I walked into headquarters, it caused quite a stir. Someone said that 'There is a Ranger lieutenant here.' They didn't know me from Adam, but they could tell I was a Ranger. I walked up to whomever was in command, a full-bird colonel, and I said we had a huge number of casualties, we were almost out of ammunition, and needed help. He looked at me sternly and said, 'You go back to Major Williams, and you tell him to hold that hill at all costs!' I said, 'Yes sir,' and went back to Major Williams."

★ ★ ★

As night engulfed the hill, the fighting grew sporadic but didn't stop. "The Germans would try to keep in contact with one another with whistles. 'BAAH! BAAH!' They were whistling with each other. By this time, it was pitch black, and this had been going on for two to three hours. We just held our positions. Of course we didn't shoot constantly, we just gave it a spurt and a burp and throw a couple grenades now and then. The Germans kept coming up between us and try to get to the pillbox, because once they got to the pillbox, they figured they were home," Stein explained.

The American artillery, along with small arms fire and grenades, finally halted the Germans' nighttime attack. Instead of the sounds of advancing Germans getting closer to the crest of the hill, the Rangers heard the welcome noise of a withdrawal. Once the artillery stopped, "you could hear . . . their whistles and 'BAAHs' going back down the hill," recalled Stein.

CHAPTER 37

Final Assault on Bergstein

As part of the enemy's December 8 counterattack, a diversionary force had struck companies B and C, located in Bergstein near the base of Hill 400. "Under covering fire of three towed antitank guns and one self-propelled gun, another self-propelled gun attempted to penetrate the position but was blocked from the entrance to Bergstein by a wrecked vehicle roadblock, which it attempted to blast off the road without success. The fire of the supporting American tank destroyers and mortars forced the withdrawal of these enemy guns. This attack was stopped at 8:37 AM."

After the attack, Doc Block began the evacuation of the wounded from the church. Earlier that day, he had eerily predicted his own death. He had remarked in the morning that he would not live out the day. A short time later, while supervising the evacuation, Doc Block was struck and killed by a German shell.*

Using a Jeep marked with red crosses to designate they were non-combatants, Zyrkowski and other men evacuated the wounded, dodging heavy machine gun and tank rounds on each run. "The sons of bitches were firing at us. It was a miracle we made it across with the

*The Ranger after-action report noted Doctor Block's premonition, "This officer had remarked that morning that he had a premonition that he would not live out this day."

Jeep," Zeke recalled. He somehow made several trips unscathed, even as the German machine gunners zeroed in on the vehicle.

After Zyrkowski survived the hailstorm of small arms and artillery fire, Joe Stevens tasked him with transporting several German prisoners who had valuable intel. "Hey Zeke, we have two prisoners who know where the German tanks are." Stevens added, "We've got to get the prisoners back so they can reveal the intelligence about where the tanks are."

Zyrkowski followed orders, making several more dangerous runs. He recalled that when he and other Rangers approached a house, some concealed Germans began firing. "A GI dashed across the road, and the German tank opened fire on him. But he made it across the road. We ran after him, and we made it through, and that was the third time we made it through the opening. Someone was watching out for us." On Zyrkowski's fourth time making the perilous journey, he saw a German tank lying in wait outside the church.

"Holy Christ!" shouted one of the officers.

Zeke recalled, "Two guys ran outside with a bazooka and fired a round and missed the tank."

⋆ ⋆ ⋆

The fifth and final counterattack began when, in the words of the official after-combat report, "Large-caliber guns to the east of the Roer River concentrated on the area at 1630 [4:30 P.M.]. The enemy came from the southeast and, at 1702 [5:02 P.M.], engaged Dog Company in a firefight."

Of the five counterattacks the Rangers withstood on Hill 400, this one was the strongest of all—and it came closest to success. As Stein noted, "The Germans came within thirty yards of the bunker before being stopped by small arms fire."

After the Rangers stopped the German advance, Lieutenant Kettlehut drove the remaining paratroopers off the hill with a tremendous artillery barrage. "He called down all the artillery available in the corps, eighteen battalions in all."

The colossal firepower of eighteen battalions fell on Rangers and Germans alike. Scores of 105 mm, 155 mm, and 203 mm guns fired their rounds, exhausting the ammunition bearers loading the guns but halting the paratrooper attack on the hill. By 5:50 P.M., the overwhelming fire forced the Germans to withdraw.

As they climbed down the hill, "the enemy... was blocked by this curtain of fire, and in their demoralized state proved easy targets for the men on the hill."

Back in Bergstein, the Germans once more hit the town with an all-out attack. "At that time, they threw another counterattack at us. I thought the roof was going to cave in," Zeke explained. "A shell came through one window and out another. One of the statues fell down. Things were so severe, we thought the church would be overrun by the Germans. So [one of the men] said bluntly, 'If you have any German souvenirs on you, get rid of them. If they break through, the last thing you want is German souvenirs on you.'"

Due to the tremendous number of wounded, there was a shortage of medical supplies, and the men had to improvise. Zyrkowski emotionally recounted the scene: "We were in a Catholic church, and they had these vestments. One of the men was ripping up the vestments, and I said, 'You really shouldn't be doing that.' He said, 'We have no choice, we have no bandages left.' At that point, another outfit came into the church and set up a machine gun near the sacristy. I lay behind the altar, and I started to cry because I thought the roof was going to collapse because the shelling was so intense."

CHAPTER 38

Relief Finally Arrives

As the sun went down, a heavy snow fell on the hill as men from the 13th Infantry Regiment finally relieved the Rangers who held Hill 400 and Bergstein. By then, December 8, 1944, Hill 400 marked the furthest penetration into Germany by any American or British unit—and the Rangers had paid a terrible price for it. Almost every man in Dog and Fox was killed or wounded.

Herman Stein recalled the arrival of the 13th Infantry. "They immediately went inside the safety of the pillbox. When they got up there, they kept piling into the pillbox." As more men of the 13th poured in, Stein was anxious to leave. "I got hold of the platoon sergeant."

"No, you've got to wait for the lieutenant," he was told.

Herm acidly retorted, "Where is he?"

"Well, he's in the back there, in the back part of the pillbox."

Impatiently, Stein waited for the sergeant to find the lieutenant. Moments later the sergeant sent the lieutenant to Stein. Nonchalantly, the lieutenant shrugged his shoulders and said to Stein, "The sergeant will take you out."

About to explode, Stein snorted, "Christ, I just talked to the sergeant, and he said I had to see you."

The lieutenant responded, "Well, you see him and tell him I told you to go out."

Herm could hardly move around in the pillbox, with soldiers "piled in there like sardines." In the darkness and confusion, he could not find the sergeant. "Fuck this! If this is the way they want to play, let them stay here! So I left."

Around 10:30 P.M., Stein left the hill to the grunts of 13th Infantry. Herman Stein, Bud Potratz, and Morris Webb were the last Rangers to leave the hill that night.

From Hill 400's commanding heights, the GIs who relieved the Rangers could see into Germany and observe preparations for Hitler's most secret operation: the upcoming Ardennes offensive. On December 13, the 13th Infantry reported the "considerable moving of troops in the enemy's rear." Incredibly, the information was logged, but apparently no one in the chain of command connected the dots. The 8th Division's intelligence summary doesn't mention it. On December 16, the Battle of the Bulge began with a furious assault on Allied lines, and the total surprise caused a degree of alarm not experienced in America since December 7, 1941.

CHAPTER 39

The Bulge

"Rack up! We're moving out!"

"We can't move out, we only have eighteen guys!" thought Vince Hagg.

Reduced to just a handful of men, Dog Company practically died on Hill 400. Most of the core members from the summer days at Camp Forrest were gone, killed or severely wounded in the fighting. The injured included the man who was, in many ways, the heart of the company, Lieutenant Leonard Lomell.* However, Dog still retained solid NCO leadership. Lomell's best friend, Jack Kuhn, rejoined the unit as Dog's first sergeant after recovering from the trauma of war, which prevented him from fighting alongside his men on Hill 400.**

Still, Hagg and the other Rangers moved around listlessly, in a fog of disbelief, as they boarded the trucks. "Our minds were blank," Hagg reflected. "It was so cold out. We had no idea where we were going."

---

*While recovering from surgery at Valley Forge General Hospital, Lomell spoke at war bond rallies. He was finally discharged from the Army because of his wounds on December 30, 1945.

**The strain of war affected even the bravest of men, including Kuhn. "He tried so hard to contain it. He'd get frustrated, and you'd see it," recalled Ruggiero. Eventually Kuhn overcame his condition and effectively led Dog Company as its first sergeant for the rest of the war.

The men of Dog Company sensed in their guts that they would face yet another difficult mission.

★ ★ ★

In the very early morning of December 16, 1944, Hitler launched his last great offensive of the war. At 5:30 A.M. sharp, a tremendous barrage from over 1,600 artillery pieces bombarded the American lines thinly spread amidst the Ardennes forest. As over a dozen German armored and infantry divisions hit the unsuspecting American troops, five U.S. divisions began to fall back in chaos. The Germans achieved nearly complete surprise as they hit a vulnerable portion of the Allied line in the Ardennes. The Battle of the Bulge had begun.

Hitler planned to drive a wedge between the British and American armies and seize the Belgian port city of Antwerp. Fancifully, he hoped to divide the Allies and force them to sue for peace, allowing him to focus on taking the eastern front.

Playing perfectly into Hitler's plan of attack, heavy overcast skies and stormy weather grounded the Allies' tank-killing planes, allowing tens of thousands of German troops and hundreds of tanks to make temporary but rapid gains deep into the Allied line. The Germans forced two regiments of the 106th Infantry Division to capitulate, achieving the largest battlefield surrender of U.S. troops in the European theater.

Dog Company and the rest of the 2nd Ranger Battalion rushed southwest to Simmerath, the tip of the spear in the northern portion of the American line. It was a crucial portion of the Bulge, and a primary focus of the German offensive. The battle-weary Rangers' mission was to help plug a hole in the vulnerable American lines.

The small German village of Kesternich, not far from Simmerath, was key to Hitler's plans for the Bulge. Kesternich, a tiny hamlet of 112 houses, sat on the German-Belgian border and also intersected an important road network. The Americans nearly disrupted Hitler's plans when the 78th "Lightning" Division seized the town on December 13.

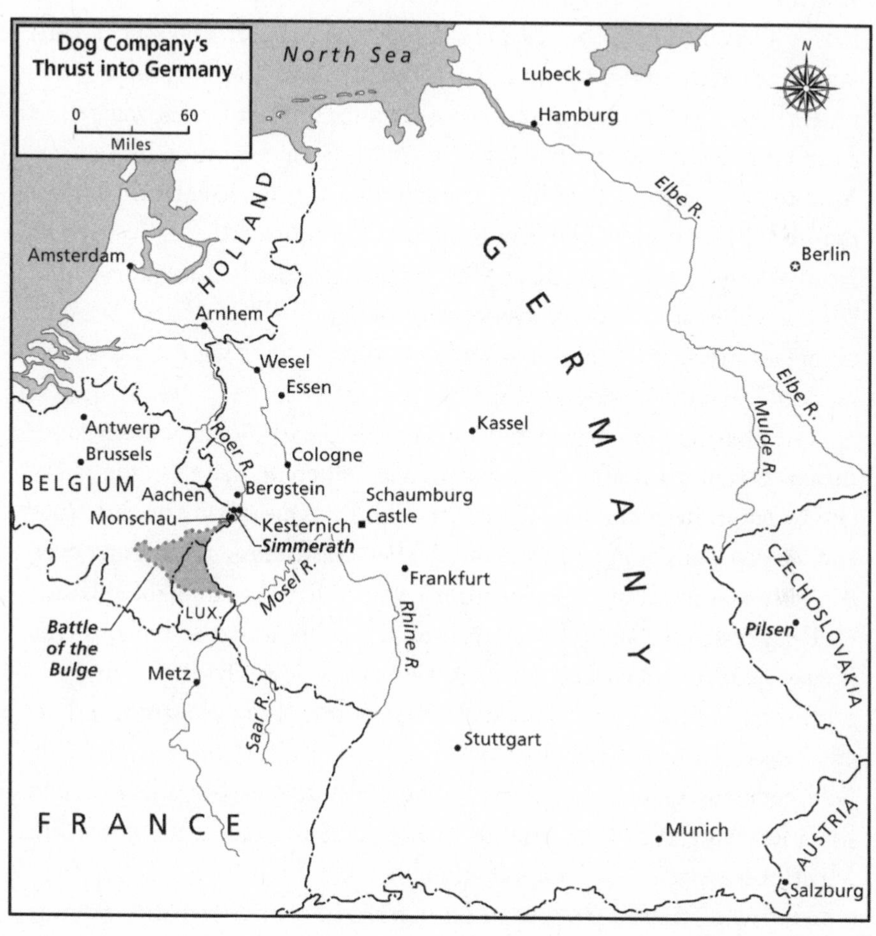

Dog Company's Thrust into Germany
0
60
Miles
North Sea
N
Lubeck
Hamburg
Elbe R.
Berlin
HOLLAND
Amsterdam
GERMANY
Arnhem
Wesel
Essen
Elbe R.
Mulde R.
Kassel
Antwerp
Brussels
Roer R.
Cologne
BELGIUM
Aachen
Bergstein
Schaumburg Castle
Monschau
Kesternich
Simmerath
Frankfurt
Mosel R.
CZECHOSLOVAKIA
LUX.
Rhine R.
Pilsen
Battle of the Bulge
Metz
Saar R.
Stuttgart
FRANCE
Munich
AUSTRIA
Salzburg

Once the 78th Division took Simmerath and Kesternich, it cut the Monschau-Düren highway, which severed the Monschau Corridor. Simmerath sat at the top of the northern shoulder of the Bulge, initially near the main thrust of Germany's advance on Antwerp. But just days before December 16, the Rangers' nemesis, the 272th Volksgrenadiers, counterattacked and recaptured Kesternich.

At 9:40 A.M. on December 16, an advance group of what was left of Dog Company rode by truck to Simmerath. Several men stayed behind in a rear area of the Hürtgen, including Captain McBride. He remained there to greet the few Rangers who returned after recovering from wounds, including Ruggiero. Although his doctor had wanted to send the wounded man away from the front, Ruggie insisted he be allowed to return to his company. "I'm going to go back even if I have to skip," he announced.

The physician finally relented and allowed the former tap dancer to return to D Company after a few days of rest. When he arrived in the Hürtgen to rejoin his comrades, at first he "didn't see everybody because they had already moved on to Simmerath." Then McBride came running over.

"Jesus Christ, Ruggie, I didn't think you were going to make it back."

Ruggie joked, "Well, I'm here, buddy, but I'm going to have to take it easy. I don't think I can eat K-Rations for a few days."

But the officer didn't laugh. At that point, Ruggerio grew serious and asked about his friends: McCrone, Adams, and others. McBride held back the tears as he shook his head. Ruggie explained, "I named five men who were close friends of mine. Every one of them got hit. Most of the men were killed by tree bursts."

McBride ordered Ruggie to rest up and recover from his wounds for several more days. After that, Ruggie was to go to Simmerath, bringing with him the crucial replacements who would help fill out the dwindling ranks of Dog Company.

When the day came, Ruggiero, along with the newly minted Rangers loaded up in a truck. As they approached Simmerath, they began to hear the sounds of war—most of them for the first time.

BOOM! BOOM!

The replacements all jumped or ducked down to shield themselves from incoming artillery they were sure were about to hit their vehicle. Unfazed by the noise, Ruggiero looked at them. "What are you ducking for?" he asked. "You can hear those things whistling. When you see me duck, you duck."

After the harrowing ride, Ruggie and the replacements arrived at Simmerath after dark.

"Everybody out!"

"Where do I go from here?" asked Ruggiero.

"Headquarters is at the top of the street. D Company is down below. You got to take those guys down there."

He found the building where Dog was holed up, but just as he got there, a round came in. This time, he knew the danger was real. He hit the dirt. So did all the rest of the men.

Standing back up and dusting himself off, Ruggie asked the Rangers standing outside the building, "Where's Captain McBride?"

"He's down in the basement," came the reply.

Looking around, Ruggiero was stunned to see so few men. "These the only guys you've got to man the mortars?"

"Yes, this is all we got left. We take turns."

Ruggerio descended the stairs into the dark cellar, where McBride greeted the veteran Ranger with a sarcastic quip: "About time you got here with somebody."

"Yeah, I've got thirteen men who are your replacements."

Counting, McBride sized up the situation quickly and said, "No, you have fifteen men." McBride asked each of the new replacements to name their former units.

Two men stepped forward and said, "We didn't volunteer to be Rangers."

"Well, you're going to spend the night here as a Ranger," said McBride. He let them go the next morning.

★ ★ ★

Now attached to the 78th Division, the 2nd Ranger Battalion took up defensive positions inside Simmerath. Dog's primary mission was to man the 81 mm mortars. "What was going on in Simmerath was actually a duel with mortars, back and forth. They were only about five hundred yards away from us. Every now and then a mortar round would come in. They wouldn't fire more than two or three," recalled one Ranger. "Near our outpost, we could hear them talking, they were that close. The 88s rained down on us. We were constantly faced with German patrols."

Besides manning the mortars, Dog Company constructed a series of two-man foxholes, which served as outposts along the perimeter of the town. As Vince Hagg hunkered down in his foxhole, the Rangers passed along constant warnings of potential attack. "We stayed out there ten or twelve hours a day," he recalled "The ground froze so hard we had trouble making a foxhole. You'd get about four to five inches in the frozen tundra, and you'd have to hack away before you got through the ground. It was colder than hell. We kept hearing, 'Be ready men; the Germans are coming. The Germans are coming; be ready for them.' There was an alert for paratroopers. They kept saying, 'Be on the watch for paratroopers.'"

During the Battle of the Bulge, the Germans launched Operation *Greif*, a special, false-flag commando operation led by the legendary German commando, SS Lieutenant Colonel Otto Skorzeny. Earlier in the war, Skorzeny rescued Benito Mussolini in a daring special operations mission. As part of Operation *Greif*, German troops wearing American uniforms parachuted or infiltrated behind American lines. They sowed chaos by changing sides to mislead American troops and capture crucial bridges. Sergeant Hoffman remembered they were warned that the Germans had captured half-tracks. "We were told to be on the watch for Germans wearing American uniforms, using American vehicles."

On December 17, the Rangers went on high alert for a German Airborne attack. "C Company of the 310th Infantry had reported observing four planes drop [German paratroopers]." The unit later confirmed that they killed one paratrooper and captured three others.

Remaining at a high level of alert, Dog and the rest of the 2nd hunkered down in Simmerath. Both the Americans and the Germans continued to probe each other's defenses with combat patrols. Dog's mortars dispatched one enemy patrol on the December 19, as the battalion's after-action report dryly noted: "Employing Company D's mortars at 10:00, Company B routed an enemy patrol which had approached too close for artillery fire."

Hagg recalled that sometimes the American patrols also ended badly. "When we would patrol, usually we had two scouts in front of us. The Germans would often let them through, go ahead. They wouldn't fire on them; they would just wait for us to come through and ambush."

As the days wore on, so did the intensity of the alerts, including an "anticipated attack by a panzer division." To counter the threat, the Americans brought up additional antitank guns to Simmerath, including "all available bazookas."

With snow blanketing the Ardennes, including Simmerath, the men of Dog spent their second Christmas together, freezing in their foxholes. Veterans and replacements huddled together in the frigid temperatures. Ruggiero recalled, "I had one of the new guys with me in the foxhole, and he was really scared." When the mortars started falling, the inexperienced Ranger started jumping.

"Take it easy," Ruggie cautioned. "You see me hugging the side of the foxhole? You do the same thing. Keep your head down."

With the constant shelling and patrols, Dog's replacements didn't stay inexperienced for long. One new Ranger, bespectacled medical student Private First Class Neil H. Shira, noticed a German creeping towards his position. "He didn't know what he was going to do, so he threw the damn hand grenade," remembered Ruggiero. "The grenade bounced. Son of a gun, the German picked it up and threw it back. Shira then picked it up again. Just as he was picking it up, it detonated.

It practically blew his hand off. Bones were sticking out. It was a bloody mess." Bravely, Shira braced his M1 against the edge of the foxhole and "just kept pulling the trigger. The German got up and ran."

Ruggiero also got hit again, this time while returning from an errand. Headquarters had made a call down to McBride, saying, "Bring a guy with you so you can get a load of mail." So McBride tagged Rugg, sending him about three hundred yards up the street to fetch the mail from headquarters around 9:00 in the morning. As McBride and Ruggiero were emerging with the day's orders and the mail, a Jeep rode in. "The Jeep was very loud, and I guess the Germans picked up on the sound," explained Ruggiero. "The Jeep damn near run me over as I was trying to get out of the way."

The Germans fired a round that just missed the vehicle. Ruggie was less lucky. "A piece of shrapnel caught me right in the nose." Blood poured down his face as his "nose swelled up the size of a football." More than sixty years later, the scar would remain visible on the one-time entertainer's face.*

Resolute, Dog remained dug in at Simmerath until the first week of January, 1945.

*"Jesus, that scar's showing even more today!" Ruggiero exclaimed while looking at his nose during the interview for this book.

CHAPTER 40

Back to Hürtgen

While the Battle of the Bulge was one of the largest and bloodiest battles the Allies fought, it was the swan song of the German Army. Hitler had denuded the eastern front of crucial men and equipment. The Russians were breaking through German lines in the east, and the irreplaceable losses suffered at the Bulge greatly weakened the German army facing the western Allies. The Germans began to retreat towards the Rhine, the last major natural waterway and defensive position in the western Allies' path to Berlin.

Placed once again in corps reserve, the Rangers moved to a rear area in the Hürtgen. In the final days of January, Dog Company would finally receive some badly needed rest and replacements. The men also went back to their all-too-familiar training regimen, just as they had following the actions at Pointe du Hoc and Brest.

On February 7, the 9th Infantry Division, followed up by the 82nd Airborne, captured the key German town of Schmidt, which had bedeviled the Allies in the Hürtgen since September 1944. With Schmidt in American hands, the Roer River's dams—the most crucial objective in the Hürtgen Forest—became the Allies' priority. Capturing the dams was a special operations mission ideally suited for the Rangers, who began planning the operation.

Their mission was "to establish a bridgehead [in the] vicinity of Dam Number Five," known as the Urft Dam. Company commanders and others scouted the area and reported finding nearby German guns that were capable of hitting the dam. More recon revealed that the dam was already stressed, making it impossible to cross over. Captain Slater and Major Williams both personally visited the massive, concrete structure.

The Rangers' planning also included interrogating a civilian German engineer who worked on the dams. The engineer revealed that the Germans had destroyed the machinery that controlled the intake and release of the water, thereby creating a continuous flow of the Roer that was flooding the area.

Preparations for the capture of the Urft Dam went forward. The officers told the men they would need to conduct the mission with lightning speed—meaning no time to tend to the wounded. "They kept telling us, 'We're going to hit the dams before they blow [them]. Be ready to jump off.' ... They told us, 'anyone that gets hit, you're not going to be able to take care of them. You're on your own. That's how fast we're going to be moving.'" Vince Hagg recalled. "I know the Marines never like to leave a guy behind, but they told us, 'If you get hit, you carry yourself. If things work out, we'll come back and get you. We're going to be running.'"

After all the planning and build-up, however, headquarters eventually scrubbed the risky mission. With the risky op canned, the Rangers shifted gears and started planning something even more important—an assault crossing of the Roer River.

CHAPTER 41

Crossing the Roer

"Take your clothes off, Rugg."

Ruggiero looked at the churning, icy waters of the Roer and replied, "Jesus, we'll freeze our asses off."

"No, you won't," McBride insisted as he began pulling off his own boots and socks.

"We got to the river, and we had to cross it. There was no damn way of crossing it without getting wet," recalled Ruggie. While most of the men kept their uniforms and boots on, McBride and Ruggiero and a few others took them off. "For most of the guys, it was up to their waists. For me, it was up to my neck. Most of the guys kept their pants and their boots on, which was the worst thing to do. You could get frostbite," Ruggiero later pointed out.

When he stepped into the cold, rushing water of the river, Ruggie's thoughts went back to the day of the landing at Pointe du Hoc. *"Jesus, I thought the water was cold on D-Day at forty-two degrees,"* he thought to himself. *"This is like ice!"*

Dog Company forded a section of the river that was about thirty feet wide. They crossed carefully, holding their weapons above their heads. Once they got to the other side, the few Rangers who decided to strip felt justified in their decision. Ruggiero recalled, "When I got across, I had all my clothes. As wet as both of us were, we put our dry clothes on, even though we were wet. The clothes felt warm."

For two weeks prior to the crossing, Dog had conducted extensive reconnaissance patrols on the other side of the river to size up German strength. The Germans were dug in but were slowly exiting the area, leaving token forces behind. Soon after the crossing, Dog encountered one such member of a remaining squad, a lone German soldier carrying a handkerchief. He offered to surrender. His unit had left him behind with a handful of other men to serve as a doomed rear guard.

As the Rangers advanced on the eastern side of the Roer, they met little resistance. One of the few casualties Dog suffered after crossing the river resulted from a mine. The esteemed Joe Stevens, known for his ever present, unlit cigar, had recently received a battlefield commission as second lieutenant. While leading a patrol, he stepped on an antipersonnel mine known as a "Bouncing Betty." When the Ranger's foot touched the mine, it triggered the device, unleashing deadly metal shot packed inside. It sprayed the air, severely wounding the newly minted Ranger officer.

★ ★ ★

After crossing the river, Dog joined Easy and Fox and once again formed into Task Force Slater, retaining the name they had used during the Brest campaign, this time attaching to the 102nd Cavalry Division.

Without infantry support clearing the way, columns of tanks are extremely vulnerable to antitank guns, mines, and infantry wielding deadly Panzerfausts. The 102nd had scouted out the positions ahead of them that needed to be cleared of German infantry equipped to destroy tanks. The 102nd was a venerable cavalry unit that had long since traded in its horses for half-tracks, armored cars, and light tanks as they advanced through Europe. The 102nd would depend on the Rangers to lead the way for the tanks.

Attached to the cavalrymen, the Rangers rode in armored half-tracks. Earlier, during several days of practice, the men had rehearsed dismounting and attacking a mock German unit, reminding them of their days working with a similar unit near Brest. Now in February, the mock exercises had become reality. Dog would speed along, and upon hitting German resistance, they would barrel out of the half-tracks and engage the Germans. After clearing the area, the men would mount back up and push deeper into Germany. The cav's light tanks utilized their main guns, and the half-tracks provided fire from .30- and .50-caliber machine guns. The unit included M5A1 Stuart tanks, M8 Greyhound armored cars, and M3 half-tracks. The 102nd was also equipped with the newest and most advanced tank in the American arsenal: the extremely fast and agile M24 Chaffee tanks, which boasted 75 mm guns.

Through the first week of March, one of the coldest European winters on record continued to torment Dog Company. Snow pelted Task Force Slater as they continued to penetrate enemy territory.

Countless times, cavalrymen and Rangers would screen ahead of V Corps' advance and dismount when they encountered German troops. "It was one town after another," recalled Ruggiero. "We'd get into a German village, and we'd see German people—not too many of them—putting up white flags. We'd tell them, 'If you have any weapons, bring them here. If we go looking through the houses, and if we find anything, you're in trouble.'"

One town in particular stood out in the former tap dancer's memory. His squad was going through the village, checking the buildings for weapons. On the way back, the street went around a bend. To ensure they wouldn't be ambushed from the rear, the veteran Ranger trailed behind. He told the rest of the men, "You guys go ahead; I'll bring up the rear."

As soon as the other Rangers made the turn, Rugg looked back and saw two German soldiers in uniform, one carrying a machine pistol. Dog's expert marksman dropped to his knee and took the hundred-yard shot. But that day, he was just carrying his carbine, which was only accurate to forty-five or fifty yards. The two rounds he fired "sailed slightly above their heads. When that happened, the taller one dropped his machine pistol and put his hands up."

Hearing the shots, the other men in the patrol came running back from around the corner.

"What's going on?"

"You see those two guys over there—go get 'em," directed the sergeant.

The Rangers quickly returned with the "soldiers" in tow. "Hey Sarge, you're going to be surprised when you take a look at these two guys," one said.

Ruggiero's jaw dropped as he saw them close up. "Oh, my God!" he exclaimed. Quickly, he asked one of the German-speaking Rangers to ask the young men some questions. The translator queried, "How old are you?" The tall one responded, "Twelve." The shorter one responded, "Nine."

"What the hell are they doing?" stormed Ruggiero.

The boys responded through the interpreter, "This is what the Führer asked us to do."*

In another town nearby, Bill Petty came upon a startling discovery:

> There was an enormous, one-story house that was large enough to billet troops. I flanked it and entered through the rear. The rooms were large, spacious, expensively furnished. It was vacant, and I walked toward the front door to get back to the outfit. As I went, I had another look at the rooms, wondering who could afford to live in such a home. When I came to the finest room near the door, I discovered a shocking surprise. At first, I thought that a beautiful little girl was asleep in a large bed. I moved closer to wake her softly so she could not be frightened. I wanted to find out where her parents were. But she could not tell me. She was not asleep, and she would never be again. Nor could I frighten her. That was all past, for she was dead. She was laid out for burial in a white dress that reached beyond her feet. Five red roses rested across her young breast. They must have indicated her age, for she looked about five. Beauty had not left her at death.

---

*Later, Ruggiero commented, "I hated to see when little boys dress up in uniform at parades. It reminded me of that experience." Two boys from his town who dressed up for parades later died in Iraq and Afghanistan.

I stood motionless and quiet by the bed, as though I too was dead. I sort of wished I was at that moment. I wished I could take her place, leave the lovely child to play, to run and jump, and to giggle and laugh. As I was having these thoughts, I saw the cause of death. Shrapnel. She must have been outside playing when the shell landed, for the house only had minor damage. Shrapnel it was. The left leg was missing from the knee down. The left arm was gone at the elbow—thus, the need for the long dress and the roses where the forearm had been.

The war had not bothered me much throughout the months of combat, except when friends were killed, and certainly not much concern for myself. To me, it was a miserable and horrible affair that involved the Germans trying to kill us and we attempting to do the same to them. No thought had ever entered my mind pertaining to the terrible results to helpless and frightened children as we struggled throughout our own madness until this day. While scrutinizing the little girl's wounds and their source, I realized the predicament that thousands of children were trapped if they were unfortunate enough to live in active battle zones. Many had already, and still more would meet the same fate as the beauty lying motionless and alone in the large bed. These facts, as I absorbed them, upset me deeply. I still think about them at seventy-four.

In another nameless town, Task Force Slater encountered more German holdouts. "They told us to go in and wipe 'em out. We went in there like hell, you know, storming in there. We had no problem taking the town. We went in maybe about 5:30 or 6:00 P.M. and kicked their ass out of there and took the crossroads," recounted Vince Hagg.

Dog Company then headed for an empty field just outside the village and dug in for the night. However, having occupied the village for some time, some of the recently displaced German soldiers had girlfriends among the civilians. What happened next reminded the Rangers of the incident at Loc Maria near Brest. "When it got dark, the girlfriends went back to the Germans and told them where we were," Hagg remembered. "We got pounded by artillery. We got hit the whole night. Men were constantly yelling, 'Medic! Medic! Medic!' They answered the call. They had to have guts to do that. When daybreak finally broke, we stuck our heads out of the foxhole. I was spitting blood from the concussion, that's how bad it was, the whole night."

Hagg continued, reflecting on the memory, "The shelling would get to you, being in battle day in and day out. Have you ever seen a shell-shocked guy? It is something to see. It's scary. They're half crying; their eyes are way open. They've just gone berserk."

The heavy shelling aggravated an old wound inside Hoffman. "I heard the shell come in. It must have triggered something." In his mind, Hoffman was back on Hill 400 where an artillery round nearly killed him. The incident in the Hürtgen had been so traumatic that he just blocked it from his memory—until now. Under the constant shelling, Hoffman relived his traumatic, devastating experience at Bergstein. With his nerves at the breaking point, his eyes grew to the size of saucers, but the stunned Ranger couldn't see anything. He sat in frozen silence. A combat medic tagged him as "severe psycho-neurosis" and brought Hoffman to a rear area.

For what seemed like eternity—it could have been hours or days—he lay on the stretcher in the back of an ambulance. Eventually, when the rear door was opened, Hoffman emerged. "The bright sunshine and cold air hit my face." To his horror, Hoffman saw a uniformed German soldier looking down at him. Jolted by the sight, the Ranger's brain took several seconds to register what was going on: The German orderly was a POW pressed into service. Hoffman realized that he and the other wounded soldiers were still in American hands. Eventually, the Army sent him back to Paris, where a psychiatrist evaluated him and stamped his papers for evacuation to the United Kingdom.

Hoffman would never return to Dog Company. Instead, he would spend most of the remaining months of the war in Britain as an MP. Recovered from the trauma, he would later retire from the U.S. Army as a master sergeant.

★ ★ ★

On March 30, the enemy suddenly ambushed trailing elements of the 102nd, seizing the cavalry's kitchen truck. Fanatical elements of the SS still had sufficient strength after multiple attempts to clean them out had failed. The attack began when "an enemy bazooka shell struck a light tank, instantly killing three Rangers." As the Rangers pursued, the Germans opened up "with machine guns, mortars, and antitank fire." Task Force Slater was facing two hundred SS troops from the 6th SS Mountain Division. The Rangers were "pinned down, and tanks had to be used to evacuate the wounded." Eventually the Rangers broke off the attack and continued pushing forward. But with their newly captured American booty, the SS undoubtedly ate well for the next few days.

Despite this brief German victory, the food-truck skirmish was not emblematic of what was happening in the rest of the Third Reich. Germany was collapsing. The enemy's resistance seemed to melt away in front of Task Force Slater as the Germans made a headlong retreat toward the last major, natural barrier on the western front—the Rhine River. The rest of the massive German army sat encircled in the Ruhr Valley, and the Russians were breaking through in the east, driving towards Berlin.

Task Force Slater pushed further and further into Germany, traversing via the infamous autobahn network of highways. Along the way, Dog, Easy, and Fox captured a German airfield, including several operational aircraft.

The Rangers eventually crossed the Rhine River at night on March 26. Quite anti-climactically, the Rangers rolled easily across one of the largest pontoon bridges ever created; another unit had secured the historic waterway days earlier.

The long, brutal march from Pointe du Hoc to final victory was almost over.

CHAPTER 42

The Last Act

"You forgot to duck!"

Jack Kuhn welcomed Sheldon Bare with a handshake and a hug. The Ranger, who had been wounded first on Pointe du Hoc and then on Hill 400, was once again back with his brothers, this time in an obscure German town in the heart of the crumbling Third Reich. Yet another Ranger, George Schneller, initially thought to be mortally wounded at Pointe du Hoc, miraculously recovered from his life-threatening back wound to take up arms again with his brothers in Dog Company. Such scenes would be replayed over and over again as wounded Rangers recovered and returned to fight alongside their comrades.

Bolstered by the return of a few "old timers," the men embarked on a combat mission that turned into an extraordinary sightseeing opportunity. As D Company made its way into the heart of Germany, the men happened upon the colossal walls of the centuries-old, stunningly picturesque Schaumburg Castle. The structure looked like something straight out of a Brothers Grimm fairy tale. Its inner keep contained a looming, one-hundred-foot high tower designed to protect the area's nobility from enemy attack. The ancient fortress officially lay outside of Dog's area of operations; however, reports had come in that a dozen or so Germans occupied it. On their own initiative, the Rangers decided to seize the castle. Dashing across the drawbridge-like causeway, storming the gates, they rounded up a couple of Germans stragglers. They also met the castle's elderly, dedicated caretakers, a husband and wife who, despite the war, had stayed to protect the building.

The men marveled at the medieval fortress and its ornate furnishings. They found a bed in the queen's chambers that could "hold six or seven guys." Unbelievably large, the castle housed a labyrinth of secret rooms and chambers. "They wouldn't allow us to go in the underground portion of the castle because they said we'd get lost," recalled Bare. Schaumburg also contained a collection of 300,000 Kriegsmarine books that had been moved there for safekeeping. The library was massive, filled with tomes and maps of all kinds, remembered Bare. "I kept rooting through it, and—I couldn't believe it—I found a book on Altoona."

As Task Force Slater penetrated the crumbling ruins of the Reich, they met minimal resistance. More often, the men came across displaced persons from all over Europe, as well as German civilians. Ruggiero remembered one horrific scene. He found a dead mother and a baby lying side by side. "They took cyanide capsules. They swallowed the capsules and believed in the Führer. It was horrible."

The Rangers were sent to act as a screening force for the armor located between General Courtney Hodges's First Army and General George Patton's Third Army. The Rangers sliced south towards Pilsen, Czechoslovakia, where they were given a much-needed rest and served as corps honor guard.

On May 8, 1945, Germany officially surrendered. Vince Hagg recalled, "When the war ended, the guys didn't make too much of it. We could see it coming. It was no big deal. We were focused in on Japan. There was constant talk of Dog Company deploying to the invasion of Japan, which we all thought was going to be bloody."

But in Pilsen, Dog went into peacetime mode, prompting Kuhn and Ruggiero, Dog's intrepid entertainers, to dream up a program and look for a place to perform. Whenever the men had a break or were in a rear area, these two and their volunteers always put on a show. Ruggerio recalled the slap-stick comedy:

> One of our shows included Jack coming out on the stage and saying, "Let's open the show with a bang." I had a carbine that was filled with blanks, and I fired it. A large black crow that I had killed earlier plopped on the stage.
>
> One of our skits included where I was a stand-in or a stunt guy. The stand-in always gets the beating while the hero never gets touched. The hero in this case was a big guy. Somebody beat on me with a bat filled with flour. We even had a table that we cut up and taped together. The big guy, who had big ears like Clark Gable, would pick me up and drop me over his head on the table. I had to do this three times!
>
> In the last show, Jack Kuhn and I found a massive theater, complete with floodlights and a stage. It was our biggest show. We had everything we needed. I got to pick out all the actors. The title was *Harry Goes Home from War*. The moral of the story was that when Harry got home, he always had trouble with his mother-in-law.

In one scene, the men used condoms to stand in for bubbles floating around Harry. Eventually, Harry gave his mother a gift. He said it was a music box, but it was actually a hand grenade. "I had a fifty-five-gallon drum and a small stick of TNT, which detonated during the show" Ruggie explained.

After the show, a major in the USO approached Ruggiero. "Can I ask you a question? Did you do all this?"

"Yes."

"Where'd you come up with all these ideas?"

"Hollywood."

The major looked at him incredulously and then made an offer to the former "Tommy Knight" that many soldiers would not refuse. "I can take you back to the USO and give you a couple more stripes if you want to come with me."

"What? Are you kidding me?" Ruggie laughed.

"No, I'm not," responded the USO officer sincerely.

Ruggiero looked directly into the major's eyes. "No. I fought with these guys. When I was hit they took care of me. They were always there to help me. No thanks."

Victory against Japan was finally achieved in August 1945, but the 2nd Ranger Battalion remained in Europe until October. Finally, on the sixteenth, the battle-hardened Rangers, whose journey began at Pointe du Hoc and who had fought more than halfway across Europe, departed for home, fittingly, aboard the USS *America*. Slater, Ruggiero, Kuhn, Bare, Sundby, McBride, Webb, Stein, Petty, and a few others were all that was left of the group that had trained at Camp Forrest. On October 23, the survivors finally reached American soil. Stepping ashore at Newport News in Virginia, the Rangers of Dog Company were deactivated without ceremony.

Epilogue

In the fall of 1945, the boys of Pointe du Hoc were finally reunited with their family and friends in their hometowns across America. After enduring over two years of intense training and relentless combat, the survivors of Dog Company returned home—some to children they had never met or hardly knew. Embracing their loved ones and the lives they left behind before fighting in the most deadly world war in the history of mankind, the battle-hardened Rangers of Dog proudly wore their brown wool "Ike" jackets sporting the iconoclastic, diamond-shaped golden eagle known as the "Ruptured Duck." As time passed, most of the men of Dog hung up their uniforms and did their best to assume the comparatively mundane rhythms of civilian life.

An exception was Captain Slater, who along with a few others, remained a professional soldier. He valiantly fought in Korea but was captured by the Chinese. Despite the hardships of captivity, The Duke's spirit never broke. After the war, he remained in uniform until he retired as a lieutenant colonel.

Len Lomell recovered from his wounds at Valley Forge Hospital in Pennsylvania and later gave rousing patriotic speeches to sell war bonds. At the end of the war, he resigned his commission, attended law school, and became a highly successful attorney.

Lomell's best friend, Jack Kuhn, pursued a career in law enforcement. Eventually, the people of Altoona, Pennsylvania, elected him sheriff.

James Earl Rudder's star continued to rise. He assumed the position of Texas Land Commissioner and later became president of Texas A&M University.

Bud Potratz resumed civilian life in a sleepy, small town in Michigan.

For his actions on Pointe du Hoc, George Kerchner received the Distinguished Service Cross for "extraordinary heroism," and he continued to serve his country as a member of the Maryland National Guard. After recovering from his wounds, Kerchner went home to Baltimore, where he and his wife raised four children. He also returned to the Arundel Ice Cream Company, where he had previously worked as a "soda jerk" to help his family earn money during the Great Depression. Ultimately, Kerchner worked his way up to become president and general manager of the company.

Ruggiero decided not to pursue his former dream of becoming a Hollywood tap dancer. Instead of entertaining people, Ruggie chose to focus on saving them, and he became a firefighter in his hometown of Plymouth, Massachusetts, eventually retiring as a captain.

McBride went to work for the U.S. Postal Service, serving as a postal carrier on a rural route near Bismarck, North Dakota.

Sheldon Bare returned home to children he hardly knew. After taking thirty days off, he went back to his job with the Pennsylvania Railroad and later worked to better the lives of the disabled.

Bill Petty became a director at a boys' camp and relied on the hard-won lessons he learned on and off the battlefield to help shape the lives of the young men. For many of the boys at the camp, Bill assumed a strong paternal role, becoming for them the loving, caring father he never had.

Petty stayed in close touch with his best friend and "pet ape," Herman Stein. After returning home, Stein, ever the gifted climber, became a roofer and built a successful business. Always true to his comrades of Dog Company, Stein served as a lifeline for many of them. Stein helped his friends get back on their feet when they were down on their luck, even giving a few "a roof over their heads" during hard times.

While many men of Dog Company attempted to stay in touch after the war through reunions and the Ranger Association, many simply vanished, including Bill Cruz, who was never seen again.

Pointe du Hoc and Hill 400, as well as all the other battles, created indelible, invisible scars that each veteran managed in his own private way. Morris Webb and many of the other men dealt with PTSD before the condition was clinically defined. Relentlessly shelled on Hill 400, Webb bore the brunt of most of the counterattacks. While standing in line to be discharged, he fainted. Admitted to a military hospital, Web spent an entire week recovering from the episode. "I was lying there in bed when I woke up. As I lay there, I felt my heart stop and knew that that couldn't be. So I jumped out of bed. When I got to the duty nurse, she saw what happened. My hands and wrist had drawn up like claws and turned purple."

Webb saw a psychiatrist who compared "his nerves to a rubber band, but like a rubber band that had been wound too tight. When you turn it loose, it will snap back to normal, but on rare occasions, they break. When the nerves break, they call it a nervous breakdown, shellshock, combat fatigue. That's what happened to me." Doctors subjected Webb to years of electric shock treatment in a vain attempt to remove the PTSD. However, according to Webb, his true salvation was the unconditional love of his wife, whom he credits with curing him of the devastating psychological effects of the war.

Other men suffered similar fates, including former radio operator Robert Fruhling. On June 6, 1984, he could take no more of the war. He placed a gun to his head and killed himself. That tragic day was, in fact, a very special one for others who served in Dog Company: it was the fortieth anniversary of D-Day, a powerful day of healing for many.

On June 6, 1984, as he stood atop the perilous cliffs in Normandy, President Reagan delivered one of his greatest, most famous speeches, "The Boys of Pointe du Hoc." At this historic event, many of the men of Dog

Company, then well into their sixties, reunited to commemorate the invasion that changed the course of the war. As they gathered on that sunny day at the site of one of most critical battles in WWII, Rangers Lomell, Kuhn, Sundby, Potratz, Ruggiero, Petty, Stein, and all other veterans living and dead were finally recognized for their pivotal role in assuring the Allied D-Day victory. After delivering his speech, the president visited Omaha Beach and stood silently as he read the powerful, poignant promise inscribed on the monument in the Garden of the Missing: "TO THESE WE OWE THE HIGH RESOLVE THAT THE CAUSE FOR WHICH THEY DIED SHALL LIVE."

Reagan's speech commemorating the valiant acts and heroism of the "Boys of Pointe du Hoc" profoundly inspired the nation and our troops during the Cold War. As historian Gary Wills aptly put it, the President's compelling words conjured up "the past as present." The Boys of Pointe Du Hoc were held up as the gold standard to serve as a powerful example. According to Doug Brinkley, "the message was clear: These men fought for freedom against Nazism, so don't we now have an obligation to fight against Soviet-style communism?"

Most importantly, Reagan's emotional, heartfelt speech remembered the tremendous contributions and sacrifices made by Dog Company and countless other veterans—at that time largely forgotten. Atop the windy cliffs of Pointe du Hoc that June day, the President's words thrust these heroes into the national spotlight, helping WWII veterans take their rightful place as what many consider "the greatest generation."

Now well into their nineties and down to only a handful, the men of Dog Company are fading away, but their legacy will never be forgotten. Their courage, fortitude, and spirit endure in new generations of Rangers. Many of them were regular citizens—patriotic volunteers asked to do the impossible. The Rangers of Dog Company answered the call, rose to the challenge, and, in the process, discovered the greatness within them. Together they transcended the ordinary and helped change the destiny of the world.

Notes

Twenty years ago, I began interviewing veterans—first the Airborne and then the Rangers. In 1995, I created a World War II oral history project called the Drop Zone.* The first online oral history project for World War II veterans, the Drop Zone was a virtual community comprised of oral and "e-Histories" based on my interviews with veterans. My books are an extension of this oral history project. The goal was to preserve the stories of World War II veterans. Over the course of two decades, I amassed over 4,000 interviews, creating one of the largest private collections of oral histories in the United States.

Through this process, I formed some of my earliest and strongest friendships with the men of Dog Company, especially Len Lomell, who introduced me to other Ranger legends, such as Herman Stein and Sid Salomon. Over the years, I have interviewed scores of Rangers, including most of the surviving veterans from Dog Company. I went to their homes and their reunions. And I travelled overseas to visit their places of battle, where I interviewed many German soldiers. I even spent the night camped out on Hill 400, the location of one of Dog Company's most important battles.

Three years ago, I serendipitously found myself at the Jersey shore while on a research trip and remembered that Len Lomell, the main character of *Dog Company*, lived in Toms River, New Jersey. I called him up and stopped by his house that day. I watched a Yankees game with him, while the 91-year-old Ranger and I each sipped a can of beer. I ended up interviewing Len once again about his experiences with the Rangers in WWII. That afternoon, the idea for the book came to both of us, and with Len's blessing I decided to write *Dog Company*.

---

*www.TheDropZone.org

I included a few of these oral histories in my book *Beyond Valor: World War II's Ranger and Airborne Veterans Reveal the Heart of Combat.* Similarly, *Dog Company* contains many stories drawn from my personal interviews with Ranger veterans. In the endnotes below, I have designated quotes and sections of the book taken from those interviews, using OH to signify "oral history."

Sadly, over the years, many of my close friends from Dog Company and other Ranger units have passed on. To fill in pieces of the story that I was unable to gather through interviews, I consulted a variety of archives and obtained oral history transcripts from the Eisenhower Center in New Orleans, Louisiana, which are designated EC below.

Throughout the writing of the book, I consulted numerous after-action reports, maps, and other materials on the unit, all of which reside at the National Archives and Record Administration in College Park, Maryland (NARA). As in my prior books, I painstakingly cross-checked the oral histories with the documentary record and vice versa. During this research, I found the initial file and interviews taken during the war by legendary historians Charles Taylor and Forrest Pogue. These interviews were part of a special study called *Small Unit Actions*, created by the Historical Division, U.S. War Department, 1946. I used a draft copy of the document, which was chock full of details that were missing from the final version.

Prologue

xi "We stand on a lonely, windswept point... arms." President Ronald Reagan, "The Boys of Pointe du Hoc." Delivered on the cliffs of Pointe du Hoc, June 6, 1984.

xii "Sixty-year-old Rangers... now." Douglas Brinkley, *The Boys of Pointe du Hoc* (New York: William Morrow, 2005), 180.

xii "All these younger guys... much." Ibid.; (OH, Herman Stein).

xiii their "longest day." (OH, various); numerous Rangers told the author that during Reagan's speech they thought about Hill 400, *their* longest day.

xiii "Fix bayonets!" (OH, Petty); L-Rod Petty, unpublished memoir. Petty gave a copy of his memoir to the author, and later Herman Stein also gave the author a copy of the same document. Note that this document is not paginated.

xiii "Let's go get the bastards!" (OH).

xiv "Go!" Ibid.

xiv “WA-WOO-WOOHOO!” The author interviewed several veterans who described the sound they made as akin to the “Rebel yell” and attempted to duplicate it for him in their older years.

xiv “We stood up just like in a movie.... one.” (OH, Petty); Petty memoir.

xiv “With bayonets shining... death.” Petty memoir.

1. Dog Company

1 “From here over... Battalion” (OH).

1 “The Duke.” Ibid.

1 “This is my first sergeant, Leonard Lomell.” Ibid.

1 “Find out when we can feed this bunch.” Ibid. Most of the early recollections come from Bill Hoffman, whom the author interviewed extensively.

2 “Anybody interested...”... “get a horse” Ibid.

2 “Get back to work.” Ibid.

2 “What are you doing standing out here?” Ibid.

2 “the moment of truth.” Ibid.

3 “Go on inside.” Ibid.

3 “I don’t see a problem here. Process Sergeant Hoffman.” Ibid.

3 “Get your butt.... your gear.” Ibid.

4 “I hope you... British.”... “the frontier.” Lucian K. Truscott, *Command Missions: A Personal Story* (New York: Button, 1954), 40–41.

4 Adopted by immigrant parents Personal biography provided by Lomell to the author.

5 “a beautiful spirit and cherished every moment of life.” Obituary for Duke Slater, *ABQ Journal,* April 17, 2011, http://obits.abqjournal.com/obits/show/215449.

6 The original core of Dog Company hailed from the Northeast (OH); unit records.

6 *“What did I...* us.” (OH, Sidney Salomon) Salomon and the author became close friends. The same quote also appears in the outstanding book *The Fool Lieutenant: A Personal Account of D-Day and World War II* by Marcia Moen and Margo Heinen (Elk River, MN: Meadowlark Publishing, 2000), 64. The authors did an excellent job chronicling the life of Lieutenant Robert Edlin, whom I also interviewed extensively.

7 *"Dirty Dozen."* The author has conducted over 5,000 interviews with veterans of America's elite units from the Rangers to the OSS.

7 "What they really tried... the training." (OH); Captain Robert A. Rowe, papers transcribing interviews with Leonard G. Lomell, conducted August 24, 1988. (Carlisle, PA: The United States Army Military History Institute), 42. Rowe was assembling a book on D-Day and conducted a number of interviews. Rowe's interviews nicely complemented the dozen or so interviews I conducted with Lomell. The papers reside at the U.S. Army Military History Institute in Carlisle, Pennsylvania.

7 "In those days.... the process." Ibid.

7 "You think you're pretty tough, huh?" Ibid., 3–8.

7 *"Jesus Christ.... knocking him out."* Ibid.

8 "one of those guys.... every blow." Ibid.

8 "You know, Captain, maybe.... with you guys." Ibid.

8 *"He's never going to quit.... whole company!"* Ibid.

8 "Duke Slater was the roughest.... at times." Ibid.

8 "typical day" (OH).

8 "assume position." Ibid.

8 "Ready, exercise!" Ibid.

9 "It made a man out of you." Ibid.

9 "What's up?" (OH, Webb).

9 "Pat McCrone and Larry Johnson....".. . "McCrone is dead." Ibid.

9 "You son of a bitch!... rat!" (OH).

10 "pit." (OH).

10 "They'd put a whole platoon.... sawdust in." (OH, Hoffman).

10 "Go get 'em!... Throw 'em out!" Ibid.

10 "Guys got hurt.... throw people out." (OH, Ruggiero.).

10 "It was about competition.... you could take" (OH, Hoffman).

11 As the men of Dog... Ranger Joe Camelo (OH); story also appeared in Ronald Lane, *Rudder's Rangers: The True Story of the 2nd Ranger Battalion's D-Day Combat Action* (Longwood, Florida: Ranger Associates, Inc., 1979), 21.

11 "Terrified, everyone ran in opposite directions." (OH).

11 "Shit was flying everywhere." (OH).

11 "Rangerism... the doctrine of a personal fight.... two fronts today." Robert W. Black, *The Battalion* (Mechanicsburg, PN: Stackpole Books, 2006), 10. A former Ranger who has spent a life-

time chronicling Ranger history, Black published a very well-researched book.

2. "Rangers? Bullshit!"

12 "Rangers? Bullshit!" Black, *The Battalion*, 12.
12 "Blood-in-the-Boots" Ibid; (OH).
12 "speed march" (OH).
12 "There better be blood in your boots after the march!" (OH, Bare).
13 "By midafternoon . . . like flies." . . . "Slater . . . exhausted himself." (OH, Stein); unpublished memoir, Herman Stein. Obtained through his daughter Debbie Stein-Caldwell. Note that Stein's memoir is not paginated.
13 *"If these guys . . . something about it."* Ibid.
13 "On one extended break . . . . like a zombie." Ibid.
13 "I thought judo . . . . nonsense." . . . "Bare . . . hardest punch," (OH, Bare).
13 "Come on, hit me." Ibid.
13 "I don't want to do that, staff sergeant." . . . *"I outweigh him . . . flatten him."* Ibid.
14 "I remember . . . . after that." Ibid.
14 "seemed to have nerves snipped." . . . "He was fearless." (OH, Webb).
14 "But after only a couple of months on the job . . ." (Dog Diary). The entry comes from a personal diary by Leonard Lomell and Jack Kuhn for most of Dog Company's training period up through May 19, 1944. Kuhn sent the diary was sent to his wife several weeks before D-Day. The diary was then transferred to Leonard Lomell, who loaned it to the author for the completion of this book. Other references to this diary will be designated Dog Diary. Note: the diary is not paginated, so page numbers will not be included in the notes.

3. Big Jim

15 "I've been sent down . . . . Any questions?" Lane, *Rudder's Rangers*, 22.
15 Biographical information obtained from reading Thomas M. Hatfield, *Rudder: From Leader to Legend*. Centennial Series of the Association of Former Students. (College Station, TX: Texas A&M University, 2011).

16 "ragtag orphan mob, with no military bearing or discipline." Lane, *Rudder's Rangers,* 23.
16 "Boiling mad and red-faced." Ibid.
16 "Nearing our destination... in his Jeep." Stein, unpublished memoir.
16 "pet ape" (OH, Stein).
17 "sort of waddle like a duck." Lane, *Rudder's Rangers,* 23.
17 "He would lash me... hated every blow." Petty, unpublished memoir.
17 "Sorry, son, you don't qualify.... You're in." Lane, *Rudder's Rangers,* 24. (OH, Ruggiero); The author interviewed Tom Ruggiero extensively, who graciously spent many, many hours of his time assisting with the book.

4. Fort Pierce and Overseas

21 "In the daytime... drive you crazy," (OH, Hoffman).
21 "No Swimming!" (OH).
21 "AAAUUUGGHH!" Ibid.
22 "They stung like a bastard." (OH, Ruggiero).
22 "The first thing.... Damn near drowned." Ibid.
23 "Sir, I don't want.... really don't want to leave," (OH, Hoffman).
23 "Get back to your car." Ibid.
23 "Like anything else... leave." Ibid.
23 "Hey, Charlie, Tom..."... "that's the unfairness of it all." Rowe papers, 99.
24 "Private Drodouski moved... hands on him." (Dog Diary)
25 "terrific scare" Ibid.
25 "The CO... was so fed up..."... "to the hospital." Ibid.
25 "the Rangers had something to do with trees, and that was OK by her." Black, *The Battalion*, 36.
26 "Ritchie Boys," The author has conducted much research on the topic and wrote *They Dared Return*, which featured one of the Ritchie Boys.
26 "We then moved out.... our mission." (Dog Diary).
27 propaganda films such as the classic film *Next of Kin*... "sex morality" Ibid.
27 "the big day arrived." Ibid.

27 "Pat McCrone remembers looking up at the largest ship..." (OH, Webb).

27 "bad case of laryngitis." ... "quiet at last!" (Dog Diary).

28 "stretched for miles before you could even get a Pepsi-Cola or candy." Ibid.

28 "cement foreign relations with the English girls" Ibid.

28 "full-time sport, calling them butterflies and USO ... soldiers." Ibid.

28 "If we were hit ... conditions." ... "greatly impressed." Ibid.

5. Bude

29 "We all received good billets.... English people," (OH, Lomell).

30 "on the job" (Dog Diary)"showed very well." Ibid.

30 "save argument, the score ended in a tie. " Ibid.

30 "stress was placed on scrambling much faster." Ibid.

30 Information about BARs. Ibid.

31 Colonel Thomas Trevor biographical information. Hatfield, *Rudder*, 158.

31 McBride, the freckled Scotch-Irishman, and Cruz, a smart, dark-complexioned Latino American... (OH).

32 "All right, you guys, listen up ..."... "gear packed." Lane, *Rudder's Rangers,* 50; Dog Diary.

33 "take the breach mechanism ...." ... "fire mission." Ibid.

33 "The company.... taken prisoner." Ibid.

33 they washed it all down with some English ale. Ibid.

33 "the feeling when one gets.... raring to go." Ibid.

6. The Needles

34 Account of Raymond Reindeau's fall. (OH) ; (Dog Diary).

34 "Tough Guy." Ibid.

35 "bouncing against the cliffs" ... "miraculously." Ibid.

35 "What the hell happened to you?" ... "everybody what you're wearing!" (OH, Ruggiero).

36 "January 31, Blue Monday—SNAFU ...." ... "named Doris." (Dog Diary).

7. The Mission

37 Scene with James Earl Rudder and Max F. Schneider in Bradley Omar's office was drawn from Hatfield, *Rudder*, 93 and Lane, *Rudder's Rangers*, 71.

38 Description of the guns of Pointe du Hoc taken from Gordon A. Harrison, *Cross Channel Attack* (Department of the Army, 1951), 196.

38 "the most formidable." Ibid, 176.

38 "the most dangerous mission of D-Day." Brief provided by Leonard Lomell; General Omar Bradley, *A Soldier's Story* (New York, NY: Henry Holmes, 1951), 269. Bradley recounts his conversation with Rudder.

38 *"You've got to be kidding. This is just to scare me."* Black, *The Battalion*, 59.

39 "festering sores as the internal shell fragments worked their way through the skin." Hatfield, *Rudder*, 97.

39 "suffered from Neurasthenic condition . . . mental crackup." Ibid.

39 "interceded in order to utilize [Schneider's] services in the initial invasion of the continent." Ibid.

39 "It can't be done . . . . that cliff." Samuel Eliot Morison, *History of the United States Naval Operations in World War II, vol. 11, The Invasion of France and Germany* (Edison, NJ: Castle Books, 2001), 126.

39 "Sir, my Rangers can do the job for you." Lane, *Rudder's Rangers*, 72.

39 "No soldier in my command . . . . Provisional Ranger Force." Bradley, *A Soldier's Story*, 269.

40 General details on the Normandy invasion were drawn from a variety of sources including Harrison's *Cross Channel Attack*.

41 "Praise the Lord." . . . "Tilt." (OH, Eikner); James Eikner, "Ranger Signal Plan: Notes on Signal Communications June 6–June 8, 1944," (College Park, MD: National Archives, U.S. Army Operations Reports, 2nd Ranger Battalion, record group 319, stack 270, row 19, boxes 1 and 2, backup for small unit actions).

8. Final Preparations

42 "Fire in the hole!" (OH).

42 "We learned how to handle . . . . before." (OH); Rowe papers, 10.

42 "Fights were an everyday affair with us, if anyone dared challenge us" Ibid., 11.

43 "You didn't earn those boots!" . . . "We were so proud . . . anything." Ibid.

43 Account regarding Staff Sergeant Jack Kuhn and another Ranger traveling to London is derived from the Dog Diary.

44 "that . . . could be successfully done from LCAs." Ibid.

44 "all the beer they could drink" and "A good time was had by all." (OH); (Dog Diary).

44 "Company D's commander has displayed . . . . known as Robin." (Dog Diary).

44 "Foot me, Jack . . . very helpful training," (Dog Diary).

45 "habit of trying the hardest cliffs." Ibid.

45 Kerchner's biography comes from the author's interview with the veteran.

45 "Sigurd Sundby was about . . . " ..."kept to himself." (OH).

45 "big show," (Dog Diary).

45 "If one looked seaward, he would have seen huge geysers spouting skyward." Ibid.

46 "it was a full-scale dress rehearsal. ...a firing exercise in which the Navy shelled" (Kerchner, EC).

46 "Above the roar . . . top of his lungs." (Dog Diary).

46 "That's all right. All first sergeants get their due in combat. I'll see you in combat." (OH, Lomell); the author interviewed Lomell about this particular subject and obtained the dialogue.

9. A Tough Spot for a Landing

47 "That's It! . . . " . . . "that is, the seaside." Dr. Walter Block, letter chronicling the meeting, from the 2nd Ranger Battalion history entitled *The Narrative History of the 2nd Ranger Battalion*, National Archives (NARA), record group 407, entry 427, stack 270, INB5.0-5.1.31, Operation Reports, 2nd Ranger Infantry Battalion, boxes 1 and 2.

49 "casualties will be high; we already filled out 517 death certificates." The author obtained the quote from Sheldon Bare, who remembers the incident. While the author cannot confirm the number 517, paperwork for death certificates was readied by the battalion.

10. "Into the Valley of Death"

51 *"I have a hell of a hot hand."* (OH, Lomell).
51 "Father Lacy is aboard!" Ibid.
51 "Jewish boys, Protestant boys. . . ."; "protection for tomorrow." (OH, Lomell); Rowe papers, 31.
51 "Hell, no. . . . to ask for it." (OH, Lomell); Rowe papers, 10–11.
51 "fat little Irishman" (OH, Lomell).
51 "When you land. . . . you do the fighting." (OH, Kerchner); (EC).
52 "You fellas have broken. . . . one of you." Lane, *Rudder's Rangers*, 60.
52 "our newly appointed commander. . . . complaining loudly about it." (OH, South).
53 "The process of arresting. . . and shouting [men in] uniforms." Ibid.
53 "Get out of here." Ibid.
53 "never wanted to hear anything about Rangers or the name 'Ranger' again." (OH).
53 "We're not going to risk you getting knocked out on the first round." Stephen Ambrose, *The Victors: Eisenhower And His Boys The Men Of World War II* (New York, NY: Simon & Shuster, 1998), 144.
53 "I'm sorry to have to disobey you, sir, but if I don't take it, [the mission] may not go." *Ibid.*
54 "You know, I'm worried about tomorrow. . . . and all reassuring one another" (OH, Lomell); Rowe papers, 33.
54 "let it all come out" . . . "a silent oath" Petty, unpublished memoir.
56 *"'Onward, onward rode the four hundred. . ." " [Rangers] into the Valley of Death].'"* Ibid.
56 "Rangers, man your craft" (OH); Patrick K. O'Donnell, *Beyond Valor* (New York, NY: The Free Press, 2001), 145.
56 "We'll get you another one" . . . "OK, I'll do that, Rugg." (OH, Ruggiero).

11. "The Sky Was Burning"

57 *"Alles kaput! Alles kaput!"* The unique German perspective on Pointe du Hoc came from Helmut Konrad von Keusgen's book *Pointe du Hoc* (Garbsen, Germany: Hek Creativ Verlag, 2006). I highly recommend the book. The actual oral histories were painstakingly translated from French and German into English by D-Day histo-

rian and tour guide Paul Woodadge and his wife, Myriam Woodadge. Paul, an expert on the area, graciously reviewed this section of the book and is the man to see for anyone wanting to tour Normandy's battlefields. For more info, see his website at http://www.ddayhistorian.com/.

57 "It seemed like the sky was burning . . . killed." von Keusgen, *Pointe du Hoc*, via Woodadge.

57 RAF bombers dropped 635 tons of ordnance as part of Operation Flashlamp. Historian Steven Zaloga tabulated the tonnage in his book *Rangers Lead the Way: Pointe du Hoc, D-Day, 1944* (New York, NY: Osprey Publications, 2009), 17.

58 "the first Allied bombardment" . . . "attaché for London." Nigel Stewart conducted research on this gallant member of the resistance who later became an OSS spy. Material was forwarded by Paul Woodadge.

59 "When the bombers arrived . . . over half an hour." von Keusgen, *Pointe du Hoc*, via Woodadge.

59 "The bombing during . . . The sky was on fire." Ibid.

59 "They can go to fucking hell!" Ibid.

60 "My unit was untouched . . . ."; " happen to us that day?" Ibid.

60 "After the fog lifted, we couldn't see the water any more—only vessels." Ibid.

60 "There were so many landing craft. . . . about to start right now." Ibid.

12. The Landing

61 "We were close enough . . . . sheet of fire." (OH, Kerchner); (EC).

61 *"How can anybody live through that?"* Ibid.

62 "Hey, Jack! . . . That's C Company's target." (OH, Lomell); Rowe papers, 47–48.

62 "Are you sure you are right about this?" Ibid.

63 "We were taking on water . . . . I know I did." (OH, Hoffman).

63 "That's one less group we have to compete with. We've only got Kerchner now." (OH, Lomell); Rowe papers, 49.

64 "Crowbar" . . . "receipted" (OH, Eikner).

65 "Rangers, lead the way!" Author's interviews with several members of the Fifth Ranger Battalion, which landed on the beach near General Norman Cota.

65 "bayonets and their bare hands" (OH, Salomon).
65 "The American landing craft.... out in the open," von Keusgen, *Pointe du Hoc*, via Woodadge.
66 "From the Pointe.... no protection there at all" Ibid.
66 "radio and telephone operators.... how many times I fired." Ibid.
66 "As we approached these cliffs.... photographer vomited on me." (EC).
67 "Bare, I lost my Thompson!" (OH, Bare).
67 "Here you go, Jack," Ibid.
67 "the grapnels seemed like a lifeline.... on top of the cliff." (OH).
67 "Don't fire those things until I give the word! We've got plenty of time." Lane, *Rudder's Rangers*, 95.
67 "You drop those gates or let those charges go before I give the order, and I'll put a bullet in your head." Ibid; (OH from various members of Fox Company).
67 "All right, everybody out!" (OH).
67 "We had amphibious DUKWs.... too close to the cliff." Ibid.
68 "Ow!"... "He didn't do it!" (OH, Lomell); Rowe papers, 48–49.
68 *"Holy hell...."*... "dumping me in this eight feet of water,." (OH, Kerchner); (EC); Kerchner's diary also consulted.
69 "Until that moment.... red hot," von Keusgen's, *Pointe du Hoc*, via Woodadge.
69 "presumed capsized"... "climb that rope!" (OH, Kerchner); (EC)

13. The Climb

70 "I thought I was kicking up.... the dirt around me." (OH, Lisko); (EC)
70 "I stopped firing because I didn't want to hit our men on top of the cliff." (OH, Bare).
70 "The ropes were slippery.... dropped grenades," Ibid.
70 "Further to my left...."... "but kept trying" von Keusgen, *Pointe du Hoc*, via Woodadge.
71 "The rope was wet.... hands still burned." (EC, Sundby)
71 "What's the matter, Sundby, you chicken? Let me—I'll show you how to climb." Ibid.
71 "I was assigned to a specific.... got up the cliff." (OH, Hoffman).
71 "roller mines." Backup interviews and notes for *Small Unit Actions*, NARA, record group 319, stack 270, row 19, Boxes 1 and 2; The

author found the original backup for the *Small Unit Actions* report from Pointe du Hoc. A draft copy of the document was chock full of interesting details that did not make it into the final published version. It included numerous interviews with the participants and French civilians. In that material, roller mines were mentioned. Throughout the book, the author primarily relied on the draft, unpublished version of the report, which will be referred to as *Small Unit Actions* from here on.

72 "Hold on. I can't help you!" (OH, Lomell).

72 "excellent athlete with a powerful build," Ibid.

72 "Medic! Medic!" (OH).

72 "superb enfilading position" . . . "its field of fire." (OH); Patrick K. O'Donnell, *Beyond Valor*, 145.

73 "top monkeys" (Lomell, OH).

73 "Hey, L-Rod, you're going the wrong way!" L-Rod Petty, unpublished memoir.

73 "Soldier, get up that rope to the top of that cliff! It's *up* you're supposed to go." Ibid.

73 "pissed off" . . . "trying to do?" Ibid.

73 "pet ape" (OH, Stein).

73 "Cole's been hit! Hit the dirt!" Stein, unpublished memoir.

73 *"God damn it. . . . gonna regroup here."* (OH, Lomell).

14. Atop the Fortress

74 "A sniper got me." . . . "Son of a bitch!" (OH, Bare).

75 "It blew his hand off, or most of it." (OH, Lomell).

75 "We'll send back a medic." (OH, Lomell); confirmed in Rowe papers located a USAMHI, Carlisle, Pennsylvania.

75 *"Well, I better cut them just in case."* (EC, Sundby).

75 "I must have gotten scared. . . . took a crap," Ibid.

75 "kept to himself." (OH, Ruggiero, Lomell).

75 "I see two of them" (EC, Sundby).

75 "shot up the two Jerries" Ibid; *Small Unit Actions*, NARA.

76 *"He must have put his head up, and they got him."* Ibid.

76 "You know what it was? . . ." . . . "so I could see him." Ibid.

76 *"Jesus Christ, there's no guns here. They gotta be somewhere."* (OH, Lomell); Rowe papers, 66.

77 "We were gonna charge across.... what the hell was there." Rowe papers, 64-66.
77 "Webb jumped the gun," Rowe papers, 59.
77 "Webb, you stay here," Ibid.
78 "Our mission.... hold the line." (OH, Lomell).

15. Bunkers and Farms

79 "What are you doing, Len?"..."We're gonna hit 'em hard." Rowe papers, 67.
79 "We were hooting and hollering,... scared the shit out of them" (OH, Lomell).
80 "It's a creeping barrage!" (OH, Lomell).
80 "Why'd you do that?" (OH, Lomell); Joanna M. McDonald, *The Liberation of Pointe du Hoc* (Redondo Beach, CA: Rank and File, 2000), 109. The book includes the voices of many of the Rangers who assaulted the Pointe and provides a great viewpoint of the other companies' actions during the battle. I highly recommend it.
80 "Didn't you see that Jerry kneeling on the road, aiming at us?" Ibid.
81 "I was by myself.... German or not." (OH, Kerchner); Kerchner diary; (EC).
81 "I realized as soon as I saw him.... he was dying." Ibid.
81 "Bill, we'll send a medic to look after you." Ibid.
82 "Go after it." *Small Unit Actions*, NARA.
82 "for fear of drawing 88 [mm] fire." Ibid. Interviews related to *Small Unit Actions*, NARA.
82 "Somebody [in our group] came up.... mortar fire hit." Backup interviews for *Small Unit Actions*, NARA; and interviews with William Cruz by Pogue and Charles Taylor, NARA.
82 "Is anybody there?"..."and four Thompsons." Ibid.
83 "I managed to get over...."..."no Germans here, just me." (OH, Hoffman).
83 "Follow me."..."You're lucky; you've got a souvenir here." (OH, Lomell); Rowe papers, 70.
84 "Three men against thirty-five.... let them pass." (OH, Lomell).
84 "My slugs must have cut.... steps and dropped." John C. McManus, *The Americans at D-Day: The American Experience at the Normandy Invasion* (New York, NY: Forge Book, 2004), 300.

84 "I had no way to protect myself and felt I was about to be shot." Ibid.

85 "There [was a field] on our left.... split up into twos." (OH); Rowe papers, 74; O'Donnell, *Beyond Valor*, 147.

85 "We figured we ought to take a look." Ibid.

16. The Guns of Pointe du Hoc

86 "You could have [hidden] a column of tanks in it, that's how deep it was," O'Donnell, *Beyond Valor*, 147. Also see notes by Taylor: "Sgt. Speen (Story of)" I found it buried behind the Draft copy of *Small Unit Actions*.

86 "Leapfrogged," Ibid.

86 *"My God, there they are!"*... "My God. Look at them. They're ready to go." Ibid.; (OH).

87 "The Germans were in various.... eight in the morning," O'Donnell, *Beyond Valor*, 147.

87 "The thermite grenade was... movable gears in the guns." (OH, Lomell).

87 "I didn't know if I was going to get back, so I wanted to do as much damage as possible." O'Donnell, *Beyond Valor*, 147. Leonard Lomell was a good friend of the author and participated in numerous interviews with him over a fifteen-year period.

88 "We've got to get more grenades." Ibid.

88 "Hurry up! Hurry up!" Ibid.

88 "the whole world blew up"... "fell around us." (OH, Lomell); Confirmed in Rowe papers, 76.

88 "What the hell just happened?" Ibid.

88 E Company's Rupinski and his patrol are certainly forgotten heroes of D-Day. As the official history notes, "Failing to notice the fact that some disabling work had already been done, Rupinski's patrol dropped a thermite grenade down each barrel and removed some of the sites. After throwing grenades into the powder charges and starting a fire, the patrol decided the guns were out of action and withdrew.

89 "Should I send a message, sir?"; "Yes." (OH, Eikner).

89 "Blow 6." Eikner, James, Ranger Signal Plan, backup for *Small Unit Actions*, NARA.

89 "Eikner threw pebbles at the bird..." McDonald, *The Liberation of Pointe Du Hoc*, 115.

89 "No reinforcements available—all Rangers have landed on Omaha." *Small Unit Actions*, (OH, Eikner).

90 "The men were turned.... smoke of that shell." (OH); (E.C.).

90 "He had no head and no blood.... death in the war." (OH, Hoffman).

90 "Praise the Lord" (OH, Eikner); Eikner, Ranger signal plan, NARA.

90 "Hold 'til duly relieved." (OH, Kerchner); (E.C.).

17. Swimmers

91 "Keep moving your legs!" (OH).

91 "We were bailing water....".. "until we land?" (OH, Ruggiero).

91 "You damn fool!..."... "Abandon ship!" (OH, Ruggiero).

92 "Baby, it's either you or me," (OH, Lomell).

93 "I squeezed it as soon... not going anywhere right now." (OH, Ruggiero).

18. The First Counterattack

95 "Hold 'til duly relieved." (OH); (EC); Kerchner Diary.

95 THUD! THUD! THUD! (OH).

95 "The twenty men [of Dog Company]... foot of the embankment." *Draft version—Small Unit Actions*, NARA.

96 "no messages from Pointe du Hoc," Zaloga, *Rangers Lead the Way*, 49.

96 "From this area.... observation had been excellent." *Draft version Small Unit Actions*, NARA. The draft version was used from here forward.

97 *"[They look] just like the chariot race from* Ben Hur."... "inseparable friends." Petty, unpublished memoir.

97 "Looking over the five-foot wall.... to hold their fire." *Small Unit Actions*, NARA; notes from interview with Lomell conducted by Pogue and Taylor.

98 "Is that the best you can do?" Interview with D-Day historian Paul Woodadge, who interviewed Trevor's son regarding the story.

99 "They started shelling.... looking for that sniper." (E.C.).

99 "It was the prettiest firing I ever saw." *Small Unit Actions*, NARA.
99 "Stay down! You guys get down!" Ibid. Lane, Rudder's Rangers, 46.
99 "Withdraw! Every man for himself!" Ibid. (OH).
100 "Come on, George, I'm going to carry you back." . . . "We can go in that bunker." (EC).
100 "Are you hit?" . . . "will ya?" Lane, *Rudder's Rangers*, 138.

19. Nighttime Attacks

102 "Very few U.S. grenades . . . . three German machine guns." *Small Unit Actions*, NARA.
102 "plus a captured loaf of bread and one can of chicken " Ibid.
102 "We were beginning . . . . our D-Day mission." (EC); (OH, Kerchner).
103 "This was . . . Germans running toward us," Ibid.
103 "Carty, we gotta get the hell outta here!" *Small Unit Actions*, NARA.
103 "close enough to shake hands with." Ibid.
103 "He gave his BAR to Hornhardt, and they started for the corner." Ibid.
104 "Once we heard the familiar . . . . better soldiers than us." von Keusgen, *Pointe du Hoc*, via Woodadge.
104 "Look, this is what we're gonna do . . . ." . . . "the men didn't hear them." (OH, Kerchner); Kerchner, personal diary; *Small Unit Actions*, NARA.
104 "You don't know how many or where they are!" (OH, Lomell).
104 "an immense sheet . . . German 155s." *Small Unit Actions*, NARA.
105 "Hans!" . . . "Klaus!" (OH); *Small Unit Actions*, NARA.
105 "Much of the fire was [from] tracers . . . ." . . . "thrown in by hand." *Small Unit Actions*, NARA.
105 "Branley, wounded, had gone . . . . came a lull." Ibid.
105 *"Kamerad!"* Ibid.
106 "Nobody north or east . . . . what the situation was." Ibid.
106 "pitch black"; "spare ammunition room." (OH, South).
106 "At times there were so . . . maybe to fight," Ibid.
106 "We carried stimulant drugs . . . . syrette packet." Walter Block, "Medical Observations on Pointe du Hoc Operation, June 6–8," handwritten report, NARA record group 319, stack area 270, row 19, boxes 1 and 2.

107 "He is not going to need it. He's going to be dead in a couple of hours." (EC).

107 "What do you think...." ... "casualty by morning." *Small Unit Actions*, NARA.

107 "We motioned for a young...." ... "to have them killed." (EC).

107 "I think we've been overrun!" ... "cut us off!" *Draft Small Unit Actions*, NARA; Lane, *Rudder's Rangers*, 166.

108 "rolled up the Ranger line from there westward." *Small Unit Actions*, NARA.

108 "The western half of E Company's position was overrun a short time after the attack opened." Ibid.

108 "One foxhole east ... were wounded." From an unpublished draft copy of *Small Unit Actions* found by the author buried in a box at the National Archives. *Small Unit Actions*, NARA. Draft copy contains many handwritten notes and additional nuggets of information deleted from the final report.

109 "They started attacking, ..." ... "got him up on his feet." Ibid.

110 *"Kamerad! Kamerad!"* Draft copy, *Small Unit Actions*, NARA.

110 "Then they marched us on out...." ... "that was just all bones." (EC).

110 "The Germans have broken through .... killed everywhere!" Lane, *Rudder's Rangers*, 169; *Small Unit Actions*, NARA.

110 "reporting that the unit had been wiped out." *Small Unit Actions*—unpublished draft version, NARA.

110 "The message was...." ... "OK, you're the rear guard." Petty, unpublished memoir.

113 "lay in the lane...." ... "soon fell asleep in deep exhaustion." Petty, unpublished memoir.

115 "We didn't know.... the brush and deep holes." Kerchner diary; (E.C.); (OH).

115 "We in Dog Company didn't even move.... what were told to do," (OH, Lomell); Rowe papers, 117.

115 "duly relieved." (OH, Kerchner).

20. June 7

116 "it was well past eight" ... "tremors had ceased." Petty, unpublished memoir

118 "After taking care.... a wounded man." (OH, South)

119 "an unidentified Ranger...retaken the Pointe." Zaloga, *Rangers Lead the Way*, 56.

119 "When the colonel asked me....right off the ground." (Vermeer, EC).

120 *"Kamerad!"* Ibid.

120 "We moved out...to the ammo dump." Ibid.

120 "We gave cover...along that area," (EC); Schneller's account is also recorded in the backup for *Small Unit Actions*, NARA.

120 *"There is no way this guy can be alive."* (Sundby, EC).

121 "even cockier than L-Rod Petty." Stein, unpublished memoir.

121 "It seemed like..."..."It's going to blow!" Petty, unpublished memoir.

121 "They also brought some bread, and Doc Block issued out jam sandwiches." (Vermeer, EC).

121 "I was scared....in the hole with me." Kerchner diary; (EC); (OH).

122 "A shell would land...coming to me on D-Day." Ibid.

21. The Relief of Pointe du Hoc

123 "Hey, is everybody alright?" Kerchner diary; (Kerchner, OH).

123 "almost kissed Kerchner." Ibid and McDonald, 155.

124 *"We're about to be overrun by the Germans."* (OH, Lomell).

124 "Right up behind....'Where are the Americans?'" Kerchner diary; (EC); (OH).

125 "A lieutenant of the 2nd Rangers, ran out of cover, jumped up on one of the tanks"

125 Raaen, John Jr. *Intact: A First Hand Account of the D-Day Invasion From A 5th Rangers Company Commander*, (Reedy Press, St. Louis, Missouri, 2012) p. 100-101. Raaen's book is an outstanding account written by a participant and true hero of the war.

125 "Again Colonel Rudder displayed....past few days." (EC).

125 "Are you being fired on?"..."Yes." Pogue, *Pogue's War*, 122.

125 "And then finally..."..."could still bear arms." (OH, South); (EC).

22. Survivors

126 "CRACK!" (OH).

126 “The road was lined.... some up ahead.” Backup detail from Draft *Small Unit Actions*, NARA.

127 “I could not help... dead lost.” (OH).

127 “I sat in silence... lay before me.” Petty, unpublished memoirs.

128 “Happy birthday, Jack!” (OH, Hoffman and others; however, the exact details were blurry in Hoffman’s mind.).

128 “whatever made them happy.” Petty, unpublished memoirs.

128 *“La boche!”*... “a good set of balls.” Ibid.

131 “Where you from?”... “we were one of them.” (OH, Hagg).

132 “We got an occasional.... meant for us,” (OH, South).

132 “We all had cigarettes.... he liked Camels.” Ibid.

133 “Len, this is your Medal of Honor.” (OH, Lomell) .

133 After the awards ceremony, the 2nd Ranger Battalion remained in Corps reserve, ready for special operations missions related to the Normandy breakout. The movement and dates came directly from *The Narrative History of the 2nd Ranger Battalion*, NARA.

133 “There is an end....”... “you’re getting into.’” (OH, Hagg).

134 “The mission was discharged.... through this enclosure.” *Narrative History of the 2nd Ranger Battalion*, NARA.

134 "When you’re actually fighting, when you’re shooting at them and they’re..." (Kerchner, EC)

135 “repel any enemy attempts to withdraw... from the area.” Ibid.

135 “I will never forget...” “brings it back quickly.” (OH, Potratz).

23. The Assault on Brest

136 “When there’s no wire... in Jerry territory!” (OH).

136 “Hold your fire!” Ibid.

136 “As Dog Company approached....“ ... “the shells started to come in..” (OH, Ruggiero).

138 “I went ahead with the costly siege... no other solution.” Bradley, *A Soldier’s Story*, 367.

140 Details on fortifications at Brest are from the author’s personal research.

141 “Fürst’s brother immigrated to America, becoming a citizen and a successful businessmen.” Hatfield, *Rudder*.

141 Dog Company formed part of Task Force Slater... FFI (Forces Françaises de l’Intérieur). Small Unit Actions, NARA.

142 "1st platoon surprised [a] large . . . exceptionally well." George Kerchner, personal diary. This is the first time the Brest portion of Kerchner's diary has been published.

142 The U.S. Office of Strategic Services (OSS) had dropped several Jedburgh Teams into the area. The author has written three books on the OSS, including *Operations, Spies, and Saboteurs* (New York, NY: The Free Press, 2004), which references the operations of the Jedburghs.

143 "Boy," they said, "Do we have a job." . . . "was the same way." (OH, Hagg).

143 "While awaiting orders . . . . several casualties." Kerchner, personal diary.

143 "We were starting to get shelled . . . . got with the rest of the guys." (OH, Hoffman).

144 "first time under canvas . . . . did a lot of good." Kerchner, personal diary.

24. Hill 63

145 "Before we knew it . . . ." . . . "but we got them all." (OH, Ruggiero).

147 "[We] settled down to what promised to be long stay on Hill 63." Kerchner, personal diary.

147 "It was the last time we ever saw him," (OH, Ruggiero, Kerchner).

147 "My God, the damage . . . . coming at you." (OH, Hagg).

147 "Ruggie, get over this hedgerow . . . " . . . *"Why him and not me?"* (OH, Ruggiero).

149 "fucked up, he would hammer you" . . . "most vivid things I can remember." (OH, Hagg).

149 "you couldn't tell . . . ." . . . "come on over here," (OH, Ruggiero).

25. The Fabulous Four

151 "I believe I see a passage . . . ." . . . "up to that pillbox." (OH, Edlin); O'Donnell, *Beyond Valor*; Moen and Heinen, *The Fool Lieutenant.*

151 "Fabulous Four" (OH, Edlin).

151 "instructions to move . . . organize his defenses." *Narrative History of the 2nd Ranger Battalion*, NARA.

152 "We could hear them talking and laughing inside." O'Donnell, *Beyond Valor*, 175.

152 *"Hände hoch!"* Ibid.

152 "Talk to somebody. See who's in charge here."; "Sir, I speak fluent English. I went to college in America." Moen and Heinen, *The Fool Lieutenant,* 161.

152 "You guys seem like . . . ." . . . "lose a lot of men too." (OH); O'Donnell, *Beyond Valor*, 175.

152 "Will you lead us to . . . ." . . . "in case they were lying to me." Ibid.

153 "Get on the radio and contact Colonel Rudder to lift all artillery fire and planes, all fire on the fort." Moen and Heinen, *The Fool Lieutenant,* 161.

153 "The fool lieutenant of yours is up there already!" Ibid., 162, quoted from Lewis Gannett, a reporter from a New York newspaper.

153 *"Hände hoch!"* (OH).

153 "They were yelling at us . . . . end the situation." O'Donnell, *Beyond Valor*, 175.

154 "Don't knock! Don't touch the door! Just step back!" (OH); Moen and Heinen, *The Fool Lieutenant,* 163.

154 *"Hände hoch!"* (OH).

154 *"This is one of the coolest characters I've ever seen."* Ibid.

154 "What do you want?" Moen and Heinen, *The Fool Lieutenant,* 163.

154 "Fine. Why don't you just . . . . whole thing over with." Ibid; (OH).

154 "You're completely surrounded . . . . going to bomb you." Ibid.

154 "I'm not going to surrender." Ibid.,164.

154 "Ah!"; "Well, there's only four of you, so you're my prisoners." O'-Donnell, *Beyond Valor*, 176.

155 "The thing that happened . . . ." . . . "die without a sound." Ibid.

156 "Initially, I thought . . . . stacking their arms." (OH, Edlin); O'Donnell, *Beyond Valor*, 176.

157 "Let me see your credentials." . . . "These are my credentials." Charles Whiting, *Hunters from the Sky: The German Parachute Corps, 1940–1945* (London, England: Leo Cooper, 1975), 154–155.

26. Interlude

158 Pat McCrone scene about his growing anger. (OH, Webb).

158 The battalion movements come from after-action reports, NARA.

159 "It was a proud moment." (OH, Lomell).

159 "These sixty men... if so directed." *Narrative History of the 2nd Ranger Battalion*, NARA.

159 Scene with Taylor and Pogue is reconstructed from oral histories and interviews the author found in the National Archives, as well as oral histories from the veterans.

159 "he had come with the idea... for a book!" *Narrative History of the 2nd Ranger Battalion*, NARA.

159 "see firsthand the job they would have to do...."... "toughest mission." *Narrative History of the 2nd Ranger Battalion*, NARA.

27. A Factory of Death

161 The opening scene regarding Hürtgen Forest is derived from several veteran interviews conducted by the author.

161 The intact aid station was recalled by 82nd Airborne veteran Robert Piper, as well as other veterans the author interviewed—see *Beyond Valor*.

161 For background on the Hürtgen Forest, please refer to Edward Miller, *A Dark and Bloody Ground: The Hürtgen Forest and the Roer River Dams,* 1944–1945 (Texas A & M University, 1995).

162 "Get out of there, you son of a bitch!" (OH).

162 Background and casualty information from Charles B. MacDonald, *Siegfried Line Campaign* (Washington, D.C.: Center Of Military History United States Army, 1990).

162 "For us the Hürtgen... ever fought." Charles Whiting, *Battle of the Hürtgen Forest* (Conshohocken, PN: Combined Publishing, 2000), preface.

162 "Passchendaele with tree bursts" Ernest Hemingway, *Across the River and Into the Trees* (New York, NY: Simon & Shuster, 1950), 232.

162 40,000 casualties. Miller, *A Dark and Bloody Ground;* MacDonald, *Siegfried Line Campaign.*

164 "The mission assigned...."... "freely during the operation." *Narrative History of the 2nd Ranger Battalion*, NARA.

167 "At night, the 300... approximately 25,000."... "counterattack force in the Vossenack area." Miller, *A Dark and Bloody Ground.*

167 "it could have been a cow or a German patrol. We had to go out and reset it again," (OH, Hoffman).

168 "the land of six-foot trees. Tree bursts and artillery just chopped up everything." Ibid.
168 "We laid the guy.... I drove."... "Purple Heart Corner" Ibid.
168 "Tell that new medic...."... "put you in for a medal." (OH, Ruggiero).
169 "We lived a dog's life.... Trees were coming down." (OH, Hoffman).
169 "The living conditions were terrible"... "but don't shit on them." (OH, Ruggiero).
171 "pulled up a handful of teeth and brains." (OH, Webb).
171 "determine the exact location... 121st Infantry Battalion." *Narrative History of the 2nd Ranger Battalion*, NARA.
171 "you had to put your hand.... hard time seeing." O'Donnell, *Beyond Valor*, 279.
172 "He was supposed to guide us in..."... "a bash to the jaw." Ibid.
172 "received intense mortar and artillery fire." *Narrative History of the 2nd Ranger Battalion*, NARA.
172 "[including] one [that] was fatal"; "their right flank." Ibid.
172 "When dawn came.... names of your comrades." O'Donnell, *Beyond Valor*, 279.
173 "For almost forty-five minutes.... top NCOs were hit." *Narrative History of the 2nd Ranger Battalion*, NARA.
173 "With men laying... any more mines." (OH, Ruggiero).
173 "The other men...."... "we all [got the runs]." O'Donnell, *Beyond Valor*, 280.
173 "Reconnoiter areas taken.... by day or by night." *Narrative History of the 2nd Ranger Battalion*, NARA.
174 "Hold Here."... "I've had enough, let's get back to the battalion as quick as we can." Moen and Heinen, *The Fool Lieutenant*, 211.
174 "old man received his summons," *Narrative History of the 2nd Ranger Battalion*, NARA.

28. Moving Out

175 "Rack it up! Get ready in twelve minutes!" (OH, Hagg and Ruggiero).
175 "Battalion alerted for movement to Bergstein."; "The battalion is to move.... take and hold Hill 400." *Narrative History of the 2nd Ranger Battalion*, NARA.

175 "They had a special mission for us . . . lights out." (OH, Lomell).
175 "Mount up!" (OH, Potratz).
175 "We had gotten a new . . . That was our section." (OH, Lomell).
176 "We rode through darkness, lights out." Ibid.
176 "Good luck." . . . "Harry, I understand . . . make sure of that." (OH); Hatfield, *Rudder*, 216.
176 6,184 casualties. Hatfield, *Rudder*, 218.
177 "We had our packs on . . . . trudged through that darkness," (OH, Potratz).
177 "If you didn't see the guy . . . It was deep mud." (OH, Hoffman).
177 "Spread out! Keep it spread out!" (OH).
178 "I will never forget . . . . charred in the tanks." (OH, Potratz).
178 "The first tank . . . . draw artillery fire."; "You don't get immune . . . . German soldier." (OH, Hoffman).
178 Combat Command R background is derived from original after-action reports from the unit.
179 "Possession of the two villages . . . . Roer River Dams." MacDonald, *Siegfried Line Campaign*, 451.
179 1,247 American dead and wounded MacDonald, *Siegfried Line Campaign*, 450.

29. Bergstein

180 "The companies plowed . . . . platoons were disorganized." After-action reports CCR, NARA.
181 "raised his gun to fire on the advancing infantrymen . . . . aim his gun." Richard Gardner, *Paths of Armor* (Nashville, TN: Battery Press, 1986), 167.
181 Biography information on Hauptmann Thomae and the location of the bunker was compiled from the author's interviews with veterans who fought on an around Hill 400 and from Douglas E. Nash, *Victory Was Beyond Their Grasp: With the 272nd Volks-Grenadier Division from the Hürtgen Forest to the Heart of the Reich* (Bedford, PN: The Aberjona Press, 2008). Nash's outstanding book, assembled from years of painstaking research with primary sources, provides invaluable insights on the German unit. The author's research and knowledge are impressive; a must read for anyone wanting the often untold German perspective on the battle.

181 "jeopardize the execution of the Ardennes Offensive." MacDonald, *Siegfried Line Campaign,* 440.

30. The Counterattack

182 "Tank against tank...." ... "although he was blinded." Nash, *Victory Was Beyond Their Grasp*, 93.

182 Nash's research reveals that the 272nd carried the Sturmgewehr-44, which was confirmed later by interviews with Ranger veterans.

183 "A brave heart.... developed [in combat]." Nash, *Victory Was Beyond Their Grasp*, 25.

183 "Assault companies are to be.... individual strong points." Ibid, 87.

184 Scenes from the battle are culled from CCR after-action reports.

184 "My eye could see.... My heart sank." Miller, *A Dark and Bloody Ground,* 165.

185 "Virtually all the men in the CCR...." ... "never been able to hold Bergstein." MacDonald, *Siegfried Line Campaign,* 456–457.

31. The Church

186 "We sat down.... Our morale went up in a hurry." Forrest C. Pogue, *Pogue's War: Diaries of a WWII Combat Historian* (Lexington, KY: University of Kentucky Press, 2001), 286.

187 "I was given that patrol...." "Halt." (OH, Lomell)"upside down ice cream cone." (OH, Potratz and Webb).

187 "most commanding terrain in the vicinity." MacDonald, *Siegfried Line Campaign,* 451.

188 "When we got there,... to the base of the hill."; "offer the best chance of success." (OH, Lomell).

188 "we surprised a number.... thirteen prisoners." *Narrative History of the 2nd Ranger Battalion,* NARA.

188 "It was like a swimming pool.... dark it was in there."; "Where am I going to go... threw that away." (OH, Hoffman).

189 "We took off our packs," ... "We're going to attack something called 'Sugarloaf Hill' [Hill 400]." (OH, Potratz).

189 "The basement was flooded.... legs were in water." (OH, Zyrkowski).

189 "Let's go!" (OH, Potratz).
189 "When the guy opened.... take care of Harsch.'" (OH, Hagg).
189 "The minute that we came out...." ... "ready as I'm gonna be." (OH, Ruggiero).
189 "There it is." ... "Bergstein was like a finger," (OH, Potratz).
190 "Captain Slater was dashing up and down.... the right decision." (OH, Stein).
190 "one guy who was bleeding.... holding onto it." (OH, Hagg).
190 "I asked him if he was hurt...." ... "That was close!" (OH, Zyrkowski).
191 "We lost a lot of men in the cemetery...." ... "gutted from shellfire." (OH, Potratz).

32. The Charge

192 "Just like *All's Quiet on the Western Front.*" Sigurd Sundby, letter to Leonard Lomell, given to the author by Lomell.
192 "a level table-top field that was filled with snow and ice." (OH, Lomell).
193 "Keep firing as you walk.... watch out for the mines." (OH, Webb).
193 "The first mortar burst.... I know I was."; "Send out a scout!" Petty, unpublished memoir.
193 "Why? Are they nuts—sending a scout into the face of obvious fire?" (OH, Stein); Stein, unpublished memoir.
193 "Fuck you..." ... "explosion of the Ranger charge." Petty, unpublished memoir.
194 "Fix bayonets!" Petty, unpublished memoir; Stein, unpublished memoir; (OH).
194 "Let's go get the bastards!" Petty, unpublished memoir.
194 "Go!" (OH).
194 "would have mowed us down." ... "We went over the field as one." (OH); Petty, unpublished memoir.
194 "WA-WOO-WOOHOO, WA-WOO-WOOHOO!" In interviews, many of the surviving Dog veterans performed a Rebel yell.
194 "dry as cotton'" "Heigh ho, Silver" (OH, Potratz); and e-history. E-history was an e-mail history obtained by the author through his online oral history project at www.thedropzone.org. The

Drop Zone is the first oral history project dedicated to preserving the stories of World War II veterans. It also serves as a virtual museum.

194 *"How do I get across this field and onto the hill in the woods?"* (OH, Lomell).

194 BOOM! BOOM! BOOM! (OH).

195 "It became a disarrayed assault.... impossible to do so." ... "didn't make the charge." Petty, unpublished memoir.

195 "We were running...." ... "right up the hill." (OH, Lomell).

195 *"Kamerad!"* Numerous veterans recall this scene.

195 "You son of a bitch!" (OH, Webb).

195 "I got about halfway...." ... "shot him through the head." (OH, Webb and Stein).

196 "McCrone shot him.... It shouldn't be." (OH, Webb). "I guess if you see.... the 'Rebel yell.'" ... "With bayonets shining... to be a Ranger." Petty, unpublished memoir.

196 "It was something straight out of...." ... "when I threw up all over him." (OH, Ruggiero).

33. Hill 400

198 "It was one wave of shooting, screaming Rangers." *Narrative History of the 2nd Ranger Battalion*, NARA.

198 "As we entered the forts...." ... "hesitant to move forward." Petty, unpublished memoir.

198 "I was so damn scared... God only knows." Potratz e-history.

199 "Everyone was screaming... thirteen of them." Sundby letter to Lomell.

199 "Then I saw... 'Stay down.'" (OH, Potratz).

199 "I'll beat you to the top of the hill." Sundby letter to Lomell.

199 "Each man... D-Day [carried the assault]." Petty, unpublished memoir.

199 "Get to the top of the hill as fast as I can and run the Germans off." (OH, Lomell).

199 "I was using my rifle as a staff because the hill was so steep," (OH, Potratz).

200 "Ranger officers... lead the charges," (OH, Lomell).

200 "went for it." Petty, unpublished memoir.

200 "like a mail flap." Ibid.
200 "As I clutched . . . him down." Ibid.
200 "bravest men of the battalion" Stein, unpublished memoir.
201 "big foot against that pillbox door . . . a pineapple grenade." *Narrative History of the 2nd Ranger Battalion*, NARA.
201 *"Kamerad! Kamerad!"* (OH).
201 "Go over the forward slope . . . we couldn't dig in." (OH, Potratz).
201 "belt-fed like a machine gun," Robert W. Black, *The Battalion,* 220.
201 "The entire hill shook" (OH, Lomell).
201 "knocking us helter-skelter. Amazingly, neither of us was hit." Petty, unpublished memoir.
202 "hysterical." Ibid.
202 "The tree saved our lives," (OH, Potratz).
202 "could hear our comrades . . . hearts." Ibid.
202 "I'm going up to the top to see who's left, and I will get some help," (OH, Lomell).
203 "When the Jerries counterattack . . . higher ground." (OH, Potratz).
203 "He was on his knees . . . brain was exposed." Ibid.
203 "Are we the only survivors?" Ibid.
203 "We got to the top . . . at the time." (OH, Lomell).
204 "L-Rod . . . never seemed to stop." Petty, unpublished memoir.
204 "I had the dubious . . . an hour's time." Ibid.

34. Their "Longest Day"

205 "Here come the Krauts!" (OH, Potratz).
206 "In some instances . . . to the bunker," (OH, Lomell).
206 "There were a lot of gray uniforms coming up, with that distinctive German helmet," Stein, unpublished memoir; (OH, Potratz).
206 CRACK! (OH, Webb).
206 "smashed and useless" *Narrative History of the 2nd Ranger Battalion*, NARA.
206 "With a captured machine pistol . . . close-in enemy." Ibid; S-2 Journal of 2nd Ranger Battalion, NARA.
206 "He stood up . . . repelling that attack." (OH, Webb).
207 "[Secor] turned the tide of the battle." *Narrative History of the 2nd Ranger Battalion*, NARA.
207 "They came right . . . outnumbered tremendously." (OH, Lomell).

207 "Jesus, where are the guys from D Company?" Stein, unpublished memoir; (OH, Stein).
207 "Well, they're right down the hill there." Stein, unpublished memoir.
207 "half dropping off" Ibid.
207 "I took my survivors . . . we had left." (OH, Lomell).
208 "Along comes a German patrol . . . back up the hill." Stein, unpublished memoir.
208 "enemy forces advanced . . . out of the bunker." *Narrative History of the 2nd Ranger Battalion*, NARA.
209 "The Germans were either . . . in the excitement," Petty, unpublished memoir.
209 "They're firing from the trees! . . . What am I going to do with two BARs?" Petty, unpublished memoir; Stein, unpublished memoir.
209 "eighty-two direct hits" *Narrative History of the 2nd Ranger Battalion*, NARA.
210 " [Kettlehut] performed superior . . . on their positions." Ibid.
210 "I was never a smoker . . . to the aid station." (OH, Bare).
210 "I can still see Len . . . we would do anything for." Sundby letter to Lomell.
210 "We had outposts . . . to cover everything." (OH, Lomell).
211 "One guy would see . . . caught or heard." Ibid.
211 "These were pretty smart troops . . . take us by surprise," Ibid.
211 "The outposts . . . from every angle." Ibid.
211 "looks and demeanor of Lee Marvin." (OH, Hoffman, Ruggiero).
212 "Only seventeen men of Company F and fifteen men of Company D were still in fighting condition." *Narrative History of the 2nd Ranger Battalion*, NARA; official log of radio communications, NARA.
212 "The artillery fell . . . don't get you." (OH, Lomell).
212 "Pat, no one ever . . . Bulge breaks out." Ibid.
212 "A large enemy tank . . . We felt helpless," (OH, e-history, Potratz).
213 "Counterattacks on hill . . . we are surrounded." Official log of radio communications, NARA.
213 "Mother . . . for hours," (OH, Lomell).
213 "Don't worry . . . shrapnel was dumped on us." Ibid.
214 "the attacking enemy force withdrew in the face of these on-rushing reinforcements." *Narrative History of the 2nd Ranger Battalion*, NARA.

214 "Everything is quiet on the hill." Official log of radio communications, NARA.

214 "Brown got straight.... were lucky." (OH, Potratz).

35. Nightfall

216 "There were several bodies in the hole, crimson blood all over them." (OH, Zyrkowski).

216 "After the injection, I was high as a kite and feeling no pain," Petty, unpublished memoir.

216 "Trees were knocked down... Run you son of a bitch, run!" (OH, Zyrkowski).

217 "By 9:40 P.M., all Ranger casualties were off the hill..." S-2 and S-3 Journal, 2nd Ranger Battalion; *Narrative History of the 2nd Ranger Battalion*, NARA.

217 "After descending... after forty-three years." Petty, unpublished memoir.

217 "Pipe down and be careful where you're walking. There are three dead Rangers next to us." (OH, Potratz).

217 "stone quiet" Ibid.

36. December 8

218 "At dawn, all hell... morning of the eighth," (OH, Potratz).

218 "The artillery fire... next approaching shell." *Narrative History of the 2nd Ranger Battalion*, NARA.

218 "I'm hit in the leg!... I'd burnt out my M1." (OH, Potratz).

219 "only ten men left." S-2 and S-3 Journal.

220 dealer's table at a gun show. Stein, unpublished memoir.

220 "came to our... uplifting sight that was," (OH, Potratz).

220 "Another German attack... us all night." Stein, unpublished memoir.

220 "When I... to Major Williams." (OH with Colonel Frank Kennard, ret.).

221 "The Germans would... they were home," Stein, unpublished memoir.

221 "BAAHs" Ibid.

221 "You could hear them with their whistles and 'BAAHs' going back down the hill," Ibid; (OH).

37. Final Assault on Bergstein

222 "Under covering fire...stopped at 8:37." *Narrative History of the 2nd Ranger Battalion*, NARA.

222 "The battalion...out this day." Ibid.

222 "The sons of bitches...and could hear it." (OH, Zyrkowski).

223 "Large-caliber guns...in a firefight." *Narrative History of the 2nd Ranger Battalion*, NARA.

223 "The Germans came within thirty yards of the bunker before being stopped by small arms fire," Stein, unpublished memoir.

223 "He called down all...withdraw at 1750." *Narrative History of the 2nd Ranger Battalion*, NARA.

223 exhausting the ammunition bearers loading the guns. Black, *The Battalion*, 230.

224 "The enemy, attempting to retreat...men on the hill." *Narrative History of the 2nd Ranger Battalion*, NARA.

224 "At that time, they threw...was so intense." (OH, Zyrkowski).

38. Relief Finally Arrives

225 "They immediately.... So I left." Stein, unpublished memoir.

226 "considerable moving of troops in the enemy's rear." Nash, *Victory Was Beyond Their Grasp*, 102 quoting "Thirteenth infantry report of enemy action, December 1-31, 1944," NARA, 4.

39. The Bulge

227 "Rack up!"... *"have eighteen guys!"* (OH, Hagg).

227 "He tried so hard to contain it. He'd get frustrated, and you'd see it," (OH, Ruggiero) Kuhn wrestled with his nervous condition, but later got it under control, as recalled by several veterans, including Ruggiero and Hagg.

227 "Our minds were blank...where we were going." (OH, Hagg).

228 "1,600 artillery pieces" and background on the Battle of the Bulge obtained through numerous sources, including Hugh M. Cole, *The Ardennes: The Battle of the Bulge* (Washington, D.C.: U.S. Government Printing Office, 1964) and Danny Parker, *Battle of the Bulge: Hitler's Ardennes Offensive, 1944-1945* (Cambridge, Mass.: Da Capo Press, 2004).

230 For the Battle of Kesternich, see Miller, *A Dark and Bloody Ground.*
230 "I'm going to go back…here as a Ranger," (OH, Ruggiero).
232 "What was going on in Simmerath…two or three," Ibid.
232 "Near our outpost…with German patrols." (OH, Hoffman, Hagg).
232 "The Germans are coming! Be ready!" (OH, Hoffman).
232 "We stayed out…'Be on the watch for paratroopers.'" (OH, Hagg).
232 "We were told…using American vehicles." (OH, Hoffman).
232 "C Company of the 310th Infantry had reported observing four planes drop [para]chutists." (February after-action reports, NARA).
233 "Employing Company D's…for artillery fire." Ibid.
233 "When we would patrol…through and ambush." (OH, Hagg).
233 "anticipated attack by the German Sixth Panzer Division." (After-action reports, NARA); the report is likely incorrect about the designation of the German Panzer division.
233 "all available bazookas." Ibid.
233 "I had one of the new guys with me…size of a football." (OH, Ruggiero).
234 "Jesus, that scar's showing even more today!" Ibid.

40. Back to Hürtgen

235 "establish a bridgehead" (After-action reports, NARA).
236 "They kept telling us…We're going to be running." (OH, Hagg).

41. Crossing the Roer

237 "Take your clothes off…The clothes felt warm." (OH, Ruggiero).
238 Joe Stevens incident was recalled by various Rangers.
239 "It was one town after another…This is what the Führer asked us to do." (OH, Ruggiero).
240 "I hated to see when little boys dress up in uniform at parades. It reminded me of that experience." Ibid.
240 "There was an enormous one-story house…still think about them at seventy-four." L-Rod Petty, letter to Herman Stein, obtained by the author through Deborah Caldwell Stein.
241 "They told us to go in and wipe 'em out…They've just gone berserk." (OH, Hagg).
241 WOOSH!…"shell-shocked." (OH, Hoffman).

242 "The bright sunshine and cold air hit my face." (OH, Hoffman).
243 "An enemy...outpost into the woods." March after-action report of 2nd Ranger Battalion, NARA.
243 "pinned down, and tanks had to be used to evacuate the wounded. The Rangers broke off the attack and continued pushing forward." Ibid.

42. The Last Act

244 "You forgot to duck!" (OH, Bare).
244 "old timers," Ibid.
245 "hold six or seven guys...on Altoona." Ibid.
245 "They took cyanide...It was horrible." (OH, Ruggiero).
245 "When the war ended...going to be bloody." (OH, Hagg).
246 "One of our shows included Jack...No thanks." (OH, Ruggiero).

Epilogue

250 "a roof over their heads" Deborah Stein Caldwell, interview with author.
251 "I was lying...happened to me." (OH); O'Donnell, Beyond Valor, 338.
251 Robert Fruhling's tragedy recounted by several of the men.
252 "the past as present." Douglas Brinkley, *The Boys of Pointe du Hoc* (New York, NY: William Morrow, 2005),187.
252 "the message was clear...Soviet-style communism?" Ibid.

ACKNOWLEDGMENTS

No book is ever created in a vacuum, and I want to thank many people for their contributions to *Dog Company*.

Dawn Hamilton, for her tremendous editorial advice and for spending hours of her time tirelessly helping me with this project and putting her Ivy League literature degree to fine use. To my friends: Ben Ibach, for his numerous ideas and keen eye as well as creative mind. Many thanks to Charles Pinck, President of The OSS Society, for his unconditional support for more than a decade. David Mindock for his friendship and encouragement. To Cyndy Harvey for her editorial comments, advice, and other input on the manuscript. Several readers helped flesh out my narrative. I want to thank David Mitchell, for his time and for sharing his keen WWII knowledge and comments. Travis Aldous and Theana Kastens, both graciously lent their time and expertise to the reading the manuscript. Paul Woodadge, a WWII historian and expert on the Normandy battlefield, who painstakingly translated several German oral histories and examined the manuscript. I'm grateful to special operations historian, Troy Sacquety for reviewing the book and suggesting edits.

Michael Edwards at the Eisenhower Center was very helpful, along with the staffs at the Military History Institute and National Archives.

To the staff at the Da Capo Press, including the best publicist any author could have, Lissa Warren.

To the men of Dog Company who opened up their hearts to me and entrusted me with their memories. In particular, I'd like to thank the late Len Lomell, a great hero and dear friend since I started the Drop Zone oral history project back in the early 90s, for helping me in countless ways over the years. I am especially grateful that he had faith in me to tell the stories of these remarkable men. I also appreciate the assistance I received from Len's, wife, family, and daughter Renee, who generously helped me with various aspects of the research. I am also grateful to Debbie and Herman Stein, and the late L-Rod Petty, for their invaluable contributions. I'm indebted to Thomas Ruggiero who graciously allowed me to pester him repeatedly about Dog Company's history. My dear friends, Dog Company Rangers Bill Hoffman, Vince Hagg, Sheldon Bare. Special thanks to Ranger legends: Frank Kennard, Jim Eikner, Dr. Frank South, and Major General John Raaen, Jr. I am especially indebted to General Raaen, a legend and hero of Omaha Beach, whose eagle eyes expertly reviewed the book. I have treasured and lost many great Ranger friends from WWII whose stories also inspired and informed this work, including: George Kerchner, Sid Salomon, Morris Webb, Bud Potratz, and Hank Zyrkowski.

To Andy Zack, a great friend whose wisdom I value. My deepest appreciation and thanks to my editor and friend, Robert Pigeon, for his ability to capture the otherwise forgotten pieces of history and allowing me the opportunity to honor the men of Dog Company and the 2nd Ranger Battalion. Bob's vision and guidance shaped this book from the beginning, and his peerless editorial skills and support brought this chapter of WWII to life.

Last but most definitely not least, I'm thankful to my parents—who have always been there for me.

INDEX

A Company, 743rd Tank Battalion, 124–125
Adams, Pop, 203
All Souls' Day Battle, 166–167
Anderson, Bill, 120–121, 200–201
Anderson, Jack, 200, 204
Andrusz, Ed, 172
Arlon, Belgium, 159
Arman (lieutenant), 105, 107, 110–111, 153
Army, U.S., training center for, 2
Arthur, Lester, 203
Atlantic Wall, 40
Auguay, France, 114
Aurand, Lester, 181
Avranches, France, 134

Baker Company, 2nd Ranger Battalion, 171–172, 173
Bangalore torpedoes, 42, 120–121
Bare, Sheldon, 12, 250
  Baugh bandaged by, 74
  Dog Company's climb and, 70
  Kuhn and, 13–14, 244
  Lomell sending medic for, 75
  on MG-42 bullets, 70
  on Schaumburg Castle, 245
  on Schneider's presentation, 49
  sniper shooting, 74–75
  Sundby taking care of, 210
  Thompson retrieved by, 67
Barnett (Ranger), 105
Barowski, Whitney, 208, 209
BARs. *See* Browning Automatic Rifles
Battle of Balaclava, 55
Battle of Hürtgen Forest, 178–179
Battle of the Bulge, 163–164, 181, 183–184, 212, 226–235
Baugh, Gilbert, 74, 75
Beever, Colin, 62, 65
Begetto (Ranger), 108
Bergstein, Germany, 164
  CCR fighting to, 178
  Dog Company moving to, 175, 176–177, 178, 186
  Germans counterattacking at, 181–185, 222–223, 224
  importance of, 179, 181
  2nd Battalion, Grenadier Regiment 980 defending, 181
  2nd Ranger Battalion marching to, 176–177, 178, 186
  Task Force Hamberg attacking, 180–181
  Thomae defending, 181
Berthier, Raymond, 58
Big Jim. *See* Rudder, James Earl
Big shows, 45–46

Big Stoop. *See* Masny, Otto
Bill (Ranger), 216–217
Block, Walter
  description of, 25
  on Harwood, 106
  hunting party organized by, 159
  jam sandwiches issued out by, 121
  Lytle punching, 53
  Petty and, 72–73, 117–118
  Rangers treated by, 106
  Schneider and, 39, 47–49
  on stimulant drugs, 106
  28th Infantry Division men aided by, 171
  Webb on, 171
Bloody Bucket. *See* 28th Infantry Division
Bouncing Betty, 238
Bourchard, Gerald, 193–194
"The Boys of Pointe Du Hoc," xi–xii, 251–252
Bradley, Omar, 37, 39, 134, 138
Branley, Mike, 103, 105, 123, 203
Braunton Camp, 42–45
Brest, France, 135, 137, 138–140, 142–143, 152–157
Brinkley, Doug, 252
Britain, 28
British Commandos, 30–32
Brown, James, 214, 218
Browning Automatic Rifles (BARs), 30, 97
Bude, Cornwall, England, 29–33
Burgberg. *See* Hill 400
Burmaster, Warren, 151, 153
Burnett (Ranger), 108

Camelo, Joe, 11
Camp Forrest, 5–6, 7–11
Camp Ritchie, Maryland, 25–26
Camp Shanks, New York, 27
Canham, Charles, 124, 156–157
Carr (bazooka man), 199
Carty (Private First Class), 103
Castle Hill. *See* Hill 400
CCR. *See* Combat Command Reserve, 5th Armored Division
"The Charge of the Light Brigade," 55
Cherbourg, France, 133, 138
Christmas, training on, 33
Church of Moorish Martyrdom, 187, 191, 211, 217
Circumcision, 35
Clark, Bill, 125
Coastal road. *See* GC32
Cold War, xii
Colden, Garness, 54–55, 209
Cole (Ranger), 73
Combat Command Reserve (CCR), 5th Armored Division, 178–179, 184–185, 186
Conaboy, Jack, 83–84, 192
Corona, Johnny, 36, 46, 92
Courtney, William J., 151, 152–153
Crew quarters, 79–80
Crimean War, 55
Crook (Ranger), 108
Crouch, Raymond, 59
Cruz, Bill, 31–32, 81–82, 150, 250–251

D-5 (staging area), 50
Darby, William O., 4
Darby's Rangers, 4
D-Day, anniversary of, xi–xiii, 251–252
Delasandros, Augie, 23–24
Department of Miscellaneous Development, 43

The Devil's Garden, 64
Distinguished Service Cross (DSC), 132–133, 156, 250
Dix, Frederick, 216–217
Dog Company, 2nd Ranger Battalion
  battalion review held by, 158–159
  Bergstein moved to by, 175, 176–177, 178, 186
  Brest and, 135, 142–143
  casualties of, 203–204, 225, 227
  deactivation of, 247
  defenses of, 167
  description of, 6–7
  driver fixated on by, 161–162
  Easy Company men joining, 121
  82nd Airborne Division men joining, 126
  English artillery unit's scuffle with, 32–33
  German patrol fired on by, 136
  Germans at barn fighting, 146
  Germans attacking, 167–168, 169
  Germans counterattacking, 147
  Germans spotted by, 145
  Germans tipped off to, 137, 241–242
  girlfriends causing shelling of, 137, 241–242
  Hill 400 approach prepared for by, 188–189
  Hill 400 approached by, 189–191, 192
  Hill 400 attacked by, 194–201
  Hill 400 defended by, 205–214
  Hill 400 positions of, 204, 205
  Hill 64 seized by, 146–147
  at home, 249–251
  Hürtgen Forest moved to by, 160, 162
  Isigny Road marched down by, 126
  Japan deployed to by, 245
  Kuhn rejoining, 227
  LCA 860 survivors returning to, 132
  Le Conquet positions probed by, 141–142
  Loc Maria Plouzané as objective of, 136–137
  157 mm guns searched for by, 78
  101st Airborne Division men joining, 126
  orders and, 13
  paratrooper boots and, 42–43
  in Pilsen, 245–247
  Pogue interviewing, 159
  Pointe du Hoc climbed by, 70–73
  recruits of, 6–7
  reunion of, 251–252
  roadblock held by, 114–115, 123–124
  Roer River crossing of, 237–238
  Schaumburg Castle seized by, 244–245
  Schneller rejoining, 244
  2nd Battalion, Grenadier Regiment 980 charged by, 198–200
  at Simmerath, 228, 230–234
  tank destroyers firing on, 202
  Taylor interviewing, 159
  13th Infantry relieving, 225–226
  training of, 1–3, 7–11
  Ty Baol advanced on by, 145
  USS *Texas* bombarding area around, 121–123
  VIII Corps subsuming, 135
Dorchester, England, 50
Dorset, England, 45–46
Double daylight savings time, 102
Double Summer Time, 102
Dreher, William, 151

Drill Call, 8–9, 10
Drodouski (private), 24–25
Drugs, stimulant, 106
DSC. *See* Distinguished Service Cross
Duck (DUKW), 43
The Duke. *See* Slater, Harold K.
Dunning, Bob, 59
Durrer, Mack, 199

Easy Company, 2nd Ranger Battalion, 89, 107–110, 121, 188
Eberle (Ranger), 119
E-boats, 49–50
Edlin, Bob, 151, 152–153, 154–155, 156, 174
8th Division, 173, 217, 220
89th Infantry Division, 166
82nd Airborne Division, 126, 235
Eikner, James, 64, 89–90, 118
Eisenhower, Dwight D., 4, 39, 40
Equipment, Pointe du Hoc, 43–44

Fabulous Four, 151–157, 174
Falaise Gap, 135
Fallschirmjägers, 205, 208
Fate, Harry
  Kerchner's counterattack and, 104
  Lomell and, 46, 68, 89
  Rudder and, 90, 95, 177
FFI. *See* French Forces of the Interior
5th Ranger Battalion, 119
First Army (German), 135
First Army (U.S.), 134–135, 174, 177, 245
1st Battalion, Grenadier Regiment 980, 184
1st Platoon, Dog Company, 2nd Ranger Battalion, 80, 81, 175–176
506th Parachute Infantry Regiment, 59
Flanagan, Joe, 147–148
Force A, 41, 61–62, 63, 65, 70–73, 125
Force B, 41, 65
Force C, 41, 62, 64–65
Forrest, Nathan Bedford, 5
Fort Dix, New Jersey, 23–25, 26–27
Fort Meade, Maryland, 1–3
Fort Pierce, Florida, 21–23
445th Antiaircraft Battalion, 173, 175, 176
Fox Company, 2nd Ranger Battalion, 78, 193–201, 202, 204, 205, 225–226
Foy, Belgium, 158
French and Indian War, 3
French Forces of the Interior (FFI), 142, 148
French Resistance, Pointe du Hoc and, 52, 58
Fruhling, Robert, 71, 72, 100, 251
Fulton, James E., 101
Fürst, Martin, 141, 154–157

Gavin, James, 162
GC32, 83
Geitz, Bill, 68, 173
Genther, Henry, 89–90
German Military Academy, 207
Germans
  boys, 239–240
  Brest fortified by, 138–140
  Cherbourg port facilities blown up by, 138
  V Corps piercing lines of, 173
  counterattacking at Bergstein, 181–185, 222–223, 224
  counterattacking at Hill 400, 202–214, 219–221, 223–224

counterattacking at Pointe du Hoc, 80–81, 96–98, 118
Dog Company, tipped off to, 137, 241–242
Dog Company at barn fighting, 146
Dog Company attacked by, 167–168, 169
Dog Company counterattacked by, 147
Dog Company spotting, 145
Easy Company rolled up by, 107–110
8th Division mauled by, 173
FFI forced to retreat by, 148
Fox Company attacked by, 96
girlfriends of, 241–242
Guernsey Islands garrisoned by, 134
Hagg on, 241
headless, 162
Hill 400 fired from by, 180
Hill 64 shelled by, 147–148
Hitler, fighting to last man for, 137–138
Hoffman's run-in with, 143–144
Kerchner attacked by, 103–110
Kuhn killing, 84
Lomell and, 84, 97
Masny captured by, 203
McHugh capturing, 128–131
Nebelwerfer used by, 196–197
at 157 mm guns, 87
patrol, 136
Petty attacked by, 111–112, 209
Petty capturing, 128–131
Petty observing, 208
Petty running away from, 113, 114, 116–117
Petty surprising, 96–97
planes, 132
powder charges, 104
Rangers captured by, 109–110
Rangers detected by, 97–98
Rangers hating, 169
Rangers overwhelmed by, 105
Rangers preparing for counterattack of, 95–96
retreating, 137
Roer controlled by, 163
roll call of, 105
Ruggiero and, 145–146, 239–240, 245
2nd Ranger Battalion and, 167, 192, 193
Secor capturing, 148–149
sniper shooting, 107
Spleen shooting, 75–76
Stein capturing, 128–131
Stevens capturing, 148–149
surrendering, 119–120, 152–157, 195, 199, 238
Task Force Slater encountering, 241, 245
Webb noticing, 191
white phosphorous used by, 191
Winsch killing, 112, 113
Germany, surrender of, 245
Gerow, Leonard, 185
Goat, 132
Goodgall, Leonard, 59
Goreman, Johnny, 176
Graf Spee Battery, 138–141, 142, 147, 148, 151
Grandcamp-Maisy, France, 119, 126
Grapnel hooks, 43–44, 67, 70
Guernsey Islands, 134

Hagg, Vince
on Dog Company's approach to Hill 400, 189

Hagg, Vince (*continued*)
on Dog Company's attack on Brest, 142–143
on German holdouts, 241
on Germany's surrender, 245
on Graf Spee Battery, 147
on Huff, 190
on Jakubiak, 149
Kuhn and, 131–132, 142–143
on Lomell, 142–143
on patrols, 233
on Rudder, 133, 143
on shelling, 242
on Simmerath, 232
Stevens consoling, 149
on Urft Dam mission, 236
Zyrkowski berating, 190
Hand-to-hand combat training, 13–14
Harris, Lester, 69
Harry Goes Home from War, 246
Harsch, Kenny, 189, 190
Harwood, Jonathan, 90, 106
Hemingway, Ernest, 163
Herm, 32
Hill 400, 164, 175
charge at, xiii–xiv, 194–200
description of, 188, 192
Dog Company approaching, 189–191, 192
Dog Company attacking, 194–201
Dog Company defending, 205–214
Dog Company preparing to approach, 188–189
Dog Company's positions at, 204, 205
evacuation of, 216–217
forward observer at, 220
Fox Company attacking, 194–201
Fox Company's positions at, 205
Germans counterattacking at, 202–214, 219–221, 223–224
Germans firing from, 180
importance of, 181
Kettlehut's artillery hitting, 209–210, 223–224
Lawson defending, 204, 219
Lomell and, xiii, 199, 210–211, 212, 213–214
Masny and, xiii, 202
Potratz at, 214, 217, 218–219
Secor defending, 206–207, 219
Slater and, 188, 211–212
Stein at, 219
Thomae's artillery hitting, 201–202
Volksgrenadiers moving back to, 185
Webb's advice on attacking, 192–193
wounded at, 215, 216
Zyrkowski at, 215–216
Hill 64, 142, 143, 144–145, 146–148, 149
His Majesty's Independent Company of American Rangers, 3
Hitler, Adolf, 40, 134, 137–138
counteroffensive of, 163–164, 181, 183–184, 212, 226–235
HMS *Amsterdam*, 45, 51–52, 53–56
HMS *Warspite*, 141
Hodges, Courtney, 132–133, 245
Hoffman, Bill
in bunker, 83
on cellar, 188–189
on Dog Company's climb, 71
on flares, 167
on Force A's approach to Pointe du Hoc, 63
on Fort Pierce, Florida, 21
Germans' run-in with, 143–144

on Hürtgen Forest, 167, 169–170
Kuhn receiving gift from, 128
on Operation *Greif*, 232
on pit, 10
Rangers and, 2–3, 168
on 2nd Ranger Battalion's Bergstein march, 177, 178
shell-shocked, 190–191, 242
Slater approached by, 23
Slater's Cutty Sark bottle and, 127, 128
on USS *Texas*'s marker shell incident, 90
Horace (Jedburgh Team), 142
Hornhardt (Ranger), 103
Huebner, Clarence, 53
Huff, Ollie, 190
Hürtgen, Germany, 178–179
Hürtgen Forest, 160, 162–164, 167, 169–170

Iron Cross, 138, 148, 181
Isigny Road, 126

Jabos (fighter-bombers), 134
Jäger, Karl, 59
Jakubiak, Jake, 149
Japan, 245, 247
Jedburgh Teams, 142
Johnson, Larry, 11, 33, 42, 84
McCrone and, 9–10, 123

K Company, 121st Infantry Battalion, 12th Infantry Regiment, 171–172
Kall River, 162, 166
Karl, Rudolf, 60, 66
Kelley (BAR man), 100
Kennard, Frank, 220–221
Kerchner, George, 250
Branley discovered by, 123
counterattack of, 104
description of, 44–45
false sense of security of, 102–103
Fate told of counterattack by, 104
Germans attacking, 103–110
on Hill 64, 143, 147
on Lacy, 51–52
Lomell advising, 104
MG-42 shooting, 147
on Omaha Beach bombardment, 61
116th Infantry Division meeting, 123–124
praying, 122
Rudder and, 69, 114–115, 133
2nd Platoon, A Company, 5th Ranger Battalion welcomed by, 102
submersion of, 68
supplies of, 102
on tents, 144
37 mm antiaircraft gun and, 81, 95
on USS *Texas*'s bombardment, 122
Vaughan found by, 81
weapons of, 102
Kesternich, Germany, 228, 230
Kettlehut, Howard K., 209–210, 223–224
King Philip's War, 3
Kinmuth (medic), 213
Kirchhoff, Wilhelm, 59, 60, 65–66, 69, 70
Kleinhau, Germany, 176, 178–179
Knight, Tommy. *See* Ruggiero, Antonio J.
Knight's Cross, 138, 181
Knudson, Dean H., 12
Komits, Al, 199
Kommerscheidt, Germany, 166

Korean War, 249
Kuhn, Jack, 44, 249–250
Bare and, 13–14, 244
on Bude training, 33
Dog Company rejoined by, 227
Duck learned of by, 43
German killed by, 84
Hagg and, 131–132, 142–143
Hoffman giving gift to, 128
incendiary grenades provided by, 87, 88
on inter-service rivalry, 28
Lomell and, 27, 54, 80
nervous condition of, 227
157 mm guns and, 84–86
Pointe et Raz de la Percée and, 62
shows of, 54, 245–246
Silver Star received by, 133
Thompson lost by, 66–67

Lacy, Joe, 51–52
Landing Craft, Assault (LCAs)
858, 61, 68
860, 63, 91–94, 127, 132
914, 93
668, 61–62, 63, 67
training, 22, 45–46
Landing Ship, Infantry (LSI), 49–50
Lapres, Ted, 79, 106, 107, 113
Lawson, Ellis, 204, 219
LCAs. *See* Landing Craft, Assault
Le Conquet peninsula, 140, 141–142
Le Devin, Louis, 59
Le Finistére (the end of the earth). *See* Le Conquet peninsula
Le Fret, France, 156
Le Normand, Gerette, 57
Leaggins (lieutenant), 108, 110
Leopold (king), 159
Lewis, Frank, 203
Lisko, Louis, 106, 107
Loc Maria Plouzané, 136–137
Lochrist Battery. *See* Graf Spee Battery
Lomell, Leonard G., xii, 175, 249
Bare's medic sent by, 75
Baugh's medic sent by, 75
on Braunton Camp, 42–43
on Bude, 29
chalk hitting, 45
Conaboy treated by, 84
on counterattack at Hill 400, 207
crew quarters attacked by, 79–80
Delasandros's letter and, 24
description of, 1, 4–5
discharge of, 227
on Dog Company's casualties, 203–204
on Dog Company's roadblock, 115
on Drodouski, 24–25
on Edlin, 153
Fate and, 46, 68, 89
Flanagan driven by, 148
Fruhling's near fall and, 72
GC32 headed to by, 83
German Military Academy class met by, 207
Germans and, 84, 97
grapnel hooks and, 67
Hagg on, 142–143
Hill 400 and, xiii, 199, 210–211, 212, 213–214
on Hill 400 charge, 195
Hodges pinning DSC to, 132–133
Kerchner advised by, 104
Kuhn and, 27, 54, 80
laryngitis of, 27
Lunning dispatched by, 89
Morris treated by, 77
on mountain capture exercise, 26

157 mm guns and, 76–77, 78, 84–86, 87–88
patrol of, 187–188
Pointe du Hoc climbed by, 71–72
Pointe et Raz de la Percée and, 62
poker game of, 51, 52
on Ranger officers, 200
Rudder pinning lieutenants' bars on, 158–159
Ruggiero's lifebelt and, 55–56
on 2nd Ranger Battalion's mission, 77–78
Shanklin and, 36
Slater and, 7–8, 187, 214
Stein directed by, 207
submersion of, 67
tank treads heard by, 123–124
on training, 7, 44
Webb treated by, 77
Lunning, Gordon, 89, 90, 95
Lytle, Cleveland A., 52–53, 118

M1918 Browning Automatic Rifles. *See* Browning Automatic Rifles
Mad Russian (Ranger), 220
Maimone, Salva, 108–110
Main, Harold D., 82
Maine (Ranger), 108
Marion, Jean, 58
Marshall, George, 4
Martin, Dick, 203
Maschinengewehr 42 (MG-42), 26, 69, 70, 103–104, 147
Masny, Otto, xii
bunker entered by, 201
description of, 19
Germans capturing, 203
grapnel hooks and, 67
Hill 400 and, xiii, 202
Petty reunited with, 117
Rudder pinning DSC to, 133
sniper decoy of, 101
37 mm antiaircraft gun and, 98, 99–101
McBride, Morton, 18, 19, 250
British Commandos and, 31–32
fall of, 34–35
rotation names submitted by, 174
Ruggiero and, 35, 145–146, 150, 169, 197, 230, 231
sniper shooting at, 196
Sparaco launching rifle grenade for, 146
at Weymouth, 46
on wires, 136
wounded, 203
McClure (lieutenant), 187
McCrone, Pat, 9–10, 27, 123, 158, 203
McDonald, L. E., 14
McHugh, William, 128–131
Meade, George Gordon, 5
Medal of Honor, 133, 156
Medals, 132–133, 138, 148, 250
Mercader, Guillaume, 58
Merryweathers Ltd., 43
Meslin, Eugène, 58
Meyer, Charles R., 14
MG-42. *See* Maschinengewehr 42
Middleton, Troy, 135
Model, Walter, 182–183
Montgomery, Bernard, 40
Morgan, Daniel, 3
Mortain, France, 134–135
Morvin. *See* Meslin, Eugène
Mosby, John S., 3–4
MP-40s, 206
MP-44s, 183, 206
Mulberries, 137
Mussolini, Benito, 232

Navy, U.S., 118, 121
Nebelwerfer, 196–197
The Needles, 34–35
Newport News, Virginia, 247
Next of Kin (film), 26–27
Nigohosian, Kegham, 93
Ninth Air Force, U.S., 57–58
Ninth Army, 158, 159–160
9th Infantry Division, 235
Normandy, France, plans regarding, 39–40
Norton, Kenneth, 89–90

Office of Strategic Services (OSS), 142
Omaha Beach, 61, 62, 64–65
101st Airborne Division, 126
102nd Cavalry Division, 238–239, 243
106th Infantry Division, 228
109th Infantry Regiment, 28th Infantry Division, 171, 177
112th Infantry Regiment, 28th Infantry Division, 166–167
116th Infantry Division, 119, 123–124
116th Panzer Division, 166
121st Infantry Battalion, 12th Infantry Regiment, 171
157 mm guns, 75
  description of, 38, 47–49
  Dog Company searching for, 78
  Easy Company eliminating, 89
  Fox Company searching for, 78
  Germans at, 87
  Kuhn and, 84–86
  Lomell and, 76–77, 78, 84–86, 87–88
  manning of, 87
  Rupinski placing grenades in, 88
Operation Cobra, 134
Operation Flashlamp, 57–58
Operation *Greif*, 232
Operation Lüttich, 134
Operation Merkur, 138
Operation Neptune, 40
Operation Queen, 171, 173
Operation *Wacht am Rhein*, 163–164, 181, 183–184, 212, 226–235
OSS. *See* Office of Strategic Services

P-47 Thunderbolts, 90
Pacyga, Francis, 69
Palmer (Ranger), 108
Parker, Ace, 102
Patton, George, 245
Pennsylvania Keystone Division. *See* 28th Infantry Division
Petty, William, 250
  Anderson, B., tackling, 121
  Anderson, B.'s, Bangalore torpedoes and, 121
  Arman's argument with, 110–111
  BAR of, 97
  Block and, 72–73, 117–118
  bunker entered by, 200–201
  at Church of Moorish Martyrdom, 217
  Colden carried by, 209
  Colden's conversation with, 54–55
  description of, 16–17
  on Fox Company's casualties, 204
  German POW and, 129–131
  Germans attacking, 111–112, 209
  Germans captured by, 128–131
  Germans observed by, 208
  Germans ran away from by, 113, 114, 116–117
  Germans surprised by, 96–97
  girl discovered by, 240–241

on Hill 400 charge, 194, 195, 196, 198
Masny reunited with, 117
McHugh talking to, 130–131
morphine administered to, 216
on mortars, 193, 194
Pointe du Hoc climbed by, 72–73
on Pointe du Hoc mission, 55
on Ranger replacements, 131
Rangers rejoined by, 117
as rear guard, 112–113
Rudder interacting with, 17
Rudder reunited with, 117
Silver Star received by, 133
South giving pill to, 118
on surrender, 113–114
survival mechanisms of, 111
on training, 131
Pilsen, Czechoslovakia, 245
Pit, 10
Pogue, Forrest, 159
Pointe du Hoc, Normandy
bet regarding, 63
bombing of, 57–58, 59–60
briefing on, 37–38
defenses of, 58–59
Dog Company climbing, 70–73
equipment for, 43–44
5th Ranger Battalion battling towards, 119
1st Platoon coming up side of, 80
Force A approaching, 63
Force A assault delay at, 65
Force A climbing, 70–73
Force A's plans regarding, 41
Force C's plans regarding, 41
French Resistance on, 52, 58
Fruhling climbing, 71, 72
Germans counterattacking at, 80–81, 96–98, 118
Lomell climbing, 71–72
observation post at, 119
116th Infantry Division battling towards, 119
P-47s at, 90
Petty climbing, 72–73
Petty on mission at, 55
planning for mission at, 39, 40–41
Reagan, R., at, xi–xiii, 251–252
relief of, 124–125
Rudder landing at, 63–64
Rudder securing, 98, 119
Schneider's presentation on, 47–49
Stein climbing, 73
Sundby approaching, 100–101
Sundby climbing, 71
2./Werfer-Regiment 85 defending, 65–66
See also 157 mm guns; 37 mm antiaircraft gun
Pointe et Raz de la Percée, 41, 61–62, 65
Portuguese man-of-war, 21–22
Post Traumatic Stress Disorder (PTSD), 39, 251
Potratz, Bud, 9, 250
on counterattack at Hill 400, 212, 220
on Dog Company's approach to Hill 400, 190, 191
on Falaise Gap, 135
on 1st Platoon, Dog Company, 2nd Ranger Battalion's replacements, 175–176
at Hill 400, 214, 217, 218–219
on Hill 400 charge, 194, 198, 199–200
on Hill 400 preparations, 189
line of fire set up by, 201

Potratz, Bud (*continued*)
on 2nd Ranger Battalion's Bergstein march, 176, 178
Prisoners of war (POWs)
Easy Company taking, 188
Ranger shooting, 129–130, 195
Rangers as, 109–110
Rangers rescuing, 156
2nd Ranger Battalion as escort of, 134
Provisional Ranger Force, 39, 41
See also Force A; Force B; Force C
PTSD. *See* Post Traumatic Stress Disorder
Purple Heart Corner, 168

Raaen, John, 125
Rafferty, Joe, 52–53
Ramcke, Hermann-Bernhard, 138, 156–157
Rangerism, 11
Rangers, U.S. Army
Auguay arrived at by, 114
Block treating, 106
A Company, 743rd Tank Battalion killing, 124–125
German counterattack prepared for by, 95–96
Germans capturing, 109–110
Germans detecting, 97–98
Germans hated by, 169
Germans overwhelming, 105
on high alert, 232–233
history of, 3–4
Hoffman and, 2–3, 168
June 7 situation of, 118
Le Fret cleared by, 156
Lomell on officers of, 200
MG-42s used by, 103–104
Petty rejoining, 117
POW shot by, 129–130, 195
as POWs, 109–110
POWs rescued by, 156
as quick reaction force, 167
Reagan, N., hugging, xiii
Reagan, R., and, xi–xiii
replacements, 131
roadblock of, 95–96
Ruggiero saving, 168–169
shell-shocked, 169
South assisting, 72
training, 7, 9, 131, 208
28th Infantry Division relieved by, 167
Webb found by, 120
Webb saving, 168
Reagan, Nancy, xiii
Reagan, Ronald, xi–xiii, 251–252
Rhein (captain), 185, 194
Rhine River, 243
Riendeau, Raymond J., 34, 35, 56, 93
Riley, John, 93
Ritchie Boys, 25–26
RMS Queen Elizabeth, 27–28
Robertson, William, 81
Roer River, 163, 179, 181, 235–238
Rogers, Robert, 3
Rogers (major), 14
Roller mines, 71
Rommel, Erwin, 40
Rowland, Thomas, 208–209
Royal Air Force (RAF), 57–58
Rubin, Leonard, 72
Rudder, James Earl, 14
ammunition depot task given by, 120
Bradley and, 39
Burmaster contacting, 153
command post of, 81, 106
description of, 15

Eikner and, 89, 90, 118
Fate and, 90, 95, 177
First Army (U.S.) reported to by, 174, 177
flag held up by, 125
Hagg on, 133, 143
Kerchner and, 69, 114–115, 133
Lomell's lieutenants' bars pinned on by, 158–159
Lunning and, 90, 95
Lytle replaced by, 53, 118
at Lytle's arrest, 53
Masny pinned with DSC by, 133
Navy and, 118, 121
Petty and, 17, 117
Pointe du Hoc landed at by, 63–64
Pointe du Hoc secured by, 98, 119
Ruggiero meeting with, 20
2nd Ranger Battalion and, 128, 133, 177
37 mm antiaircraft gun attack orders from, 82
Thorson briefing, 37–38
training of, 15–16
transfers of, 159–160
Trevor asked by, 106–107
USS *Texas* and, 90, 125
Vermeer on, 125
Ruggiero, Antonio J., 250
on boat-handling skills, 22
circumcision of, 35
Cruz retrieving company with, 150
on Dog Company's approach to Hill 400, 189–190
Flanagan and, 147–148
Germans and, 145–146, 239–240, 245
on Hill 400 charge, 196
on Hill 64 attack of 2nd Ranger Battalion, 149
on hummock, 196–197
on Hürtgen Forest living conditions, 170
on LCA 860, 91–92
LCA 860 abandoned by, 92–93
lifebelt of, 55–56, 92
on Loc Maria Plouzané women, 136–137
McBride and, 35, 145–146, 150, 169, 197, 230, 231
on mines, 173
on Portuguese man-of-war, 22
Ranger saved by, 168–169
replacement cautioned by, 233
rescue of, 94
on Roer River crossing, 237
Rudder meeting with, 20
2nd Ranger Battalion joined by, 18–20
shows of, 44, 53–54, 245–246
Simmerath approached by, 230–231
Slater asking, 170
toilets and, 170
USO major's offer to, 246–247
wounding of, 233–234
Rules of Ranging (Rogers), 3
Rundstedt, Gerd von, 40
Rupinski, Frank, 78, 88, 105, 110

Saffrons, William C., 14
Salomon, Sid, 171–172, 173
Saving Private Ryan (movie), 64
Schaumburg Castle, 244–245
Schelper, Lawrence, 190
Schmidt, Germany, 164–166, 174, 235
Schneider, Max F., 37–39, 47–49, 64–65
Schneller, George, 98, 99, 100, 120, 244

Schutzstaffel (*SS*), 232, 243
Scotland, 28
Scouts and Raiders School, 21–23
2nd Battalion, Grenadier Regiment 980, 181, 198–200
2nd Platoon, A Company, 5th Ranger Battalion, 102
2nd Ranger Battalion
  in Arlon, 159
  assembling, 127
  awards ceremony for men of, 132–133
  Bergstein marched to by, 176–177, 178, 186
  CCR reinforced by, 178, 186
  Cherbourg assigned to, 133
  in corps reserve, 133, 185, 235
  description of, 6
  First Army (U.S.)'s flank secured by, 134–135
  as First Army (U.S.)'s POW escort, 134
  445th Antiaircraft Battalion transporting, 176
  friendly shelling of, 198
  Germans and, 167, 192, 193
  Graf Spee Battery approached by, 151
  Graf Spee Battery as objective of, 140–141, 142
  Hill 64 attacked by, 149
  home departed for by, 247
  honor guard formed by, 159
  Horace working with, 142
  Kleinhau reached by, 176
  Lomell on mission of, 77–78
  Ninth Army receiving transfers from, 159–160
  as Ninth Army's mobile counterattack force, 158, 160
  Pogue interviewing, 159
  as POW escort, 134
  reconnoiter orders of, 173–174
  Roer River crossing of, 236–238
  Rudder and, 128, 133, 177
  Ruggiero joining, 18–20
  Schmidt as objective of, 164–166
  at Simmerath, 228, 230–234
  Taylor interviewing, 159
  Urft Dam mission of, 235–236
  at Valognes, 134
Secor, Edward, 14, 148–149, 206–207, 219
Seventh Army, 135
76th Division, 2
78th Division, 228–230
Shanklin (training area), 35–36
Shannon (Ranger), 209
Sharik, Mike, 175–176, 189, 201, 218
Shell shock, 169, 190–191, 242
  See also Post Traumatic Stress Disorder
Shira, Neil H., 233
Silver Star, 133
Simmerath, Germany, 228, 230–234
Simmons (Ranger), 108
6th SS Mountain Division, 243
Skorzeny, Otto, 232
Slapton Sands, 49–50
Slater, Harold K., 249
  at Bude, 30
  Cutty Sark bottle of, 127, 128
  Delasandros's letter and, 23–24
  description of, 1, 5, 44
  Herm mission and, 32
  Hill 400 and, 188, 211–212
  Hoffman approaching, 23
  LCA 860 abandoned by, 92
  Lomell and, 7–8, 187, 214
  march of, 12–13

patrols sent by, 187–188
Portuguese man-of-war biting, 22
Ruggiero asked by, 170
Stein on, 190
on USS *Texas*, 94
volunteers of, 2
Small Unit Actions (monograph), 87
Snipers
Bare shot by, 74–75
Fruhling shot by, 100
Fulton killing, 101
German shot by, 107
in Grandcamp-Maisy, 126
Jakubiak killed by, 149
Masny's decoy for, 101
McBride shot at by, 196
Sundby going after, 76
Trevor shot by, 98
South, Frank
Clark recognized by, 125
description of, 25
on German planes, 132
on goat, 132
Lytle and, 52–53
in perimeter defense, 118
Petty given pill by, 118
Rangers assisted by, 72
on Rudder's command post, 106
28th Infantry Division men aided by, 171
Sparaco, Dominic, 44, 91–92, 93, 146, 149
Speed marches, 12–13
Spleen, Richard J., 75–76, 82
SS. See Schutzstaffel
Stecki (Ranger), 105
Stein, Herman, 250
climb reenacted by, xii, xiii
on counterattack at Hill 400, 221, 223
description of, 13
Fallschirmjägers spied by, 208
on Fox Company's scout, 193
Germans captured by, 128–131
at Hill 400, 219
Lomell directing, 207
on map-reading exercise, 16
Pointe du Hoc climbed by, 73
on POW shot by Ranger, 195
on Slater, 190
on Slater's march, 12, 13
13th Infantry Regiment and, 225–226
Stevens, Joe, 148–149, 223, 238
Stüttgen, Günter, 166
Summers, John W., 142
Sundby, Sigurd, 192
Bare taken care of by, 210
crap taken by, 75
description of, 45
on Hill 400 charge, 199
mortar landing near, 99
Pointe du Hoc approached by, 100–101
Pointe du Hoc climbed by, 71
Schneller and, 99, 100, 120
sniper gone after by, 76
Vermeer receiving cover fire from, 120
wires cut by, 75
Supplies, 102, 137, 224
Surrender
of Brest garrison, 152–157
of Fürst, 155–157
of Germans, 119–120, 152–157, 195, 199, 238
of Germany, 245
of 106th Infantry Division regiments, 228
Petty on, 113–114

Surrender (*continued*)
of Rupinski, 110
of Spleen's men, 82
Swanage, Dorset, 49–50

Task Force Hamberg, 180–181
Task Force Slater
airfield captured by, 243
as corps honor guard, 245
description of, 141
Germans encountered by, 241, 245
Hill 64 set off for by, 144–145
102nd Cavalry Division, attached to, 238
in Pilsen, 245
Rhine River crossed by, 243
as screening force, 245
Taylor, Charles, 159
Tennyson, Alfred Lord, 55
Third Army, 245
13th Infantry Regiment, 225–226
37 mm antiaircraft gun, 79, 80–81, 82, 95, 98, 99–101
Thomae, Adolf, 181, 201–202
Thompson (Ranger), 103
Thorson, Truman, 37–38
352nd Infantry Division, 58
Tough Guy. *See* Riendeau, Raymond J.
Training
Army, U.S., center for, 2
boat-handling skills in, 22
at Braunton Camp, 42–45
British Commandos augmenting, 30–32
at Bude, 29–33
at Camp Forrest, 7–11
at Camp Ritchie, 26
at Camp Shanks, 27
on Christmas, 33
demolitions, 11
of Dog Company, 1–3, 7–11
at Fort Dix, 25, 26–27
Fort Pierce infiltrated in, 22–23
hand-to-hand combat, 13–14
intelligence courses in, 26
LCA, 22, 45–46
Lomell on, 7, 44
map-reading exercise in, 16
at The Needles, 34–35
Petty on, 131
of Rangers, 7, 9, 131, 208
of Rudder, 15–16
at Shanklin, 35
at Swanage, 49–50
at Weymouth, 45–46
Trevor, Thomas, 31, 43, 98, 106–107
Trout, Jack, 203
Truscott, Lucian K., 4
12th Infantry Regiment, 171
28th Infantry Division, 166–167, 171
2./Werfer-Regiment 85, 58, 65–66
272nd Volksgrenadier Division, 183–184
Ty Baol, France, 142, 145

United Service Organization (USO), 28, 246–247
Urft Dam, 235–236
USO. *See* United Service Organization
USS *Ellison*, 124
USS *Satterlee*, 89
USS *Texas*, 90, 94, 121–123, 125

V Corps, 119, 173, 179
V-1s, 169
Valognes, France, 134

Vaughan, Bill, 81
V-E Day, 245
Vengeance, 169
Vermeer, Elmer, 119–120, 121, 125
VGDs. *See* Volksgrenadiers
Vierville Draw, 64–65
VIII Corps, 135, 137
Volksgrenadiers, 183–185
Vossenack, Germany, 173

Weaver, William G., 185
Webb, Morris
  on Block, 171
  boot kicked by, 161
  description of, 9
  Germans noticed by, 191
  Hill 400 attack advice given to, 192–193
  Lomell treating, 77
  on POW shot by Ranger, 195
  PTSD of, 251
  Ranger saved by, 168
  Rangers finding, 120
  on Secor, 14, 206–207
Wegner, Karl, 104
Weymouth, 45–46
Wheezers and Dodgers. *See* Department of Miscellaneous Development
Williams, George, 175, 220–221
Wills, Gary, 252
Winsch, Carl, 97, 112, 113
Wintz, Richard A., 67, 120

Zyrkowski, Hank, 189, 190, 191, 215–217, 222–223, 224

Combat historian, bestselling author, and renowned leadership speaker Patrick K. O'Donnell has written eight critically acclaimed books that recount the epic stories of America's wars.

His books include *Give Me Tomorrow: The Korean War's Greatest Untold Story–The Epic Stand of the Marines of George Company*; *Beyond Valor*; *Into the Rising Sun*; *Operatives, Spies, and Saboteurs*; and *The Brenner Assignment*. He also wrote *They Dared Return*, which provided the inspiration for the film *The Real Inglorious Bastards*. In addition, his book *We Were One: Shoulder to Shoulder with the Marines Who Took Fallujah* was selected for the USMC Commandant's Professional Reading List, and all of his books have been selections of the History, Military, and/or Book-of-the-Month Clubs.

A frequent contributor to the *National Review* and other major publications, O'Donnell has provided historical consultation for Dreamworks' award-winning miniseries *Band of Brothers* and for scores of documentaries produced by the BBC, History Channel, and Discovery Channel.

During the Battle of Fallujah, he served as a combat historian and war correspondent in a Marine rifle platoon. He is also an expert on WWII espionage, special operations, and counterinsurgency on the modern battlefield.

He is a recipient of the Colby Award, which is awarded to nonfiction "that has made a major contribution to the understanding of intelligence operations, military history, or international affairs," and he received the 2012 OSS Society's Waller Award for outstanding scholarship in special operations and espionage.

He is also the founder of The Drop Zone, the first online oral history website for WWII veterans. Over the past twenty years, O'Donnell has interviewed more than 4,000 veterans who fought in America's wars, from WWI to Afghanistan.

www.dogcompanybook.com
www.facebook.com/patrickkodonnell
www.thedropzone.org
www.patrickkodonnell.com